SERVICE REBELLION™

THE WOLF PACK STANDARD

Why Customers Leave, Teams Drift and the Behavioural System that Stops Both

JUSTIN HERALD

First published by Hembury Books in 2026
hemburybooks.com.au
hello@hemburybooks.com

Paperback ISBN 9781923765030
Ebook ISBN 9781923765047

Typeset by Lorena Susak

A catalogue record for this book is available from the National Library of Australia

CONTENTS

INTRODUCTION

EASY TO LEAVE

There's a point in a business where nothing looks broken, but something doesn't feel quite right. From the inside, everything appears to be working. The work is getting done. Customers are still coming through. The team is busy, and busy tends to create a sense that things must be moving in the right direction. But from the outside, the experience can feel different.

Customers don't always say it out loud, and they rarely make a formal complaint about it, but they start to behave in ways that suggest something has shifted. They take longer to decide, they ask a few more questions than they used to, they hesitate before referring, and they keep their options open. They might still use you, but something isn't as solid as it once was.

From the inside, nothing looks broken. From the outside, confidence has started to thin. That's the part most businesses don't see, because they are measuring what is happening internally, while customers are responding to something completely different.

Most businesses are built around what they do, but customers judge them on how it feels. Those two things overlap, but they are not the same, and when they drift apart – even slightly – the impact shows up in ways that are easy to misread.

You can be very good at what you do and still be easy to leave. That's what makes this hard to spot. It's not about being bad. It's not about people not caring. It's happening inside capable businesses, with good teams, strong products, and solid reputations, whether that's a single operator, a growing team, or a larger organisation with layers of people and process. And yet something feels slightly off. Growth feels heavier than it should. Retention doesn't feel as stable. Referrals aren't as consistent. Things still work, but not as smoothly as they used to. Even inside the business, something feels slightly off, but it's hard to put your finger on exactly what it is.

Sometimes the signs are small enough to miss. A follow-up that takes longer than expected. A conversation that feels slightly rushed. A customer who says everything was fine but doesn't come back as quickly as they used to. Individually, none of those feel like a problem, but together, they start to change the experience.

So the natural reaction is to push harder. Do more. Add more activity. Increase marketing. Try to drive momentum from the outside. And sometimes that works for a while. But it only works if what people experience once they start dealing with you actually holds up, and for a lot of businesses, that's where things have quietly shifted. Somewhere along the way, what it feels like to deal with the business has stopped being something actively managed and started being something that just happens. It varies depending on who you deal with. It changes when things get busy. It gets explained away as personality, or style, or "just the way things are now". Inside the business, it feels normal, but outside the business, from the customers' or clients' perspectives, it feels inconsistent.

That gap is easy to miss when you are inside it every day. Customers aren't inside it. They experience it in moments. And those moments shape whether they trust you, rely on you, or quietly start looking elsewhere.

This book you are about to read is about that. It's about understanding what's really going on when a business looks fine on the surface but feels harder to grow than it should. It's about the gap between how a business operates internally and how it's experienced externally, and what that gap does to how customers feel, decide, and behave. It's also about what happens when that gap is left alone for too long.

You'll see the idea of the Wolf Pack Standard throughout this book. Not as imagery, and not as a slogan, but as a way of operating where the standard holds, even when things are busy and pressure would normally cause it to slip. Because in most businesses, that standard moves more than people realise. And when it moves, so does everything else. The problem is, by the time you notice it there, it's already been happening for a while.

What follows will help you see it clearly and understand what needs to change.

— PART 1 —

THE DRIFT

Chapter 1

EASY TO LEAVE

Most businesses don't fall apart in dramatic fashion. There's no big moment where everyone looks around the boardroom table and says "Well, that escalated quickly". What actually happens is quieter and far more dangerous. The business slowly becomes easier to leave, easier to replace, easier to forget. Yet from the inside nothing feels broken enough to trigger the alarm.

Staff are still working hard, customers are still coming through, jobs are still getting done, and even the odd review is being posted online somewhere. Everyone feels busy, and when people feel busy, they mistake activity for progress. Busy feels like movement, and movement feels like safety. The problem is that activity and customer experience are not the same thing. A business can be running flat out while the experience of dealing with it is quietly becoming more effort than it should be.

That's the part leaders rarely see clearly because leaders are trained to look at outputs. Revenue, margins, productivity, marketing performance, pipeline, growth charts . . . all of that matters, of course it does, but customers are not sitting there making decisions based on your internal dashboard. They're making decisions based on how it feels to deal with you, and feelings are shaped in moments, not metrics.

Moments don't look important when you're in the middle of a day that already feels overloaded. The tone of a reply, the speed of a response, whether someone felt properly listened to or just processed, whether a problem was owned or quietly passed along, whether a follow-up happened without being chased, whether the customer had to repeat themselves, whether someone sounded distracted, whether the interaction left them feeling certain or slightly unsure. All of these matter to the customer and client yet most are never measured by a business.

Nobody wakes up and decides standards are slipping today. What happens instead is pressure increases, time feels tighter, and behaviour shifts to cope with the day rather than protect the experience. Shorter communication feels efficient. Faster handovers feel practical. Fewer updates feel understandable because everyone is juggling. Inside the business this looks like survival. Outside the business it feels like uncertainty. Customers feel it before leadership even sees it.

"AVERAGE" CHANGES BEHAVIOUR

Picture a business that is technically solid: the product or service works, the team is capable, the reputation is decent enough that new customers still come in. There are no dramatic complaints, no social media disasters, nothing that makes leadership sit up and think there's a serious issue here. From their perspective it's not perfect, but it's steady.

Inside the business, everyone is under pressure. Emails get shorter because there's no time. Calls are returned, but sometimes later than is ideal. Handovers between team members are functional but realistically rushed. Everyone assumes someone else explained the next step to the customer because surely someone did . . . didn't they? The job still gets done, which for the business feels like success.

Now look at the same situation from the customer's side. They feel like they have to check in more than they expected. They're not always sure what stage things are at. They get answers, but not reassurance. They sense people are flat out, which makes them hesitate to ask questions because they don't want to be a hassle. They don't feel mistreated, but they don't feel confidently looked after either.

They don't complain. They adjust.

Next time they need the service or product, they get another quote just to compare, or they shop online because if they aren't going to get any form of service they may as well do it from the comfort of their own home. They hesitate before referring a friend because it's their own reputation on the line. They pay closer attention to price. From the customer's perspective, they simply don't feel safe enough to rely on the business without checking alternatives.

Nothing dramatic happened. No one made a huge mistake. The business didn't become incompetent. It just drifted into "average" for the customer experience, and average quietly changes behaviour.

Here in Australia, there is a large retail chain that once sat at the pinnacle of customer service. Now the numbers are falling, complaints are rising, foot traffic is down, and the lived experience does not match the marketing. Over time the focus on customer experience gave way to fewer staff on the floor and departments segmented by brand instead of running as one business. On paper it probably made sense. On reports it probably looked efficient. On the shop floor it created confusion. Customers needing help in one section were told staff from another brand could not assist. Internally that is structure. Externally that is frustration. What made sense at head office made no sense to the person simply trying to spend money.

Inside any organisation, people adapt to their environment. They get used to delays. They normalise short communication. They accept messy handovers. They tolerate uncertainty because that's what they live in every day. It becomes the water they swim in, and once something becomes normal internally, it stops feeling like a problem.

UNCERTAIN CUSTOMERS PROTECT THEMSELVES

Customers, however, don't live in your environment. They visit it. And like any visitor, you have to make them feel welcomed otherwise they will leave. What you have normalised they experience as friction.

Leaders see the effort the staff are putting in but sometimes through rose-coloured glasses – they know how hard the team is working, they see the staffing gaps, the pressure and the complexity. The customer, on the other hand, doesn't see that behind-the-scenes effort. They *feel* what happens in the interaction, and if that interaction feels rushed, vague, or slightly chaotic, their brain registers risk.

You may be incredibly proud of how much your team is doing, but meanwhile customers are quietly losing confidence in how it feels to deal with you. That gap is one of the biggest blind spots in business. Most customers will never say it out loud, but it runs quietly in their head: the need to check whether messages were received, follow up to make sure nothing was missed, get another price in case something feels off, hold back from recommending until they're sure.

That internal dialogue isn't aggression, it's risk management. When customers feel uncertain, they protect themselves by keeping their options open. That's logical behaviour from their point of view. Businesses often interpret this as customers being slow, fussy, or price focused. In reality, customers are responding to how safe or unsafe the experience feels. If the experience creates confidence, the internal dialogue relaxes. If the experience creates uncertainty, the internal dialogue stays active and eventually will get in the way of the business's desired outcome. Active risk management from customers has consequences for the business, whether anyone connects those dots or not.

Consider the moment after a customer commits. Payment is made and the agreement is signed. The business quite naturally shifts into delivery mode: the team focuses on tasks, logistics, timelines, and getting the work done properly. From their point of view, this is where the real effort begins. From the customer's point of view, though, this is the most emotionally sensitive part of the relationship. Money and trust are now on the line and the quiet question in their head is no longer "Should I buy?", it's "Did I make the right choice?"

If communication drops during this stage, if updates are vague, if no one checks in, the customer doesn't interpret that as efficiency or focus. It *feels* like distance. It *feels* like the business cared right up until the payment went through and then moved on to the next thing. The emotional experience between commitment and completion *feels* uncertain, and uncertainty leaves a mark.

Later, when that customer describes the experience to someone else, they might say the work was good – which sounds positive on the surface – but then add that they had to stay on top of things a bit. That sentence is the sound of loyalty leaking. When customers feel like they have to supervise, they don't relax into the relationship. A small part of their brain stays switched on, just in case.

Always remember . . . Just because the sale has been done, it doesn't mean the customer has been won! People don't stay loyal to relationships that feels like supervision. They stay loyal to relationships that feel like relief and value.

MAKING CUSTOMERS DO THE WORK

This is where the gap between capability and experience becomes obvious. The business might be very good at the technical side of what it does yet still create an experience that feels harder than it should. Leaders often assume that if the outcome is right, the experience must have been good enough. Rarely do they do a stocktake on the customer's journey. Customers don't separate those two things so neatly. They remember how it felt to get there just as much as they remember what they got in the end.

When customers and clients feel like they have to work too hard, confidence fades. And when confidence fades, loyalty goes with it. The customer might still buy again, but they'll take longer to decide. They might still speak well of the business, but they won't actively recommend it. They might still come back, but they'll compare prices first. None of those shifts look dramatic in isolation, but together they change the economics of the business: referrals slow down, marketing has to work harder to fill the gap, and more leads are needed to achieve the same sales. That increases pressure on the team, which makes service behaviours even more rushed, which then feeds back into the experience feeling harder. The business feels busier, but the loyalty engine is weakening.

From the inside, this feels like the market is tougher and customers are more demanding. From the outside, customers are simply responding to the level of certainty the experience creates. When people feel safe, they stop looking around. When they feel unsure, even slightly unsure, they keep their options open. That's not customers being difficult. That's humans managing risk.

One of the reasons this problem hides so well is because most businesses treat service as an attitude rather than a system. They believe if they hire good people and tell them to look after customers, the experience will take care of itself. That works when everything is calm. It falls apart under pressure.

PERSONALITY-BASED SERVICE

This is something I see constantly through my work with my business, Customer Culture. Businesses hire people based on what their resume says about customer service then give them no clear behavioural standards for how customers should actually be treated in the business.

That is not culture. That is hope.

Any business that does this is putting their culture at major risk. It becomes a "ready – fire – aim" way to run a business and create a customer-focused culture.

Under pressure, behaviour defaults to survival mode. Survival mode focuses on clearing tasks, not creating reassurance. It focuses on what needs to be done next, not on how the customer is feeling in the middle of it. The team isn't being careless. They're coping with the environment they're in.

Without clear behavioural standards that are reinforced consistently, service becomes personality based. Some staff naturally create strong experiences. Others prioritise efficiency. The customer experience then depends on who they happen to deal with that day. From the customer's perspective that feels inconsistent. One interaction feels smooth and reassuring, the next feels rushed and transactional. Inconsistency creates uncertainty, and uncertainty leads to comparison.

Leaders often believe service problems come from people not caring. More often they come from people caring but operating in a system that doesn't make it easy to show it consistently. When standards aren't clear and reinforced, the environment decides behaviour, not intention. That's why drift is so hard to see from the inside. Everyone feels like they're doing their best – and they probably are – but best effort without shared behavioural standards doesn't guarantee a consistent experience. It guarantees variation, and variation is what customers experience as risk.

FINE

And when that translation doesn't happen, the business doesn't suddenly fall apart. It slowly becomes forgettable. It becomes fine. Fine is one of the most dangerous words in business because "fine" never builds loyalty. It builds replaceability.

A customer who describes your business as fine isn't angry, but they're not attached either. They're not telling their friends about you with enthusiasm. They're not overlooking small issues because they trust you. They're not defaulting to you without thinking. They're keeping you in the mix, and being in the mix is not the same as being their number one choice.

The uncomfortable question isn't where are we failing badly, it's where have we drifted quietly.

- Where are the standards assumed instead of reinforced?
- Where is our behaviour inconsistent?
- Where are customers having to work harder than they should to deal with us?

Because those areas cost the most, even if they never show up in a complaint.

STANDARDS SET THE STANDARD

The good news, which we'll come back to again and again, is that this can be fixed. Not with slogans, posters, or one-off workshops. You can fix it with standards, awareness, leadership reinforcement, and a system that turns service from intention into consistent behaviour.

What makes all of this even more uncomfortable for leadership or business owners is that the business can look healthy on the surface while this drift is happening underneath. Revenue might be steady, the pipeline might look decent, marketing might still be generating leads. From a distance, nothing screams crisis. That's exactly why this problem survives as long as it does. It is like mould growing in the dark. You do not see it until the damage is already there.

Customer experience rarely collapses all at once. It thins out gradually like a slow-dripping tap. You start to see small signals that are easy to dismiss: customers take longer to decide, they ask more questions about price, or they say they're "just looking around". Referrals slow, but not enough to feel dramatic, and repeat purchases stretch out a little. None of it looks like a red alert, it just looks like business being business.

What's actually happening is that the emotional buffer you used to have with customers is shrinking. When people feel very confident in a business, they overlook small issues. They're more patient. They're more forgiving. They don't compare as aggressively. That buffer comes from consistently feeling looked after, not from one great interaction six months ago. When the experience becomes inconsistent, that buffer disappears. Customers move into a more cautious mode. They don't feel angry, they feel watchful. Watchful customers behave differently . . . they double-check everything.

Referrals are a transfer of trust. When someone refers your business, they're putting their name on you. They only do that when they feel safe that the experience the next person has will match their own. If their own experience felt average or required them to stay on top of things, they won't feel comfortable making that recommendation. And so service drift quietly chokes growth. Not by losing every customer, but by reducing the number of customers who are willing to stake their reputation on you.

At the same time, leadership often responds to slowing growth by focusing even harder on marketing and sales tactics. More campaigns, more ads, more promotions, and even more pressure on sales conversions.

This is where Service Rebellion begins. Not with slogans but with standards. The internal story and the customer's story really start to part ways here.

So the real question this chapter leaves you with isn't whether your business is good at what it does. It's whether the experience of dealing with your business makes customers feel safe enough to stop looking around.

Where have you normalised things internally that customers experience as friction? Where are small gaps being excused because everyone is busy?

Where is the experience depending too much on individual personality instead of shared standards?

Which staff members are quietly carrying the experience while others hide behind tasks? Those quiet gaps are where loyalty leaks out and comparison creeps in.

The encouraging part is that this is fixable. Not with a one-off training day or a new slogan on the wall, but with clear behavioural standards, shared awareness, leadership reinforcement, and a system that makes the right behaviours normal, not optional.

The businesses that win won't simply work harder. They'll create certainty. Certainty builds confidence. Confidence builds loyalty. Loyalty fuels referrals. And it all starts by seeing the drift most businesses ignore.

This is why the Wolf Pack Standard exists. Not to motivate people, but to remove variation when pressure hits.

Chapter summary

- Internally, the narrative is that everyone is stretched because the business is busy and trying to grow.
- Externally, the customer narrative is that the business doesn't feel as on top of things as it used to.
- Both stories can be true at the same time, but only one of them drives behaviour.
- Customers make decisions based on feeling safe and certain, not on how hard you are working.
- Certainty is emotional – it comes from feeling that someone has you covered.
- When certainty drops, even slightly, customers move into self-protection mode.
- Bad experiences trigger complaints and force action.
- Great experiences create loyalty and referrals.
- Average experiences create quiet drift.
- A pattern of small behaviours that have been allowed to become normal determines if customers feel safe.
- Motivation alone will not solve the problem – people already care.
- That care has to be translated into visible, repeatable behaviours, especially when pressure is high.
- Without that translation, the environment decides behaviour, and the environment under pressure defaults to speed and task completion, not reassurance.

Chapter 2

WHAT CUSTOMERS REALLY WANT BUT RARELY SAY

Most customers don't know how to explain what they actually want. They'll talk about price, speed, features, options, value, turnaround times, and discounts. That's the language available to them. But those words are usually a surface translation of something deeper. What they're really looking for isn't another feature or a slightly sharper price.

They're looking for a feeling. Yet most businesses optimise for the words instead of the feeling.

If you take customer requests at face value, you end up optimising for the wrong things. You start tweaking pricing models, adjusting offers, adding extras, speeding up processes, all in the hope that the next improvement will finally tip the scale.

Sometimes it helps, but often the impact is smaller than expected, and the reason is simple. Most of what customers say is a translation of how they feel, not a technical specification of what they need. People are not walking around scoring businesses on a spreadsheet in their head. They are making emotional safety decisions first and using logic later to explain it.

CUSTOMERS DECIDE USING FEELINGS

Think about the last time you chose one provider over another when both seemed capable. On paper they might have looked similar, maybe one was even slightly cheaper, but one just felt more solid, more on top of things, easier to deal with. You probably didn't say "I'm selecting them because they create a stronger sense of emotional certainty". You probably said something like "They seemed more professional", or "I just had a better feeling about them", or "They were clearer". Those phrases are emotional triggers. They sound logical, but underneath them sits one consistent driver. What customers are really responding to is certainty.

Recently we had to get a few quotes for some work to be done to our house. I went online and found various companies in our area and checked out their websites. Every single one of them highlighted how good they were (you would hope they were good), how the client is always their priority, how they have five-star Google reviews, and how they treat all customers like family.

Then came the time for me to try and have a talk with them about my job. Two of the websites didn't have any phone numbers listed, so there was no chance of calling them, and all of them had a "contact us" form to be filled out. As our job was a big one – and one that would require a lot of money – I wanted to speak with them first to make sure we weren't going to waste our time and also to see if the company would be a good fit and give us a sense of certainty.

I rang two of the businesses I selected. The first conversation was so stupid it made my decision easy. The lady I spoke to on the phone said that I needed to fill out the form before someone could talk to me. I casually asked if she would be the person who would ring me after

I filled out the form, to which she replied yes. I get that she had a set process to follow, but from my side all it felt like was another hoop to jump through when I was already trying to spend money.

The second company I rang was over-the-top helpful. The owner made a time to come out that afternoon and the deal was done. We just wanted reassurance, and making things easy was all it took.

THE BENEFITS OF REASSURANCE

Reassurance doesn't mean exaggerated friendliness or forced enthusiasm. It means clarity, follow-through, visible ownership, and consistency. It means the customer doesn't have to wonder what's going on. When people don't have to wonder, they relax. When they relax, they commit more easily.

This is where logic takes a back seat. A customer might say "We went with them because their price was competitive". But if you dig deeper, the real reason often sits underneath that explanation. The price was acceptable, yes, but what tipped the scale was how confident they felt in the experience. How painless it was, or how uncomplicated.

When confidence is high, price becomes less dominant. When confidence is low, price becomes a bigger factor because customers are mentally adding a risk buffer. Uncertainty makes price matter more. That's why two businesses can offer almost identical services at different prices, and both still win customers. The one that creates more certainty can often charge more because customers feel like they're reducing risk.

This also explains why businesses sometimes lose work to competitors that don't appear objectively better. From the inside, the business owner or management team looks at the outcome and says

"But we're more experienced", or "Our product is stronger". From the customer's side, the other business simply felt easier to deal with, clearer, and more on top of things. Emotional safety wins more often than technical superiority. Customers rarely admit that directly because it doesn't sound rational, but behaviour shows it all the time.

Another thing customers won't say is how much they value not having to think. When a business communicates clearly, sets expectations, follows up, and closes loops, the customer's mental load decreases. They don't have to remember to chase, they don't have to keep checking, they don't have to manage the process in their head.

That reduction in mental effort is a huge part of perceived value. When dealing with a business feels mentally heavy, customers describe it as "hard work". When it feels mentally light, they describe it as "easy to deal with". Easy often wins over technically superior but mentally heavy.

THE DISADVANTAGES OF UNCERTAINTY

If you look back at situations where customers became frustrated, you'll often find the core issue wasn't the outcome, it was the uncertainty along the way. Delays that weren't communicated, changes that weren't explained, or silence where there should have been updates.

That stress comes from not knowing, not from the work itself. People can handle problems. It's the uncertainty that messes with their head. A clear delay with communication is less stressful than silence where nothing is explained. Yet many businesses default to silence when they're busy, not realising that silence is interpreted as loss of control.

We saw this play out recently in our own life. My wife and I use brokers across different areas – property, finance, insurance – because when they're good, they make life easier. That's the whole point of a broker. They sit between you and a complex industry. They understand the systems, the language, the processes, and they're meant to carry that load, so you don't have to. You don't use a broker just for access. You use them for certainty.

We ran into a situation where something needed attention. Nothing dramatic, just one of those moments where the reason you have a broker in the first place becomes real. This was the moment for them to step in, take ownership, manage the process, and be the buffer between us and the back-end complexity. Instead, we found ourselves chasing updates, reminding them to follow up, checking whether things had moved. Technically, things were happening. But emotionally, the experience shifted. The certainty we normally feel dropped in a big way. It started to feel like we were managing the process instead of being supported through it.

That's the turning point. Because when certainty drops, behaviour changes. We didn't suddenly get angry. We didn't write complaints. What happened was quieter. The referrals we would normally make without thinking stopped. Not because we didn't like them, but because referring someone is putting your own reputation on the line. If you're not confident about how the experience will feel for the next person, you hesitate.

From their side, they were probably busy, and they were probably working hard. They might have thought things were progressing fine. But from our side, the experience felt uncertain, and uncertainty changes behaviour faster than most businesses realise. That emotional experience in the middle changed the relationship, and it's the part many businesses miss. People don't just judge you on whether the thing eventually gets done. They judge you on how safe they feel while it's getting done.

PREDICTABILITY AND THE MENTAL LOAD

Customers don't want perfection, they want predictability. They want to feel like someone is on top of things, they want to know what happens next, and they want to feel like they matter, not in a dramatic way, but in a consistent, low-key way. That's what they really mean when they talk about service. And that's why the businesses that win aren't just the ones that are good at the technical side. They're the ones that consistently reduce uncertainty at every stage of the journey.

Because when customers feel safe, they stay. When they stay, they refer. When they refer, growth becomes easier. And none of them ever walks in and says, "Hi, I'm here for emotional safety."

Customers rarely explain this directly because most people aren't walking around analysing their own emotional responses to businesses. They just know when something feels easy and when something feels off. When it feels easy, they describe the business as professional, organised, reliable, good to deal with. When it feels off, they say things like "Communication could have been better", "I just had to chase a bit", or "It was fine . . . but". That word "but" is where emotional safety fell short.

What's interesting is that two businesses can technically deliver the same outcome yet create completely different levels of emotional comfort along the way. One leaves the customer feeling looked after, the other leaves them feeling like they had to stay alert. The difference isn't usually dramatic mistakes, it's how many question marks the customer carries in their head during the process.

When customers say they want fast responses, they're not just talking about speed. They're reacting to question marks. A quick reply closes one but a slow reply leaves it hanging. And when too many question marks hang around, customers start stepping in to manage the process themselves. That mental load is rarely acknowledged, but it shapes loyalty more than most features or benefits ever will.

Think about any situation where you've had to deal with multiple providers at once. The one that required the least follow up probably felt the easiest to work with, even if their offering wasn't dramatically better. You didn't have to remember to chase them. You didn't have to check whether they were still on track. You didn't have to wonder what stage things were at.

As a customer, how frustrating is it when you have to follow up a business multiple times when all you are trying to do is spend money with them? If that frustrates you, just make sure your business isn't doing the same to your customers!

When customers say they want transparency, they're often trying to say they don't want surprises. Surprises create uncertainty, even if the surprise isn't catastrophic – a change of timing without warning, a different contact person appearing without explanation, a process step that wasn't mentioned earlier. Each one makes the customer adjust mentally. Enough of those and the experience starts to feel unpredictable.

Predictability isn't boring from a customer's point of view, predictability is reassuring. It means they can relax a little because they feel like they understand how things work with you. When customers understand the rhythm of dealing with your business, they feel more in control, even though they're not the ones running the process. That sense of control reduces stress. This is why clarity often beats charm. A business can be friendly and still make customers feel uncertain if communication is vague. On the other hand, a business can be quite straight forward in tone yet make customers feel very safe because everything is explained clearly, expectations are set, and follow-up is consistent. And as I've said earlier in the chapter, customers won't usually articulate that difference. They'll just say one felt more professional – meaning, in this context, emotionally predictable.

THE EMOTIONAL LOAD

This lack of sense of control also explains why customers sometimes stay with a business after a problem but leave after a series of "nothing major" interactions. When a problem happens but is handled clearly, with ownership and communication, certainty can actually increase. The customer sees that when something goes wrong, the business steps in and manages it. That builds trust and earning trust is rare these days. But when nothing major goes wrong, and yet the experience still feels disjointed, trust doesn't grow. The customer never gets to see a strong recovery moment, and they also don't get the steady reassurance of a smooth process. They're left in a grey area where the business seems capable but not fully in control. Grey areas don't create loyalty. They quietly push people away.

What most businesses still don't see is that customers aren't really choosing between products or services: they're choosing between environments, they're choosing how it feels to deal with you over time, and they're choosing whether they have to stay alert or whether they can relax. And that choice is rarely verbalised . . . It's often felt though.

When a customer walks away from an interaction and feels like they don't have to think about it anymore, that's not luck, that's not charm, that's not personality. That's the result of behavioural signals stacking up in a way that tells their brain "You're in safe hands".

Inside a wolf pack, no one is guessing who's leading, who's covering, or whether someone is paying attention to the surroundings. The coordination is visible and the signals are constant. When terrain shifts, communication increases, not decreases. When pressure rises, formation tightens. That's what keeps the pack stable.

Customers are scanning for the same thing, not consciously, but instinctively. They're asking themselves – even if they'd never phrase it this way – "Are these people coordinated, or am I going to have to manage this myself?"

When customers start managing you, loyalty starts thinning. They might not complain, they might not even leave immediately, but they stop relaxing into the relationship. They double-check. They follow up. They keep options open. And once someone is keeping options open, growth becomes harder than it needs to be.

This is where Service Rebellion actually lives. Not in slogans, not in scripts, not in tone. It lives in the decision to stop leaving emotional load sitting on the customer's shoulders. It's drawing the line and saying "In this business, we don't let customers carry uncertainty that we could have removed". That's not softness, that's the discipline that creates certainty before customers even realise they need it.

That's the pack standard. And that's the Service Rebellion.

Not against competitors. Against drift.

Chapter summary

- Don't just listen to what customers ask for, watch for the signals that the environment doesn't feel fully stable:
  - how they behave around you
  - whether they hesitate before committing
  - whether they escalate decisions internally
  - whether they ask the same question twice in different ways
  - whether referrals slow even though satisfaction seems fine.
- In the high-functioning wolf pack, silence doesn't follow uncertainty: signals increase, communication becomes tighter, roles become clearer, and the pack adjusts before instability spreads.
- Businesses that operate like a wolf pack feel different to deal with – not louder, not friendlier, just steadier.
- If the customer has to chase, decode, or guess – you haven't delivered service, you've delivered uncertainty.
- Customers want to feel like someone competent is steering the situation and that they won't be blindsided.
- When that feeling is present, price matters less, decisions move faster, and referrals feel safer to make.

Chapter 3

THE COST OF BEING AVERAGE

Most businesses aren't trying to be average. That's what makes this problem so frustrating. No one sits in a management or staff meeting and says "Right, let's aim for forgettable". Average doesn't come from intent. It comes from drift, pressure, and a slow lowering of what people start calling "normal".

And this is exactly why Service Rebellion exists. Not because businesses are evil, not because staff don't care, but because average becomes "normal" so quietly that no one even notices the line has moved until they realise customers are leaving without saying a word. From the inside, things seem to look okay. But from the outside, the experience feels unremarkable, and unremarkable is dangerous in a world where switching businesses or suppliers is easy. Nothing is on fire, customers aren't storming the front desk, and sales haven't fallen off a cliff. Customers aren't leaving because something terrible happened. They are leaving because nothing memorable did.

Average service doesn't offend but it also doesn't attach. It doesn't give customers a reason to stay loyal when a competitor shows up with a slightly better offer, a slightly sharper price, or a slightly more convenient option. When customers describe a business as "fine" that's not a compliment, it's a warning sign. Fine doesn't mean that they are angry, it normally means that they are not invested. Fine means you're *an* option, not *the* option. When something slightly better appears, there's no resistance. They just drift. Drift is what kills businesses quietly.

BECOMING EASY TO LEAVE

And if you're reading this thinking "Yeah, we've probably become a bit like that", then good. That's not shame, that's awareness. You can't change what you keep excusing, or you keep walking past and not fixing. What a lot of business owners and large corporations seem to have missed is that when customers feel "fine" loyalty weakens. And loyalty is not a bonus. It's the backbone.

So if growth has slowed and you've convinced yourself it's just the market, or that people are more price conscious now, or you need to spend more on marketing . . . maybe. But maybe your business has simply become easy to leave, and no amount of ads will fix an experience people don't feel confident sticking with. Your customers only commit long term when the experience feels safe, smooth, and certain – and fine does not create that feeling. Fine keeps people until they see something better, whereas strong experiences create commitment even when it takes effort.

When referrals slow and you start working twice as hard for the same result, the business feels a lot busier but not stronger. That is the silent damage of average. It does not just lose a customer. It weakens the engine that brings the next one. And most businesses do not notice until they are spending more money to replace trust they used to earn naturally. That is why average is not neutral. Average feels safe, but it's not. It's expensive!

Remember the two businesses with similar offerings. The first consistently creating experiences where customers feel looked after, clear about what's happening, and confident that someone's on top of things, and the other delivering the outcome but leaving small question marks along the way. Not disasters, just moments of uncertainty. The first business builds relationships people rely on, creating loyalty. The second just completes transactions, making it replaceable.

EMOTIONAL BUFFER

When the market tightens, or a competitor rolls in waving a cheaper price, the business built on strong experience has something most leaders never factor in: a buffer. Not a legal buffer, not a financial one, an emotional one. It's the space between a customer thinking "Maybe I should look around" and actually doing it. That space exists when people feel confident with you. When they feel looked after, when the journey has been smooth enough that their brain says "We're fine here". That's the buffer.

And here's what most businesses don't realise. You don't lose that buffer with one bad day. You lose it by letting small behaviours slide for long enough that customers stop feeling looked after. They stop feeling anchored. And once they're not anchored, the next competitor doesn't have to be better, they just have to be clearer.

Inside a wolf pack, average doesn't survive. If one member drifts out of formation, it's noticed immediately. Signals increase and movement tightens. The pack doesn't tolerate neutral performance because neutral performance creates vulnerability. That's the difference between surviving and slowly weakening without realising it.

It's what makes a customer pause before leaving and give you the benefit of the doubt when something small goes wrong. It's what makes them ignore a slightly cheaper option because they don't feel like starting again somewhere else.

Most businesses don't even know this buffer exists. They only notice it once it's gone. So when pressure hits the market, those customers don't stay loyal out of principle. They leave easily because emotionally they had already loosened their grip.

The business built on average experience doesn't have a buffer. Its customers are already mentally halfway gone, and they don't need a big reason to switch. It just requires just a small nudge.

AVERAGE SERVICE AFFECTS PROFIT

What's ironic is that average service often hides inside businesses that are technically very good. The product works, the expertise is strong, and the team knows what they're doing. Leaders point to capability and assume that should be enough. Capability gets you on the list, experience keeps you there.

You think you're selling a product or a service. The customer thinks they're buying the outcome and the experience wrapped around it. Both get judged. If the experience feels neutral, it all feels neutral. And neutral is easy to replace.

Think about the last time you dealt with a business that did everything right on paper but didn't make you feel particularly looked after. Nothing went wrong, but nothing stood out either. You had no reason to complain, but you also had no real pull to go back. And you definitely weren't rushing to recommend them. That's "average" in action: technically fine but emotionally forgettable. And forgettable is dangerous because customers don't stay loyal to businesses they can barely remember.

While nothing looks broken on the inside, it's your commercial advantage slipping through your fingers. It's also contagious. When average becomes normal, small drops in standards stop being noticed, but together they lower the emotional quality of the experience. Customers don't measure these moments individually. They feel the pattern. And trust is built from patterns, not promises.

When customers can't predict how an interaction will make them feel, they stay cautious. Cautious customers compare, and comparing customers chase price, and price chasers don't build strong businesses. So average service doesn't just affect loyalty, it affects your profitability.

A business delivering average experience has to rely more heavily on marketing and sales effort to maintain revenue. More marketing spend means more pressure to close, and more pressure to close means more focus on transactions. The cycle feeds itself. It's not dramatic, it's slow leakage, and because it's slow, it's often misdiagnosed. Leaders think the issue is market conditions, competition, customer behaviour – those factors matter, but they often mask the underlying truth that the experience no longer creates enough emotional pull to counter them. No customer wakes up thinking "I'm leaving because the service is average". They just drift towards the place that feels easier.

They just drift towards the business that feels easier, clearer, safer. That's the silent damage of average.

TRANSACTIONS DON'T BUILD LOYALTY

Average service also creates a strange illusion inside businesses. If nothing appears to be going badly wrong, owners, leaders, and even board members assume things must be broadly okay. There are no disasters to fix, so attention goes elsewhere, usually towards growth tactics, new offers, marketing campaigns, or efficiency improvements. Meanwhile, the experience customers are having every day remains just good enough to avoid complaints but not strong enough to build attachment.

This is where businesses unknowingly trade loyalty for activity. You know what this means: from the inside, this increased activity looks like improvement, but from the customer's side, it can feel like the business is becoming more transactional, not more personal, even when the staff are decent people. They feel like a process being followed, not a person being served. The customer feels like they're moving through a system rather than being looked after by a business that notices them. That shift is subtle, but it changes the emotional temperature of the relationship.

My wife and I have five daughters (yep, that's why I have no hair!), and we live near a major shopping complex. I have had the utmost pleasure (insert sarcasm here) on many occasions in being invited to go with them shopping for clothes. One thing that I have increasingly noticed is the level of transactional experiences in some of these stores.

Part of the deal in me doing the whole shopping thing is there must be a "man chair" in the stores we go into. You know the one. The chair where a husband or boyfriend is staring at his phone while someone tries on a million things? Recently I was on a shopping safari with my wife, and I was sitting on a man chair just noticing what was happening. Every time a new potential customer walked into the store, the sales attendee would yell out, without looking up, "Hi, how's your day going?" The next new person would walk in the store, and the same thing happened again. "Hi, how's your day going?" It happened every single time someone walked in.

That is a transactional experience, right there. Yes, this lady has probably been instructed by her head office through her training that she needs to acknowledge everyone who walks into the store. Unfortunately, they haven't trained any further than that. Honestly, you could hire a parrot and get the same result.

When customers don't feel seen, they feel processed. And the moment customers feel processed, they start shopping like it's a transaction, not staying like it's a relationship. When customers feel like a case number rather than a person, they start behaving like shoppers instead of partners. Shoppers compare but partners stay.

That's why average service doesn't just affect whether customers like you. It affects the role you play in their mind. If you're a partner, you're part of their world. If you're a provider, you're replaceable.

Most businesses don't mean to slide into transactional mode. Things get busy and the focus turns to ticking boxes instead of looking after people. How many can we process today? How quickly can we get through this queue? What can we standardise to save time? All reasonable questions, but if reassurance and clarity aren't built into those systems, customers experience speed without safety, and speed without safety feels stressful.

You can see this in environments where processes are tight but communication is thin. Customers move through steps quickly, but they're not sure what's coming next. They get outcomes, but they don't feel guided. They get responses, but not context. The experience becomes efficient but emotionally hollow. Hollow experiences don't build stories customers want to repeat. And loyalty is a story. When someone talks about your business, they're not listing features, they're describing how it felt to deal with you. If the story is neutral, it doesn't get told. If the story includes small frustrations, it gets softened or withheld. But if the story feels reassuring and smooth, it spreads. What about average? Average doesn't travel.

This is where the emotional and commercial sides of the business are directly linked, even if they're rarely discussed together. Leaders often separate "customer service" from "growth strategy", but customers don't experience them separately. The experience they have shapes how often they come back, how confidently they refer, and how sensitive they are to price. When service feels average, customers switch their brain into comparison mode. When customers feel strong emotional confidence, they're more forgiving, more decisive, and less price driven. Neutral is risky. When people don't feel something, they analyse you, and you become replaceable. That's why average service increases competitive pressure without anyone announcing that's what's happening.

AVERAGE MAKES MORE WORK

Another thing average does is increase internal strain. When customers don't feel fully looked after, they ask more questions, they chase more often, and they need more clarification. Staff spend more time responding to follow-ups, smoothing things over, and re-explaining steps that could have been clearer upfront. That extra effort doesn't show up as a clear cost, but it adds to workload.

So average service not only reduces loyalty externally, but it also increases friction internally. Teams feel busier, and owners and management think demand is rising or expectations are increasing. In reality, part of the workload comes from managing the consequences of unclear or inconsistent experiences.

This is one of the most frustrating loops in business: experience drifts → customers feel less certain → they ask more, compare more, hesitate more → that creates more work for the team → the team feels stretched → behaviours become more rushed → the experience feels even more average. The system ends up feeding itself.

This is where Service Rebellion begins to matter. Not when things are broken. When things are just acceptable. Rebellion isn't against failure. It's against the slow normalising of average. In a world where switching providers takes minutes, average is not neutral. It's a slow loss of competitive advantage. Customers today have more visibility, more choice, and lower switching costs than ever. They have a new favourite four letter word . . . NEXT! When everything else looks similar, experience is the differentiator. Not dramatic experience, just consistent, reassuring, "on-top-of-it" experience. Average doesn't win those comparisons.

The dangerous part is that average can sit inside businesses that genuinely believe they care deeply about customers. The intention is there, and the effort is there. What's missing is the consistent translation of that care into behaviours customers can feel every time. Care that isn't visible to the customer doesn't build loyalty.

So the real issue isn't whether your business is good at what it does. It's whether the experience of dealing with your business is strong enough to make customers feel it would be a mistake to go elsewhere. If the answer is "We're fine", that's the signal. Fine doesn't protect you. Fine leaves the door open.

AVERAGE SERVICE IS EVERYWHERE

Average isn't industry specific. It pops up in shops, clinics, offices, job sites. The environment shifts, but people react the same way every time.

In a retail setting, average feels like being served without being noticed. The transaction happens, but there's no sense that anyone paid attention. The staff aren't rude. They're just not fully there. The customer leaves thinking it was fine. Not bad. Just . . . fine. That's what I call the "Ninja experience": it happened, but it left no trace. Next time, if somewhere else is closer, cheaper, or easier, the switch is effortless. If your service is average, you've just lowered the barrier for someone else to take your customers or clients. You've made switching feel safe.

In a business-to-business setting, average feels like communication that answers questions but doesn't remove doubt. Emails are sent, meetings happen, the work is technically right, but the client still feels like they have to chase updates, clarify expectations, or check progress. Again, it's not bad enough to trigger a complaint, but it's also not strong enough to build deep trust.

In direct sales or advisory environments, average feels like a relationship that revolves around transactions instead of care. The client hears from you when there's something to sell or renew, but not consistently in between. They don't feel forgotten, but they don't feel held either. When a competitor calls with a compelling offer, there's no emotional anchor holding them in place.

Across all of these settings, the pattern is the same. The experience is competent but not confidence-building. And confidence is what makes customers and clients stay still. The more confident people feel, the less they move. Uncertainty makes people shop around, average pushes them to compare, but strong service makes them stop looking.

Retail customers might scan by browsing other stores. Clients might scan by taking meetings with other providers "just to see". B2B decision-makers might scan by asking peers who else they use. It's the same behaviour expressed differently. The moment someone asks "Who do you use?" they've already stepped away from you. That's how referrals are born: when confidence drops.

AVERAGE MEANS MORE WORK TO KEEP CUSTOMERS

Average keeps customers in motion. This is why businesses sometimes lose long-term clients to competitors that don't appear dramatically better. From the inside it feels baffling. You've done good work for them for years. The outcome has always been solid, so why would they change? They changed because the relationship felt transactional, not relational. That's the real danger of average. It removes the emotional weight that keeps customers from drifting.

And it's not just about losing people. It's about how they behave while they're still with you. Average customers question invoices more. They challenge pricing more often, they need more reassurance, and they escalate small issues faster. They require more meetings, more follow-ups, more explanation. The relationship consumes more time and emotional energy.

Strong service reduces friction on both sides, but average service and experiences increases it. That's why average service quietly damages your business as it creates invisible workload. Staff spend more time clarifying, smoothing, and recovering than they would if expectations were clearer and reassurance more consistent upfront.

The big issue is that because average doesn't feel like a crisis, businesses often respond by pushing harder, but if the underlying experience remains average, all that extra effort sits on shaky emotional ground. You can squeeze a sale out of someone, or you can build something solid. This is where the real cost of average becomes visible. It forces the business to rely more on effort and less on attachment. Effort is expensive and exhausting whereas attachment is efficient and effective in the long run.

Businesses with strong service experiences don't just have happier customers. They have calmer customers. Calmer customers buy with less resistance, stay longer, and defend you when competitors appear. That stability reduces marketing pressure, sales pressure, and service recovery pressure.

Average businesses work harder every year . . . and go nowhere. The danger is that average often feels like the norm in an industry. If competitors also feel average, it's easy to believe that's just how things are. It only takes one business to do it better and suddenly average gets exposed. Customers don't need perfection. They just need to feel more certain in one place than another. And they will move for that, guaranteed. That's why average is not a safe middle ground. It's a slow erosion of advantage. It makes your business easier to compare, easier to question, and easier to leave.

The uncomfortable truth is that most businesses losing customers to "price" or "competition" aren't losing purely on price or capability. They're losing their customers or clients due to emotional confidence. Another option simply felt more reassuring, more on top of things, more certain. That's the silent damage. No explosion. No dramatic failure. Just a gradual weakening of the bond between customer and business until switching feels easy.

There's a phrase you hear in business all the time. "We're drawing a line in the sand." It sounds strong. It sounds decisive. It feels like leadership, but think about it. Sand moves. It gets kicked around, it shifts when pressure hits, and it disappears the moment things get uncomfortable. So what have you really drawn?

If you're serious about standards, you don't draw the line in the sand: you draw the line in the concrete! You set it once. It's clear, it's non-negotiable, and it doesn't depend on mood, targets, or how hard the week's been.

Service Rebellion is the line in the concrete. It's the decision that "fine" is no longer acceptable. Not because you want applause. And not because it looks good on a values poster. But because customers stay when standards don't move.

The Wolf Pack Standard is simple. Drift gets noticed; drift gets corrected. The standard holds, even when people are busy.

Because the businesses that win aren't louder. They're steadier.

Chapter summary

- Average doesn't come from intent – it comes from drift, pressure, and a slow lowering of what people start calling "normal".
- When customers describe a business as "fine" that's not a compliment, it's a warning sign that your business has simply become easy to leave.
- Average feels safe, but it's not – it's expensive.
- Building relationships people rely on creates loyalty – only completing transactions makes you replaceable.
- You create a buffer when the customer feels looked after and their brain says "We're fine here".
- You lose the buffer by letting small behaviours slide for long enough that customers stop feeling looked after.
- The business built on average experience doesn't have a buffer.
- Average service often hides inside businesses that are technically very good.
- Average service doesn't just affect loyalty, it affects your profitability – cautious customers compare and chase price.
- Businesses with strong service experiences have happier, calmer customers who buy with less resistance, stay longer, reducing marketing, sales, and service recovery pressure.

Chapter 4

BEING GOOD IS NO LONGER ENOUGH

One of the most dangerous beliefs in business is this one right here: we're good at what we do, so customers should stay.

It sounds reasonable, logical, like something you'd nod along to in a meeting, but it is completely wrong. Being good at the technical side of your business does not automatically make customers feel good about dealing with you. Capability and experience are not the same thing, despite most businesses talking like they are interchangeable.

You can be brilliant at the core thing you sell and still slowly leak customers – not because the outcome was terrible, but because the journey around that outcome felt clunky, uncertain, or just a bit too hard.

This is where a lot of "good" businesses get blindsided. They look at their credentials, their history, their product quality, their experience in the industry, and think, we're solid, we know our stuff, people should appreciate that. Don't get me wrong, customers do appreciate competence. It's just that they don't stay loyal to competence alone. Competence gets you considered, but the customer experience is what gets you chosen and chosen again.

You might have nailed the technical side, but if the customer felt like they had to chase, guess, remind, or keep an eye on things, they leave with uncertainty, not confidence. And uncertainty is the enemy of loyalty.

A lot of businesses confuse "no complaints" with "great experience". Those are not the same thing. No complaints often means that customers decided it was just not worth the effort to say anything. They got what they needed, it was fine, and they moved on. Fine is not loyalty. Fine is temporary.

Good businesses often get silence, and silence then gets mistaken for safety, when in reality silence can mean customers are quietly adjusting their expectations and their behaviour. They might still use you, but they start shopping around more, they hesitate before referring, and they take longer to come back. From the inside, it feels like nothing changed, but from the outside, confidence is quietly thinning out.

One of the biggest reasons this happens is because good businesses focus heavily on outcomes and assume the experience will look after itself. They measure what was delivered, not how it felt to get there. Was the job done, yes. Was the product correct, yes. Was the service technically right, yes. That is "outcome thinking".

Customers live in "journey thinking". How easy was it? Did I feel looked after? Did I know what was happening? Did I feel like a priority or a number? You can tick every outcome box and still fail the journey.

TOLERANCE

Here's where business owners and management get uncomfortable. A lot of this loss of customers does not come from big, dramatic failures. It comes from tiny bits of friction repeated over time: a delay here, a lack of update there, a handover that feels impersonal, or a promise that is technically kept, but only after the customer nudges you. Each one on its own seems small. Collectively, they build a story in the customer's mind. And the story is not "They're great". The story becomes "They're fine, but I have to stay on top of them".

That sentence is the beginning of the end of loyalty. The moment a customer feels like they have to manage you, instead of you managing things for them, the relationship shifts. You are no longer the safe pair of hands, you are just another supplier they need to monitor. That is not loyalty. That is tolerance.

You can see this clearly in industries like telcos or electricity providers. Their customers are often frustrated even though they know fully well that they could switch easily. They look around, but instead of feeling hopeful, they say to themselves, "They're all the same. Just another company promising great service to get my business, only to disappear into the system once I sign up." So they stay. Not because they're loyal – it's because they don't believe switching will reduce the hassle. That's tolerance! They are not choosing you. They are avoiding the pain of changing.

And tolerance is the weakest kind of customer retention there is because the moment one provider genuinely feels easier, clearer, more on top of things, customers move fast. The bar is not high, it's just rarely met.

You see the exact same thing in business-to-business relationships. A company sticks with a supplier, not because they are blown away, but because changing feels risky and time-consuming. They know the problems dealing with this supplier, but they've built workarounds. They've learned how to manage them, creating their own safety nets, double-checking timelines, sending reminder emails, and following up after meetings "just to confirm". From the supplier's perspective, the account is stable, but from the client's perspective, they are carrying extra mental load to make the relationship work. That's tolerance! They are not staying because it feels great, they are staying because leaving feels like effort.

But the moment a competitor comes along who feels organised, clear, and easy to deal with, the switch happens faster than expected. The client wasn't loyal because they were given no reason to be. They were just tired. If customers are staying because leaving feels like effort, that's not loyalty. That's just them not wanting the hassle.

Let's talk about tolerance for a minute. A lot of good businesses are surviving on customer tolerance, not customer confidence. Tolerance means the customer is putting up with the friction because the alternative feels like effort too. But the minute a smoother option appears – even slightly smoother – the customer drifts.

HOW NOT TO KEEP YOUR CUSTOMERS

Busyness is one of the biggest contributors to this problem. "We're flat out" becomes the unspoken excuse for everything. Here's the thing, though. You *should* be flat out. That's what a healthy business looks like. The difference is whether being busy affects how quickly you respond when someone is trying to give you money.

I have lost count of how many times I've made an enquiry to a new business and been told it hasn't been actioned because the team was "flat out". If you are too busy to respond when I am trying to become a customer, I already know what dealing with you is going to feel like later. You're teaching me what staying with you will feel like in the future. You will be too busy to keep me loyal.

Customers do not experience your workload. They experience your responsiveness. If busy consistently shows up as slower communication, less clarity, and more chasing, customers do not see a thriving business. They see a business that might drop the ball.

Another trap good businesses fall into is assuming their reputation will carry them. "We've been around for years, we've got experience, people know us." That may get you through the door, but it does not guarantee the experience today matches the reputation from five years ago. Reputation gets you considered, but experience keeps you relevant. Customers are not loyal to your history. They are loyal to how it feels to deal with you now.

Let's now talk about handovers because this is a silent killer. A customer talks to one person then gets passed to someone else, then someone else again. Each person does their bit, but the customer feels like they are being transferred, not looked after. From the business side, that looks like teamwork. From the customer side, it feels like nobody owns me. And if no one owns the customer's experience, the customer will. That ownership is emotional. It's not about job descriptions. It's about whether the customer feels like someone is personally making sure things are handled. If a customer ever feels like they are "in the system" instead of "with a person", you are in dangerous territory.

Communication style plays a huge role here too. Knowledgeable staff sometimes fall into the trap of talking at customers instead of talking with them. Information gets delivered, but reassurance does not. The customer understands the facts, but not the process, not the timing, not what happens next. Knowing what is happening reduces stress, but not knowing creates background anxiety. Customers rarely say "I feel a low level of uncertainty about this interaction". Instead their low comfort level influences their future decisions.

Good businesses also underestimate the power of follow-through. Not whether the thing eventually gets done, but whether the customer feels confident along the way that it will. There is a big difference between completion and confidence: completion is technical whereas confidence is emotional. And loyalty lives in confidence.

This is why you see technically excellent businesses struggling with retention while less skilled but more organised and communicative competitors grow. The competitor might not be better at the core task, but they make customers feel safer, clearer, and more looked after. Customers do not run spreadsheets on this. They remember how dealing with you felt.

YOU NEED STANDARDS TO GET BEYOND GOOD

I see the opposite of this every day in the business my wife, René, has built: The Temple Skincare & Spa, which has been named Best Day Spa in Australia numerous times. That didn't happen because of marketing campaigns, flashy promotions, or discounting. It happened because of standards that have been drilled into the business for more than twenty years. She calls it "The Temple Way".

It means every client – every single one – receives the same level of care, attention, and service, no matter who is looking after them, how busy the day is, or whether it's their first visit or their fiftieth. It's not a suggestion, it's not optional, and it's not dependent on someone having a good day. It's trained. It's reinforced. It's expected. There isn't a "depends on who you get" version of the experience. The standard doesn't move. So clients don't walk in hoping it'll be good, they walk in knowing how it's going to feel. That certainty builds trust, and trust is what builds loyalty. And over time, that loyalty turns into recognition, repeat business, referrals, and, yes, awards. Not because of marketing but because of deliberate behaviour.

Is it bulletproof? Of course not. There are hiccups and there are moments. There are team members who slip and don't follow the process like they should. But here's the difference: there is a standard. The line has been drawn in the concrete. So when something drops, it's obvious. It gets corrected, and it gets brought back to the level the business is known for.

Without a standard, mistakes become the culture, but with a deliberate and trained standard, mistakes are the exception.

Being good at what you do is the entry ticket. It is not the differentiator anymore. In most industries, competence is expected, but experience is where separation happens. Experience is not built by accident. It is built by behavioural standards, consistency, and leadership attention, not by hoping good people will naturally create it under pressure.

This is where many business owners and managers get caught out. They hire good people and assume good service will follow automatically. Good people under unclear standards and constant pressure default to survival behaviours, not experience behaviours. They focus on getting through the workload, not shaping the journey. It is not about whether your team cares – most do. It is about whether the environment makes it easy to consistently deliver an experience that builds confidence. That is a system issue, not a personality issue.

How can a business that is technically strong can still lose customers? It's simple. The outcome might be good, but the experience around it is not strong enough to make customers feel safe relying on you long term. In a market full of options, safe wins.

GOOD AND EASY TO DEAL WITH

Here is the practical part because this is not just philosophy. As a "good" business, if you want to stop losing customers, you need to start asking different questions.

- Where are customers having to chase us?
- Where do they not know what is happening next?
- Where do handovers feel like transfers instead of ownership?
- Where does busyness show up as disorganisation to them?
- Where are we assuming "fine" equals "great"?

These are not fluffy questions. They are commercial ones. Every point of uncertainty you remove increases the chance that a customer thinks "These people have got me". That feeling is gold.

This is not about being perfect. It is about being consistently reassuring, clear, and on top of things in the eyes of the customer. That is the gap good businesses need to close. That gap is not closed with more effort alone. It is closed with standards, awareness, and leadership that treats experience like a commercial priority, not a soft side topic. Because being good is no longer enough. There HAS TO be more!

Being good and easy to deal with . . . that is where the advantage sits because here is what most leaders do after reading something like this. They nod. They agree. They say "Yep, makes sense". Then they walk back into their business and nothing changes. Why? Because this problem hides in normality. It hides in what feels like "just how it is". Inside the business, this is just work. Outside the business, all this feels like is friction. And friction is the silent customer repellent.

The subtitle of my second book makes a lot of sense right here. *If Nothing Changes . . . Nothing Changes!* You can have a technically strong business that repels customers emotionally without even realising it. Nothing massive is happening, it's just that slow emotional drift away from you. That is a much more dangerous outcome. When they just drift, you tell yourself stories – the market is tough, people are price shopping, or competition is aggressive. That maybe the case, but often they simply found someone who felt easier.

Here is a brutal reality. Customers do not wake up in the morning excited to manage their suppliers. They are trying to run their own lives, their own businesses, their own problems. You might have solved their technical problem, but every time they have to follow up, clarify, or double-check you have added to their mental load. That mental load is exhausting and it takes a toll. Over time, that becomes associated with dealing with your business or your staff. "They're good . . . but dealing with them is a bit of work." That sentence should terrify you because "a bit of work" is the exact space your competitors are trying to win on.

This is why speed of response is not just operational, it is emotional. A quick, clear reply says "You're not alone in this, we've got it". A slow or vague reply says "You're on your own for now". Remember, customers rarely articulate this, they just feel it, and feelings drive behaviour.

LEAKING LOYALTY

Let's get very practical. If you want to see where good businesses lose customers, look at these moments.

- The gap between enquiry and first reply.
- The gap between promise and update.
- The gap between one staff member and the next.
- The gap between "job done" and "customer feels confident".

These gaps are where loyalty leaks. Now here's the uncomfortable reality. Most of these gaps exist because nobody owns them. Everyone assumes someone else is across it. The business has tasks, processes, systems, but it doesn't always have clear behavioural ownership of the customer's emotional experience. It has all been overlooked. The customer does not care who in your organisation is responsible. They just feel the result.

So when something slips, they're not trying to understand your systems. They're just thinking "Here we go . . . better stay on top of this. I need to keep an eye on these guys". That's when trust starts slipping. Not because of one disaster, but because of a stack of small moments that slowly add up. It's another wake-up call: being busy is not the same as being reliable. Customers cannot see your effort. They can only see your organisation from their perspective.

This is where good people get trapped in bad systems – they care and they want to do the right thing. But the way work is structured means communication, follow-up, and reassurance are the first things to drop when the pressure rises. And under pressure, humans revert to task completion, not experience creation.

If you want loyalty, you have to design for behaviour under pressure, not behaviour on a good day. Customers judge you on your worst days, not your best ones.

Here is another hard reality: a business that is technically strong but weak in experience discipline *trains* customers not to fully trust them.

The customer goes into protection mode – double-checking, asking for confirmation, sending reminders, allowing for delays that haven't happened yet – and that behaviour is a signal the customer does not feel safe handing things over fully. And if they do not feel safe, they are always open to alternatives.

CONFIDENT ENOUGH TO REFER

Let's now talk about referrals because this is where the damage really shows. Customers do not refer based purely on outcome. They refer based on confidence. When someone says "Do you know anyone?", they mentally replay how it felt to deal with you. If their memory includes chasing, uncertainty, and mild stress, they hesitate – even if the job was technically good. Referrals are emotional risk, and people only take that risk when they feel sure. No one risks their reputation on a business that felt like work. A good business with a shaky experience does not just lose repeat work. It loses word-of-mouth momentum, and that is expensive.

Here's what happens when it's done right. Imagine a business that is competent and incredibly easy to deal with. Clear updates, fast responses, obvious ownership, no guessing, no chasing, and even when things go wrong, they are proactive. Customers relax. When customers relax, loyalty grows, referrals grow, and tolerance for small mistakes grows (there's that buffer again). This is not about perfection, and it is about predictability and reassurance.

The goal is not "We never make mistakes". The goal is "Even when something happens, customers still feel in safe hands". That feeling is built long before anything goes wrong. And it is built through behaviour, not slogans, or motivational posters around the office walls.

CLOSING THE EMOTIONAL GAP

So here is the practical leadership shift this chapter demands. Stop asking only, "Did we deliver the outcome?" and start asking, "Did the customer feel confident the whole way through?" Stop measuring only what got done and start paying attention to how much chasing, guessing, and reminding customers had to do. Stop assuming your team's effort is visible, and start making clarity, updates, and ownership visible.

This is what it comes down to: good businesses lose customers not because they are bad at what they do but because they underestimate how much emotional safety drives commercial outcomes. Emotional safety is created by small, consistent behaviours that say, without words, "You don't have to worry. We're on it". And that is the gap most good businesses still have to close.

Most businesses never admit that when customers are leaving a good business the problem is almost never skill but the emotional tax of dealing with you. Every time a customer has to chase you, you've just charged them emotional tax. Every unclear next step is tax. Every impersonal handover is tax. Every moment of wondering what's going on is tax. And people don't stay where they feel taxed. Customers do not consciously say "I am paying too much emotional tax here". They just start leaning towards places where the tax is lower. The competitor does not have to be better than you, they just have to feel lighter.

That is the punch in the guts for many experienced operators. You have spent years mastering your craft, building expertise, improving technical delivery, and yet customers can still drift because someone else feels easier to deal with. That is not unfair – unfortunately that is reality. The businesses that accept this will win, but the ones that argue with it will lose.

Here is a leadership reality check. If your team is constantly saying "Customers are so demanding" or "People expect too much these days", you are not hearing the signal. You are hearing the symptom.

Expectations have not become unreasonable, the tolerance for friction has just dropped. The world customers live in outside your business is built around speed, clarity, and instant feedback. When your business feels slow, vague, or reactive, the contrast is amplified. You are not being compared to businesses in your industry. *You are being compared to every smooth experience your customers have anywhere else.*

The above sentence is something I really hope makes its way into the way you think and operate going forward. Read that sentence again. That is the standard now.

REPEATABLE BEHAVIOURS

Here is the final uncomfortable thing. Most businesses don't lose customers in the sales process. They lose them in the day-to-day stuff leadership never sees. The missed follow-ups, the updates that come after the customer has already chased, the handover that feels like being passed along without thought or care, or the delay no one bothers to explain. None of those feel big enough to cause a scene, but stack enough of them together and that's the story the customer carries about you, and that story is what decides whether they come back.

If you want to stop losing customers, it's not about some big dramatic change. It's all about what you do consistently. Every day be disciplined in communication, disciplined in taking ownership, disciplined in all aspects of follow-through, and disciplined in clarity. Not occasionally, not when there is time. Every day . . . especially when you are busy. Because busy is when standards slip. And when standards slip, confidence slips. And when confidence slips, customers start looking.

This is where the Wolf Pack Standard starts to matter. In a pack, no one says, "That part isn't mine." The outcome and the safety of the group are shared responsibilities. If one wolf drops the ball, the pack feels it. In business, if one interaction drops the standard, the customer feels it.

The pack doesn't run on big moments. It runs on repeatable behaviours. That's what most good businesses are actually missing. They're not short on talent, not short on effort, and they're not short on intention. They're missing consistency in the way the experience shows up.

The businesses that close that gap don't just keep more customers. They become less stress to deal with, and low-stress businesses are addictive. Customers come back because it feels easier. They refer because it feels safe. They forgive mistakes because the overall experience has built trust.

That is not soft, that is just commercial.

If you want the simple takeaway from this chapter, here it is: being good gets you in the game, but being easy to deal with keeps you there.

If you're a technically strong business and you are losing customers, this isn't a capability problem. It's a standards problem, and standards don't set themselves.

Chapter summary

- Customers don't stay loyal to competence alone – it gets you considered, but the customer experience is what gets you chosen.
- A lot of businesses confuse "no complaints" with "great experience".
- If a customer feels like they have to manage you, instead of you managing things for them, the relationship shifts – you are just another supplier they need to monitor, and that is not loyalty, it is tolerance.
- With tolerance, customers are not staying because it feels great, they are staying because leaving feels like effort.
- Without a standard, mistakes become the culture, but with a deliberate and trained standard, mistakes are the exception.
- Good people under unclear standards and constant pressure default to survival behaviours, not experience behaviours.
- As a "good" business, if you want to stop losing customers, ask:
  - Where are customers having to chase us?
  - Where do they not know what is happening next?
  - Where do handovers feel like transfers instead of ownership?
  - Where does busyness show up as disorganisation to them?
  - Where are we assuming "fine" equals "great"?
- Customers do not refer based purely on outcome, they refer based on confidence.
- Stop asking only "Did we deliver the outcome?" and start asking "Did the customer feel confident the whole way through?"
- When customers are leaving a good business the problem is almost never skill but the emotional tax of dealing with that business.
- Being good gets you in the game, but being easy to deal with keeps you there.

Chapter 5

THE LIE OF "WE'RE TOO BUSY"

There is a sentence almost every business says at some point, and most people genuinely believe it: "We're just flat out."

It gets said in cafés, trade businesses, salons, clinics, professional firms, call centres and corporate offices like it is a badge of honour. Phones are ringing, emails are piling up, orders are moving, people are running from one thing to the next. From the inside, it feels like momentum, it feels like demand, and it feels like proof that things are working the way they should. Busy feels like success when you are inside it. Busy even feels like protection, and it always feels like progress.

Busy may feel productive, but it does not always feel professional to the person on the other end. If something slips, busy explains it. If communication drops, busy softens it, or if a follow-up is late, busy justifies it. The story of busy keeps everyone safe internally because it means no one has to look too closely at behaviour. But customers do not experience your reasons, they experience your behaviour. And behaviour is what tells them whether they can relax or whether they need to stay alert.

What most people do not realise is that busy is addictive. It gives everyone a reason for everything. Once "busy" explains everything, behaviour stops being questioned and standards quietly bend. Not in a dramatic way, but in tiny ways that feel reasonable at the time. A message that could have had detail and context becomes one line, an update that could have been proactive and informative waits until someone asks, a handover that could have been reassuring and meaningful becomes transactional.

BUSY IS NOT THE ISSUE

The problem is not that businesses get busy. The problem is what busy quietly starts to excuse. Busy is not the issue . . . using busy as permission is!

On the weekend, I decided to take a break from writing this chapter, so my wife and I went up to the local shopping centre. She had a few gift cards for a particular clothing store and wanted to grab something for our upcoming holiday. She just wanted to have a quick look before they closed.

We walked up to the store at 4.45 pm, so we were all good as the closing time was 5pm. But the doors were already about three-quarters shut. We squeezed through anyway, thinking maybe they were just starting to pack up slowly. Inside, one staff member was already cashing up while other staff members were vacuuming the floor. Cords were stretched across the shop, and at one point we were asked to step off one of the cords so she could keep cleaning.

No one said hello. No one asked if we needed help. No one said, "Just letting you know we close in 15 minutes." It wasn't rude in an aggressive way. It was worse than that, it was indifferent. We were technically allowed in, but we weren't welcome. So we left.

From their perspective they were probably just being efficient. Getting a head start on wrapping up the day and talking about how slow it had been. From our perspective the store had already emotionally closed. That's what busy does when there isn't a standard protecting the customer. Internally, they were productive, but externally, they were pushing customers out the door before the door was even shut.

When we got back to the car my wife said, "Don't buy me any more vouchers from there." We didn't complain, we didn't make a scene, we just made a quiet decision and left.

That's how revenue disappears. Not in explosions but in moments. And that's the lie of busy. It convinces you that because you're doing things, you must be doing the right things. But if the customer feels like an inconvenience, it doesn't matter how efficient your closing procedure is. You're not too busy. You've just let the standard slip.

WHAT SLIPS WHEN YOU'RE BUSY?

When pressure rises, something has to give. And what usually gives first is not delivery. It is the experience around delivery. Communication gets shorter, updates get delayed, follow-ups become reactive instead of proactive, and conversations become more about clearing tasks than reducing uncertainty. None of it is intentional. It's about survival.

Inside the business this makes sense, as there is a lot to do, and everyone is trying to keep up. From the outside, the customer does not see survival, they feel distance. They do not experience your workload. They experience your attention – or lack of it.

This is where businesses often misread the situation. People inside are working hard and assume customers must feel looked after. Your team can be flat out and the customer can still feel ignored or like they are chasing. Yet a business can be under pressure and still make customers feel calm and confident. The difference is not effort, it is behavioural discipline.

Two businesses can be just as busy but come across completely differently. One stays organised and makes customers feel looked after. The other lets the pressure leak into every interaction and customers feel like they're in the way. The difference isn't workload, it's what happens to behaviour when things get hectic.

Busy doesn't usually lose customers because of one massive stuff-up. It's the little signals that quietly tell people they are not the priority right now: the short reply that feels rushed, the update that never quite comes, the answer that technically responds but doesn't actually give clarity, or the handover that feels like a pass rather than someone saying "I've got this". Their behaviour shifts and they stop relaxing with you. They double-check, follow up "just to make sure", hold back from referring because they're not totally sure what experience the next person will get, and compare more than they used to, even if they don't say it out loud.

WHAT DOES BUSY DO TO YOUR BRAND?

When pressure hits, behaviour becomes the brand. Not your logo, and not your mission statement. The tone of your reply, the speed of your follow-up, the clarity of your update. That's your brand! The one that customers actually experience when they deal with you on a normal Tuesday, not on your best day. Customers don't respond to what you say your brand is. They respond to how it feels to deal with you when things are busy.

This is where a lot of businesses get it backwards. They spend money telling the market who they are, while everyday customer and client experiences are quietly telling a different story. You can run ads about care, quality, and service all day long, but if the lived experience feels rushed, unclear, or hard work, the customer believes the experience, not the campaign.

Branding is what you promise, but experience is what people report back to others. And word-of-mouth always outranks advertising. That's why businesses can have great branding and still struggle with loyalty. The message is strong, but the experience doesn't back it up. When that gap appears, marketing stops being an asset and starts becoming noise. Your customers or clients don't compare your slogan to your competitor's slogan. They just compare how it felt to deal with you. And you don't want your customer experience becoming the best advertisement your competitor never had to pay for.

You see this all the time with big telcos. The ads tell you the customer is their number one priority. Happy families, smiling staff, big, bold promises about being here for you. Then you actually have an issue. You're on hold, you finally get someone, you explain the whole thing. You then get transferred, and you have to explain it all over again. Then to another department and once again start from the top.

By the end of it, you don't feel like a priority. You feel like a case moving through a system that was designed around their structure, not your sanity. From their side, the process probably makes sense. From your side, it feels like hard work just to get something sorted, especially when the problem wasn't even yours to begin with.

That's the gap. The gap that is frustrating your customers and clients more than you realise. The marketing says one thing, but the actual lived experience says something else. And customers always believe the experience. No campaign can out-argue a lived frustration.

BUSYNESS ERODES TRUST

When the two don't match, the promise doesn't just weaken. It works against them because subtle reactions shape loyalty. Guided feels safe, but chasing feels stressful, and customers do not stay loyal to stress. When people sense a business is stretched, they get cautious. They hesitate to add extra requests because they do not want to be a burden. They hold back from referring because they are not sure the experience will be consistent. From the inside, the team feels overwhelmed. From the outside, the customer feels unsure. This is the trap as busy often looks like growth, yet it can be the moment loyalty starts quietly leaking.

Under pressure, humans simplify. They shorten conversations, focus on what must be done now, reduce the explanation, or stop offering context unless asked. None of this comes from deliberate and bad intent. They care – it's just that when they are flat out, they stop thinking about how it feels and start thinking about what's next. The focus shifts to clearing the job, not calming the person. Boxes get ticked, but confidence doesn't get built. No one complains in that moment, and nothing explodes. But something changes and the customer stops relaxing. And once that happens, the relationship starts thinning, even if the work is technically fine.

There's a moment in every busy day that tells the truth about your business. It won't show up in a report, and no one will raise it in the next staff meeting. It's the customer who hesitates because the room feels frantic, or the client who rewrites their email so they don't sound like a burden, or the person who decides not to ask the next question because they can feel the pressure on the other end. Nothing blows up. No complaint gets lodged. But a quiet decision gets made: I'll manage more of this myself.

Customers shouldn't feel like the project manager in their own purchase. And yet here they are, lowering what they ask for, preparing for delays, and building buffers. They tell themselves "They are good, just busy". And every time they do that, a little trust moves from the business back onto their own shoulders.

Trust is not just believing someone is capable, trust is relaxing your guard. And busy environments slowly teach customers not to relax.

You can watch this happen across a whole day. A customer calls and gets voicemail instead of a person. They send an email and receive a one-line reply. They ask for clarification and get told someone will get back to them. No single moment is dramatic, but the emotional tone of the relationship changes. By the end of the interaction, the customer is doing more of the thinking, more of the remembering, and more of the following up. They don't leave angry, they leave guarded.

When reassurance drops, incoming communication rises. When communication rises, the team feels more stretched. And when the team feels stretched, reassurance drops further. Busy creates more busy. You feel like you're moving all day, but nothing actually feels under control. It's like being stuck in a roundabout. Plenty of motion, no real progress.

One clear, proactive update can remove ten reactive questions. Behaviour can reduce your workload, not just add to it. It is not a people problem – it is a behaviour loop, and loops do not fix themselves.

Customers do not reward effort they cannot feel because invisible effort does not build visible trust. Customers do not see how long the day was, they feel clarity. They feel responsiveness, and they feel certainty. If those feelings drop, no amount of internal effort balances the scale.

There is also a psychological shift that happens when pressure stays high. People stop aiming for excellent interactions and start aiming for acceptable ones. Acceptable feels realistic and excellent begins to feel unrealistic. It becomes a "this will do" standard. That shift is subtle, but it changes the emotional tone of the business. Customers feel when they are receiving acceptable rather than being cared for, and acceptable does not build loyalty. The business can be growing on paper and thinning out in reality. The numbers go up, but the confidence holding customers in place goes down.

This is where most businesses have a fork in the road. One path blames workload. The other owns behaviour. You can add people all day, but if the behaviour doesn't tighten up, customers still feel the drift. Busy is not the signal for you to relax standards. Busy is the signal to tighten them.

THE STORY YOU TELL

There's something else that quietly happens when busy sticks around for too long. It stops being a season and starts becoming part of the identity. "We're always flat out" gets said with a little bit of pride in it. Exhaustion becomes proof that the business is in demand. Stress becomes normal instead of temporary. And once that happens, no one really questions it anymore.

Because questioning busy can feel like questioning effort. And no one wants to accuse a hard-working team of not trying, but effort and discipline are not the same thing. You can be exhausted and still be sloppy, but also, you can be stretched and still be reactive. You can be working huge hours and still be quietly leaking trust. The danger isn't that you're busy. The danger is when busy becomes the story you tell about yourselves.

In a wolf pack, the standard doesn't drop just because the terrain gets rough. The pace might change, the environment might shift, but formation holds, position holds, and the signals stay tight. If one wolf drifts out of line because it's "flat out", the pack doesn't applaud the effort. That drift creates exposure.

Business is no different. When pressure rises, customers aren't measuring how hard you're running. They're watching whether the formation still holds, whether communication stays clear, whether ownership stays visible, and whether someone is still in control.

That's the real lie of "we're too busy". It sounds responsible. It sounds admirable. And it even sounds successful. But underneath it can be hiding something far more dangerous, a slow acceptance that behaviour under pressure doesn't matter as much as output. Customers feel that shift long before anyone inside the business admits it's happening. And they will forgive pressure, but they won't forgive unpredictability.

So when pressure rises, clarity has to rise. When workload increases, reassurance has to increase. When pace picks up, ownership has to become more visible. Because busy doesn't break culture, it exposes it! In a wolf pack, pressure doesn't lower the standard. It reveals who's holding it.

BUSY DAYS ARE THE TEST

So the real question is not "Are we too busy?" The real question is "What happens to our behaviour when we are busy?" Busy does not damage loyalty by itself, but busy *without discipline* does.

Growth without burning trust is not about working harder. It is about behaving differently when the pressure is on. Because most businesses behave better when things are calm and worse when things are intense. That is backwards.

Customers judge you on your busy days, not your quiet ones. Anyone can look organised on a slow Monday. But your real brand is revealed on the day everything goes wrong at once – when phones are ringing, emails are stacked, three people are off sick, a job runs over time, a delivery is late. That is when customers decide whether your busyness feels controlled or contagious.

Controlled busy feels like momentum, but contagious busy feels like risk. Customers do not think those words, they feel them, and feelings drive behaviour long before logic catches up. This is why busy periods are not operational tests – they are emotional tests. They test whether the customer still feels safe while you are under pressure. If the answer is yes, loyalty deepens, if the answer is no, loyalty thins. And thinning loyalty does not show up immediately. It shows up later when referrals slow down, when repeat business becomes less predictable, and when customers start saying things like "They are good, just hard to get hold of lately". That sentence should worry any business owner more than a complaint. When customers complain, they're still in the relationship, but when they go quiet, they're halfway out the door.

THE BUSY TAX

Here's where it gets interesting. Busy does not just change how staff behave, it changes what staff notice. Under pressure, attention narrows and people stop seeing small emotional cues – the confused look, the hesitation before asking a question, or the slightly unsure tone in an email. Those signals get missed because the brain is focused on clearing the next task. Everything becomes transactional. From the inside, the day feels productive, but from the outside, the experience feels thinner. And thin experiences do not create stories worth repeating, and referrals are stories.

This happens everywhere. The business changes, but unfortunately the behaviour doesn't. In a small business, busy might mean the owner answering calls between jobs and sending quick replies at night. In a corporate, busy might mean meetings stacked back-to-back and emails answered between conversations. In both cases, communication gets shorter, updates get delayed, and context gets dropped. It's different environments but the same outcome.

When a customer feels like they have to work a little harder to stay informed, that extra effort is the hidden tax of busy. Every time a customer has to chase, clarify, or double-check, they are paying that "busy tax".

Customers rarely say "I am paying too much emotional tax here". They simply start leaning towards places where the tax is lower. Where the competitor does not have to be better than you, they just have to feel lighter to deal with. That is the uncomfortable reality: you can be technically excellent and still lose to someone who is simply easier to deal with.

BEHAVIOUR UNDER PRESSURE

Now here is the leadership shift that changes everything. Stop asking only "Are we delivering?" and start asking "How does it feel to deal with us when we are under pressure?" That question changes the entire operating system of a business. Because that is the true test of your service culture. A strong culture does not collapse under workload, it becomes more deliberate. Communication gets clearer, not shorter. Updates get earlier, not later. And ownership becomes more visible, not less. Why? Because someone decided that behaviour under pressure matters more than behaviour on a good day.

That decision is not made by chance. It is made by setting standards that stick. You don't draw a line in the sand. You draw a line in the concrete, so those standards will never move or wash away.

That's what Service Rebellion is really about: behaviour that doesn't move when the pressure rises.

Standards are what protect customers from the internal chaos they never see. Without standards, customers feel the chaos you think you're hiding. Standards are what make busy feel safe instead of contagious. Without standards, behaviour follows energy, and busy energy is frantic. With standards, behaviour follows principles, and principles create calm, even when pace is high. That is the difference between a business that feels overwhelmed and a business that feels in control. One leaks trust. The other builds it.

So the lie of "we are too busy" is not about time. It is all about responsibility.

Pressure explains behaviour in some businesses, but in strong businesses, standards do. Busy is not an excuse, it is a spotlight and it shows you who you really are as a business.

Your customers are watching that spotlight more closely than you think. They are not judging how many emails you had. Instead they are judging how it felt to deal with you while you had them. If they still felt clear, confident, and looked after, you are building something strong. But if they felt rushed, unsure, or like they were adding to the strain, you are slowly teaching them to look elsewhere.

This is not about perfection as things will still inevitably go wrong. It's about how the customer feels while those things are going wrong. Do they feel informed, remembered, like someone owns their situation? If it's a yes, trust holds, but if the answer is a no, then trust thins. And trust is the real asset busy businesses cannot afford to burn.

So here is the practical takeaway. The moment you hear your team say they are flat out, that is not the cue to lower expectations, it's the cue to tighten behavioural standards. It's when clarity matters more, follow-up matters more, ownership matters more, and reassurance matters most. Because busy days are when customers decide whether they can relax with you or whether they need to stay alert. Always remember that customers and clients do not stay long where they feel they have to stay alert.

That is the real cost of busy without discipline. Most of the time there are no immediate complaints and no dramatic exits, just a quiet drift or reduced referrals.

The businesses that win long term are the ones that never let busy change how it feels to deal with them, not the ones that are never busy. That is the difference between growth that is stressful and growth that is sustainable. One burns trust whereas the other compounds it.

The question is not whether you are busy. The question is whether your customers still feel safe while you are. That answer decides everything because busy doesn't build trust. Behaviour under busy does. Customers don't care how busy you are, they care how it feels to deal with you when you are.

Remember: busy doesn't build trust, it exposes it because anyone can look professional on a quiet day. Who you become under pressure is the version your customers remember.

Chapter summary

- Busy may feel productive, but it does not always feel professional to the person on the other end.
- If the customer feels like an inconvenience, you've just let the standard slip.
- A business can be under pressure and still make customers feel calm and confident – it's not effort, it's behavioural discipline that makes the difference.
- When pressure hits, behaviour becomes the brand regardless of what the marketing says.
- When reassurance drops, incoming communication rises, meaning the team feels more stretched, causing reassurance to drop further.
- When pressure rises, customers are watching whether the formation still holds, whether communication stays clear, whether ownership stays visible, and whether someone is still in control.
- Busy does not damage loyalty by itself, but busy without discipline does.
- Customers judge you on your busy days, not your quiet ones.
- Every time a customer has to chase, clarify, or double-check, they are paying a "busy tax".
- Stop asking only "Are we delivering?" and start asking "How does it feel to deal with us when we are under pressure?"
- Without standards, behaviour follows energy, and busy energy is frantic.
- With standards, behaviour follows principles, and principles create calm, even when pace is high.
- The moment your team says they are flat out is not the cue to lower expectations. It's the cue to tighten the standard.

— PART 2 —

THE SERVICE REBELLION

Chapter 6

WHEN SERVICE STOPS BEING EVERYONE'S JOB

Here's something most businesses never notice happening, but once you see it, you can't unsee it: there was a point where service stopped being how the business worked and quietly became someone's job. It didn't happen because the leaders stopped caring. It crept in quietly as the business grew – roles became more defined, departments formed, and suddenly "customer service" existed as a function rather than a standard that applied to everyone. And that quiet structural shift changed the entire experience customers have.

This is where Service Rebellion starts drawing a line. Because the moment service becomes a job title instead of a standard, you've already lost control of how the experience feels. It won't show up in your structure, it will show up in your reputation.

The moment service becomes a department, everyone else subtly relaxes their grip on the experience side of the relationship, not because they don't care, but because in their head that part now lives somewhere else. Sales focuses on selling and moving the deal forward, operations focuses on delivery and getting the job done, accounts focuses on billing and getting paid, and suddenly the emotional side of dealing with the customer gets filed under customer service as a separate activity. It's like it became a gift with purchase, not the thing that goes before everything else.

The problem is that customers do not feel those internal handballs, they just feel the temperature change. One person is warm and explains what is happening, the next person is quick and mechanical because they are only doing their own part. The customer is left doing the stitching in their own head to make it feel like one experience. As care slowly gets boxed up, customers don't experience one relationship with your business anymore, they experience it in pieces. One conversation feels human and reassuring, the next feels like a process they're being moved through. One person takes the time to explain and calm things down, the next just pushes them to the next step. No one is trying to create that contrast, but the way the business is structured quietly produces it.

SPLITTING UP SERVICE

The problem is customers don't experience your internal set-up, who does what, or how your team is split. They only experience what it feels like to move through you. And if that feels like walking into different worlds depending on who they speak to they don't call that structure, they call it hard work. This isn't about how hard people are working. It's about whether they're working together.

In a wolf pack, no one carries "customer service" as a role. They're not thinking in departments, they're thinking in formation, in alignment, in protecting the run together, and when that formation holds the movement feels powerful and steady, but the moment it loosens, even slightly, exposure creeps in.

This shows up everywhere. In retail, energy is high until the sale, then anything outside the transaction gets redirected. In professional services, relationship-building is strong early, but delivery later feels mechanical. In B2B, pre-sale feels attentive, post-sale feels procedural. The pattern is the same. In each case the business believes it provides good service because parts of it absolutely do. The customer, however, experiences the journey as a whole, not as individual departments performing well in isolation. When care isn't everyone's standard, it becomes something that switches on and off. It shows up strongly at certain touchpoints and thins out in others. That's where the drift begins.

When service lives in a department, it often activates most strongly when something goes wrong. A complaint triggers attention, a problem triggers urgency, and care suddenly becomes very visible. But when things are running "normally", the experience runs on autopilot. Expectations are assumed rather than clarified, follow-ups depend on individual habits, and ownership is not always obvious.

Autopilot is where average grows. Tasks still get done, but reassurance disappears. The signals that tell customers someone is thinking about their experience quietly fade.

And this is the opposite of Service Rebellion because rebellion in this context isn't loud, it's disciplined. It's choosing not to drift into autopilot just because nothing is technically broken. And it's deciding that experience is never accidental. And average, as we've already seen, doesn't create loyalty. It creates customers who stay until something easier or clearer appears.

No one sat down and said, "Let's water down the customer experience." It happened because the business grew and everyone focused on their piece. The work got divided, but so did the care. Efficiency improved, but the feeling of being looked after stopped belonging to everyone and started belonging to no one. So care became something that happened in moments, not something that defined the environment. Moments matter, but environments matter more. A customer remembers how it felt overall, not which department tried hardest. If the environment feels fragmented, then care feels occasional rather than dependable.

Customers feel that immediately. They don't think in terms of departments or job descriptions, they just sense when the experience flows and when it feels like they are moving between separate worlds. When it flows, confidence builds, but the moment uncertainty creeps in, even in small ways, customers start looking around.

What makes this shift even more dangerous is that it feels efficient internally. When service becomes a department, leaders believe they have "covered" the customer experience. There's a team for that, processes for that, a channel for that. On paper it looks structured, but in reality it often means the emotional side of the relationship only gets attention at specific points, instead of being woven through everything.

OWNING THE TASK AND PROVIDING GUIDANCE

So now the business starts running on task ownership instead of experience ownership. Task ownership is "My part is done". Experience ownership is "The journey is still mine". Each team focuses on completing its part of the job. Sales hands over, then operations execute, accounts invoices, and support handles issues. Each area might perform well according to its own measures, yet no one is truly accountable for how it feels to move from one stage to the next. No one is thinking about the customers journey through all of these stages.

The customer ends up bridging the gaps without realising they are doing it. They feel like the baton in a relay race, being crudely handed from one person (or department) to another. From the inside, the business sees a process. Processes are invisible to customers unless they create clarity. If the process creates handovers without reassurance, then what looks organised internally feels disjointed externally, and from the outside, the customer feels the seams.

You can tell this is happening when customers start saying things like "I wasn't sure who to speak to" or "I thought someone else was handling that" or "I had to explain it again". None of those comments point to incompetence. They're pointing to disconnect. And disconnect makes the customer feel like the system isn't working for them, rather they are working for it.

Guidance builds trust, whereas navigation creates effort. When customers feel guided, they relax because someone else is clearly in control. When they feel like they have to navigate, they stay mentally engaged, tracking steps, remembering details, and filling in gaps the system did not cover. That mental effort changes behaviour over time.

When service is a shared standard, everyone sees the customer journey as something they are part of, not just the section that sits inside their job description. People will naturally think about what the next step looks like for the customer, not just whether their own task is complete. When service is a department, the handover mindset takes over: "That's done, now it's with them." Responsibility moves on, and so does emotional attention.

That handover mentality is one of the biggest sources of uncertainty in customer experience. Handover language often sounds neutral internally, but emotionally it sounds like detachment. Each time responsibility shifts without visible continuity, the customer feels the temperature of the relationship drop slightly. Each transition is a potential drop in reassurance. If the next person doesn't pick up the emotional thread, the customer feels the relationship cool slightly. One drop doesn't seem like much, but several drops in a row change the tone of the entire journey.

PERSONALITY ISN'T ENOUGH ON ITS OWN

This is also where personality starts doing the heavy lifting that systems should be handling. In environments where service isn't a universal standard, the experience depends heavily on who the customer happens to deal with. One person naturally communicates clearly and follows up, but another is more task focused and assumes silence means everything is fine. Both are doing their job, but the customer experience swings depending on the individual. When experience swings, confidence swings with it. Customers start assessing each interaction separately instead of trusting the whole relationship. Customers don't separate these interactions into categories in their mind. They don't say to themselves that the operations team was efficient, but the service team was great. They form one overall impression of what it is like to deal with your organisation. If that impression feels unpredictable, their trust stays cautious. Cautious trust behaves differently from confident trust. It asks more questions, compares more options, and refers less often.

That's why moving service into a department often leads to a business that is technically well organised but emotionally uneven. There are clear roles, clear responsibilities, and clear processes, yet the feeling of being looked after depends too much on which doorway the customer happens to walk through. When the experience depends on entry point, it's not a standard, it's a lottery.

Most leaders never intended this outcome. They were trying to create structure, accountability, and efficiency. What got lost along the way was the idea that service is not a function that sits alongside everything else: it is the way everything else is delivered.

Once that idea fades, the experience becomes something that is handled when needed rather than something that defines how the business behaves all the time. And when care becomes occasional instead of constant, customers never fully relax into the relationship. They stay slightly alert, slightly cautious, slightly open to alternatives. That alertness is quiet, but powerful. It is the difference between a customer who defaults to you and one who keeps scanning alternatives just in case. That's the cost of losing coordination.

WHERE CULTURE MAKES A DIFFERENCE

And this is the point where the mindset has to shift because what looks like a structural decision is actually a cultural one. When service becomes a department, the message the organisation quietly sends itself is that looking after the customer is a task to be handled, not a way of operating. It sounds like a small difference, but it changes everything because a task is something you do when it pops up, whereas a way of operating is how you behave all the time, especially when no one's reminding you.

If care only shows up when a ticket is raised, a complaint is made, or a request lands in the service queue, then care becomes reactive.

Customers get looked after when something prompts it, not because the environment is designed to make them feel looked after by default. Care that only shows up when something goes wrong feels very different from care that's simply part of how the place runs because when service only appears after a problem it feels like a reaction, not the foundation of how the business operates. Customers quickly sense whether they had to trigger attention or whether support was there before they even thought to ask.

You can see this difference clearly when comparing organisations that still treat service as a core operating principle versus those that have boxed it into a function. In the first group, the way people communicate, set expectations, follow up, and take ownership has a similar tone across all roles. In the second group, those behaviours change depending on which part of the business you are dealing with, which you experience as unpredictability.

Unpredictability isn't dramatic, but it's exhausting, and it chips away at trust. Each small uncertainty adds weight until the relationship feels heavier than it should. It forces customers to stay slightly alert. Even when the work itself is solid, the journey feels heavier than it needs to. Over time, that weight changes how people behave. They become more cautious, more likely to compare, and less willing to commit their reputation through referrals.

This is where the shift from service as a standard to service as a department gradually starts affecting growth as customer loyalty softens. Customers stay, but they don't attach. Attachment requires emotional continuity, not just functional delivery. Without that continuity, customers remain transactional even when they are satisfied. They buy, but they don't advocate. They engage, but they keep their options open.

From the inside, the business still believes it provides good service because the service team is working hard and handling issues well. From the outside, customers experience care as something that appears in bursts rather than something that defines the relationship. That inconsistency erodes confidence.

When care is integrated, customers sense a steady hand behind the experience. They don't have to think about who owns what. They don't feel the transitions between teams. The journey feels like one conversation, not a series of handovers. That feeling of continuity is what allows customers to relax, and relaxed customers stay longer, refer more, and create less friction.

When care isn't integrated, the customer becomes the glue. They repeat themselves, fill the gaps, and carry the story from one person to the next. Nothing feels broken . . . but nothing feels joined either. And that's where loyalty starts to drift.

WHO SHOULD WE BE TRAINING?

Let me show you how this looks like in the real world. With one of my businesses, Customer Culture, I'm constantly asked to come into businesses to "fix customer service" and to do some staff training. And almost every time, the brief is the same. "Can you run a customer service session for our team?" I turn up, and guess who's in the room . . . the customer service team. Not sales, not operations, not accounts. Not the people who actually shape most of the customer journey. Just the department with "service" in their title, and that, right there, is the whole problem.

Because the people in that room already care. They already try. They already deal with the complaints, the follow-ups, the frustrated customers, and the messy handovers from other parts of the business. They're the ones patching up the experience after it's already been chipped away elsewhere. Meanwhile, the departments that create most of the uncertainty for customers aren't in the room. Most of the time even the sales team aren't in the room, and they're the ones setting expectations right from the start!

You cannot train one department to carry an experience that five departments are shaping. And yet that's exactly how most businesses are set up. They treat service like the clean-up crew, not the operating system. The experience keeps breaking in the same places, and the service team keeps being asked to fix a feeling they didn't create. This is why the solution is not to strengthen the customer service department alone.

Most organisations need a different operating standard, not a better department. High-performing teams don't pass the customer around and hope care survives the journey. They move as one unit, where responsibility for how it feels never gets handed off. That's the difference between fragmented service and the Wolf Pack Standard, where the pack protects the experience together, so the customer never falls through the cracks.

This is the standard the rest of this book builds on. It's not service as a department, and it's definitely not care as a moment. It's a way of operating where the experience is protected across the whole journey, no matter who the customer is dealing with and no matter how busy things get. Because in a real wolf pack, the job doesn't change depending on who's closest. The pack moves together, and the one thing they never drop is protection. That's the shift.

THE SHIFT

If you want this chapter to land as a shift in thinking, the shift is simple. Service is not the department that cleans up the mess, service is the standard that stops the mess being created in the first place. It is the behaviours that keep the experience joined up, even when five different people touch the customer journey, and even when the business is growing. Once leaders get that, they stop asking how to improve customer service and start asking a much sharper question: Where are we handing the customer off without realising that we are also handing off responsibility for how it feels?

That question alone changes everything. To answer it is to move service out of the box and back into the bloodstream of the organisation. Not as a slogan, not as a training day, but as a shared understanding that how the customer feels while dealing with the business is everyone's responsibility. Every department and every person should be asking themselves "How does what we do here change the customer's experience out there?"

When that happens, behaviour changes in small but powerful ways. People think about what the next step looks like from the customer's side, not just whether their own task is complete. Handovers include emotional context, not just information. Follow-ups happen because they are part of the standard, not because someone remembered. That is when service stops being something the business does at certain times and starts being how the business operates all the time.

And when that shift happens, customers feel it immediately because the experience stops depending on departments and starts feeling coordinated. Coordination builds certainty. Certainty builds trust. Trust is what holds relationships steady when alternatives appear.

Without that, even good businesses with strong teams and solid processes find themselves easier to leave than they ever intended to be.

Service cannot live in a department because experience does not happen in a department. It happens in the spaces between roles. And if nobody owns those spaces, customers pay for it.

Chapter summary

- The moment service becomes a department, everyone else subtly relaxes their grip on the experience side of the relationship because in their head that part now lives somewhere else.
- When care gets handed off and boxed into roles, the customer doesn't experience one relationship anymore, just pieces of one.
- When care isn't everyone's standard, it becomes something that switches on and off, showing up strongly at certain touchpoints and thinning out in others.
- When service lives in a department, it often activates most strongly when something goes wrong.
- With task ownership, the customer ends up bridging the gaps without realising they are doing it.
- When service is a shared standard, everyone sees the customer journey as something they are part of, not just the section that sits inside their job description.
- In environments where service isn't a universal standard, the experience depends heavily on who the customer happens to deal with.
- The departments that create most of the uncertainty for customers are the ones that need the training, not the ones with "service" in their title.
- Service is not the department that cleans up the mess, service is the standard that stops the mess being created in the first place.

Chapter 7

STANDARDS ARE THE REBELLION

The word rebellion usually makes people think of noise and confrontation, like people pushing back loudly against something they don't agree with. That's not what this is about. Service Rebellion isn't dramatic, and it isn't emotional. It's disciplined, it's quieter than people expect, and it's the decision to raise the standard at the exact moment when it would be easier to let it slide.

Most people think standards drop because someone makes a bad decision. But that's rarely how it happens. Standards drop because *nobody* makes a decision! Everyone is busy, everyone is juggling, everyone assumes someone else will hold the line, and before you know it, what used to be exceptional quietly becomes acceptable.

That's drift, and drift never announces itself. It just shows up later when customers start saying things like "It's fine" or "They're good, just hard to deal with lately". That sentence right there is the sound of standards slipping. And it's not because people stop caring. The environment slowly changes what feels acceptable. Pressure builds, workload increases, and behaviours adjust to cope with reality. What used to be considered not good enough slowly becomes normal, things that once would have been followed up are now assumed to be fine, and communication that once would have been clearer gets shorter. None of it feels like a turning point at the time. It quietly sneaks in.

That's why this isn't rebellion against customers or management. It's rebellion against drift. It's the moment someone notices that the experience customers are having is starting to thin out and decides that this can't quietly become the new standard. It's not a big speech or a dramatic reset. It shows up in small decisions that most people wouldn't label as cultural, yet they are exactly that.

CHOICES UNDER PRESSURE

Under pressure, there's always a temptation to trade clarity for speed and reassurance for efficiency. These choices don't feel serious in isolation, but together they reshape how the experience feels from the customer's side. Over time, the journey becomes more procedural and less reassuring. The business is still working, yet the emotional quality of the experience has shifted.

I had an accounting firm I used to love dealing with. Nothing flashy, just solid. Over the years I had found them a good company to deal with. They were easy, informative, and on top of things most of the time. I always knew where I stood with them, never had to chase them. If something needed doing, it got done, and if something was coming up, they told me. It felt like someone was watching my back. They didn't mess up my tax, miss a deadline, or drop the ball. They just got . . . harder to deal with.

Replies got shorter, updates got vaguer, and ownership got blurry. Instead of "Here's what's happening next", it became "Yep, we're onto it". Instead of "We'll take care of that", it became "You might need to check with . . ." Instead of them staying ahead of things, I started having to follow things up. There was no drama, no blow-up, and no complaint. There was just more effort needed from my end.

And that's the shift most businesses never see. Because from their side, nothing changed. The work still got done, and the numbers were still right. From my side, everything changed. I stopped feeling looked after, and I started feeling responsible for keeping things moving. I didn't leave in anger, I didn't send an email saying I was unhappy. I just stopped relying on them. I started to compare. I asked around, and I became open. Open to maybe there could be a better option.

Once a customer becomes open, loyalty is already weakening. They didn't lose me because of a mistake. They lost me because it slowly felt like more work to deal with them.

That's drift. And drift is what kills businesses that *technically* still do a good job. Service Rebellion is what stops that drift before the customer ever feels it.

SETTING THE STANDARD

This is where the Wolf Pack Standard comes in because a real pack does not move based on mood or convenience. It moves based on shared behaviour. The front doesn't decide one thing while the back does another. Protection isn't situational. It's constant. That is the model. Not someone stepping up on a good day, and not personality-driven effort. It's behaviour that stays steady even when the environment isn't.

Service Rebellion is the refusal to let convenience set the bar. Because convenience always whispers "Just this once". Just this once we will skip the follow-up, just this once we will send a short reply, just this once we'll assume they understand. But customers do not experience "just this once", they experience patterns, and patterns are what form trust. It's the understanding that the experience customers have is not something you deliver when you have spare time. It is part of the work itself.

When that mindset takes hold, behaviours change in subtle but powerful ways. People start thinking about what the customer needs to feel confident, not just what needs to be completed operationally. This is where a lot of organisations get it wrong. They think improving service means launching a program or bringing in new tools. Sure, that stuff can help, but none of it sticks if behaviour doesn't change. This is not a systems problem, it's a standards problem, and it comes down to what the business treats as non-negotiable.

I get asked all the time to come in and "train the staff", or to "come and speak at our staff meeting". I always say the same thing to the CEO or HR lead: I can run the session, and I can do the talk, but if the way people behave the next day isn't reinforced, coached, and protected, it fades, and it's just motivation, not activation. One session doesn't build culture . . . repetition does and standards do. What gets talked about after the training matters more than what happens in the room.

That's how Service Rebellion – the Wolf Pack Standard – actually began. It started as a keynote: one conversation and one moment that made people stop and look at how their behaviour was really landing. But it became very clear, very quickly, that one talk doesn't change a culture. It can spark awareness. It can start momentum. But it doesn't set behaviour.

So we started working inside individual businesses. It became an in-house program – not just for staff, but for leadership as well. Teams and managers went through it together, over weeks and sometimes months, resetting what "good" now meant in real situations, under real pressure. The point was never motivation. It was all about behaviour, repetition, reinforcement, and drawing a line that didn't move just because things got busy.

Over time, some organisations went even further. They trained their own internal facilitators, so the standard didn't rely on an external voice. Because if a behaviour only holds when someone is watching, it isn't embedded. And if leadership doesn't reinforce it daily, no program ever sticks.

That evolution is what led to me writing this book. Not as an idea, but as the result of weeks and months of embedding behaviour into the DNA of businesses that wanted the line set in concrete, and seeing what happens when standards are deliberately built, tested, and protected inside real businesses with real people doing real work.

SERVICE NON-NEGOTIABLES

Every business has areas where standards are protected. Financial matters don't get skipped because the day is busy. Safety rules don't get relaxed because the warehouse is under pressure. Legal compliance doesn't get ignored because a deadline is tight. People understand those things are built into how the business operates. They have to be done right and all the time. Nobody says "We're too busy to reconcile the accounts this week". Nobody says "We're flat out, skip the safety checks". Because those standards are not optional.

Service Rebellion says customer experience behaviour belongs in that same category: non-negotiable. Not because it's nice, but because it protects loyalty, and loyalty protects revenue. This is where rebellion becomes disciplined rather than emotional. It's actually less dramatic than people think. It's the tone in the email, it's the extra sentence that explains what happens next, it's the check-in that wasn't strictly required. It's the level of ownership that says "I'll handle this" instead of "You'll need to speak to someone else". It's the small things that send the big signals, and that's what tells a customer whether they can relax with you or whether they need to stay alert.

I wrote a book years ago called *Forget the Elephants, Watch Out for the Fleas*. Same idea. It's rarely the big, obvious stuff that ruins the experience. It's the little things that get overlooked, that slowly erode trust. It's not about trying harder. It's about refusing to let the bar drop just because circumstances are tough. Discipline creates consistency, and consistency is what customers interpret as reliability.

When customers experience that reliability repeatedly, their confidence increases. They feel like someone is on top of things, even when the environment is busy. Those feelings change behaviour. Decisions get easier and loyalty deepens. Then referrals become more natural.

NO EXCUSES

Rebellion like this is not loud or dramatic. It's the steady commitment to protect the experience when it would be easiest to protect yourself instead. What makes this idea uncomfortable is that it removes one of the most common hiding places in business: the belief that "this is just how it is". Every industry has stories it tells itself about why service standards are hard to maintain. The work is complex, customers are demanding, margins are tight, systems are old, teams are stretched. All those things can be true, but they don't automatically explain the experience customers end up having. They explain the environment, but they shouldn't define the standard.

This is where most businesses quietly give themselves permission. Pressure becomes the excuse. "We're doing our best", "It's been a big week", "They'll understand" becomes the normal mantra, but customers don't experience your context. They experience your behaviour, and behaviour under pressure is the truest signal of what your real standards are. Anyone can be impressive when the phone isn't ringing and the inbox is quiet. Standards only mean something when they hold in the moments that test them. This is the line Service Rebellion draws. Not in the sand, remember, in the concrete.

Pressure does not get to vote on behaviour, and workload does not get to rewrite expectations. Being busy explains why things are hard. It should not explain why the experience drops in response. Rebellion, in this sense, is the moment a business stops using context as an explanation for lowered behaviours. Rebellion doesn't ignore reality, but it refuses to let reality quietly redefine what good looks like. Instead of asking "What can we get away with today because we're busy?", the question shifts to "What behaviours do we protect, even when we're under pressure?"

That shift sounds subtle, but it changes how people make decisions in the middle of a hectic day. When someone knows that clarity and reassurance are part of the job, not an extra, they build those behaviours into how they work. They explain next steps, even if they are moving quickly. They check that the customer feels confident, not just informed.

They take ownership rather than simply passing the issue along. None of this requires grand gestures. It requires consistency.

People underestimate the power of small things. Customers don't build trust from big heroic moments. They build it from repeated signals that say "These people are on top of things". There's a clear next step, a proactive update. There's someone taking ownership instead of deflecting. These are not dramatic moves, but they reduce customers' uncertainty. When uncertainty drops, confidence rises. When confidence rises, decisions get easier. When decisions get easier, loyalty follows. This is the chain reaction most businesses miss.

THE PERSONALITY LOTTERY EFFECT

This is also where Service Rebellion moves away from the idea of personality and towards the idea of standards. Many businesses rely on individual "service stars" to carry the experience. Certain people are naturally good with customers, naturally proactive, naturally reassuring, and leadership quietly leans on them as proof that the culture is strong.

The problem is that culture built on personality is fragile. What happens when those individuals are away, overloaded, or leave? The experience shifts. Same business, same systems, but a completely different feeling. The customer doesn't think, "That person is off today." They think, "This place is inconsistent." Rebellion is about making the standard strong enough that it doesn't depend on a few people carrying the emotional weight. When the standard is clear, people don't have to be extraordinary to create a strong experience. They only have to operate within the expectations of the environment.

The Wolf Pack Standard removes the lottery effect because a pack doesn't rely on one strong wolf to carry the group. Its strength is in the way they move together: if one adjusts, the others adjust; if the environment changes, the formation holds.

That's the point. The customer shouldn't feel a difference depending on who they deal with because the behaviour should be recognisable across the whole business. That's when service stops being luck and starts being culture. And that's when customers stop bracing themselves and start relaxing.

This is why rebellion is not about asking people to care more. Most people already care. It's about making it easier to show that care consistently, even when things are messy, and it's about removing the silent permission that pressure gives to lower the bar. That silent permission is powerful. No one announces it. It shows up in phrases like "That's good enough for now", or "We'll sort that later", or "They'll understand". Each one sounds harmless, but together they redraw the line between acceptable and excellent. Rebellion is the refusal to redraw that line downward.

THE WAY FORWARD

When enough people in a business start protecting the standard instead of adjusting it, the culture shifts. Customers notice it before anyone writes a new mission statement. They feel more certainty, they feel more coordination, and they feel like the business is on top of things rather than scrambling behind the scenes. That feeling is what separates businesses that customers tolerate from businesses customers trust.

And trust, once established, does more for growth than most marketing campaigns ever will. Marketing creates expectation, but experience creates memory, and memory is what people share. When Service Rebellion becomes the norm, customers don't just stay. They talk. They refer without being asked. They defend your brand in conversations you'll never hear. That is growth without chasing.

This is where Service Rebellion stops being an idea and starts becoming a filter for everyday behaviour. Tolerated businesses get compared, but trusted businesses get chosen. And chosen businesses grow without shouting.

Once you understand that drift happens through small, tolerated compromises, you start seeing rebellion not as a big change initiative but as a series of micro-decisions. In the middle of a normal day, under normal pressure, people are constantly choosing between what is convenient for the moment and what protects the standard. Those choices rarely feel dramatic, and they happen in seconds. Do I send that update now or leave it until later? Do I clarify expectations properly or assume they'll work it out? Do I take ownership of this issue or move it along because technically it belongs somewhere else? Each of those moments looks operational on the surface, but together they define how the experience feels.

Rebellion is choosing the standard in those moments and doing it consistently. Enough choices in the right direction and the experience feels solid. Enough in the other direction and it feels shaky. And shaky experiences get compared where solid experiences get trusted.

That's the quiet part people miss. It may start as a workshop, but it becomes real in the moments no one's watching. It's not about perfection, and it's not about slowing everything down or adding layers of process. It's about protecting the few behaviours that have the biggest impact on how safe customers feel. Clear communication, visible ownership, consistent follow-up, and coordinated handovers are not extras. They are the signals customers use to decide whether they can relax. When those signals are steady, customers don't need to manage the relationship. Their confidence grows quietly, and confident customers behave differently. They stay longer, they decide faster, and they refer more easily because the risk feels lower.

That's the commercial side of rebellion. It isn't soft. It directly affects loyalty, referrals, and price sensitivity. When customers trust the experience, they don't make every decision through a cost comparison lens. When trust is shaky, price becomes the safest variable to lean on.

Rebellion, then, is not against management, customers, or systems. It is against the slow acceptance of average. It is the steady insistence that how the business feels to deal with matters just as much as what the business delivers. A program can introduce it, a department can support it, but only the mindset sustains it. Leaders protect it by reinforcing standards in everyday conversations, not just in strategy sessions. Teams protect it by holding the line on behaviours, even when it would be easier to let them slide.

This isn't about being service focused, it's about being behaviour focused. Because behaviour under pressure is the real brand of a business. Anyone can look organised when it's calm. The pack is revealed when the environment is rough. Over time, this creates an environment where customers experience consistency without needing to ask for it. The experience feels coordinated, not dependent on luck. And when customers feel that kind of consistency, trust stops being fragile and starts becoming the foundation of the relationship.

That is why Service Rebellion is not an initiative. It is a stance. A quiet, disciplined stance that says the experience we create under pressure is the experience we will be known for. Because this is the uncomfortable truth. It's not the blow-ups that lower the bar. It's the quiet tolerance of "good enough" that does the damage.

Every time a business says "That's fine for now", it is voting for a lower future. Service Rebellion is the opposite vote. It is the quiet insistence that the experience customers have under pressure is the experience worth being known for, which is what separates businesses that survive from businesses that lead.

That is what Service Rebellion really is. Not noise. Not complaint. A disciplined refusal to let the bar drift downward just because the environment is pushing that way.

Chapter summary

- Standards drop because nobody makes a decision, not because of bad decisions.
- Under pressure, trading clarity for speed and reassurance for efficiency reshapes the emotional quality of the customer's experience.
- The Wolf Pack Standard is behaviour that stays steady even when the environment doesn't.
- One training session doesn't build culture . . . repetition does and standards do.
- If a behaviour only holds when someone is watching, it isn't embedded, and if leadership doesn't reinforce it daily, no program ever sticks.
- Every business has areas where standards are protected, and Service Rebellion says customer experience behaviour belongs in that same category.
- Rebellion is the steady commitment to protect the experience when it would be easiest to protect yourself instead.
- Culture built on personality is fragile.
- When enough people in a business start protecting the standard instead of adjusting it, the culture shifts.
- Clear communication, visible ownership, consistent follow-up, and coordinated handovers are not extras – they are the signals customers use to decide whether they can relax.

Chapter 8

TRANSACTIONS DON'T BUILD LOYALTY

One of the quietest but most damaging shifts in modern business is the move from relationships to transactions, and most organisations don't even realise it has happened. They still talk about customers, and they still use the language of service. They still say things like "We value our clients", but unfortunately the behaviour underneath tells a different story. The focus is on the moment of exchange rather than the experience of the relationship.

Transactional thinking is subtle. It doesn't look like poor service. It looks efficient, it looks like getting the job done. It shows up when the primary goal becomes completing the sale, closing the ticket, finishing the job, sending the invoice. Once that point is reached, attention shifts to the next task. Customers can feel that shift immediately. Before the sale, communication is quick, friendly, responsive. After the sale, communication becomes more procedural. Before commitment, there is energy and reassurance. After commitment, there is execution but less emotional presence. It isn't that the business stops caring, it's that the emotional effort drops once the exchange is secured. That drop is what customers interpret as being processed rather than looked after.

Here's the problem in plain language: transactional thinking feels efficient to the business, but it feels like abandonment to the customer.

DOWNGRADING RELATIONSHIPS TO TRANSACTIONS

You see it everywhere. Before the sale you get "Absolutely, we can help with that", "Let me explain how this works", and "Great question". After the sale you get "Your job number is 4827", or "Please refer to the website", or "We'll be in touch". Nothing is technically wrong. The job still moves forward, but the tone changes, the energy shifts, and the warmth gets replaced with workflow. Customers notice that faster than most businesses realise. And once they feel like a number instead of a person, the relationship shrinks down to the size of the transaction.

And here's the dangerous bit. Customers mirror how you treat them. If you reduce the relationship to a transaction, don't be surprised when they reduce you to a price. Treat them like a transaction and they'll treat you like a supplier. Treat them like a relationship and they'll treat you like a partner. Suppliers get compared, but partners get protected.

I'll give you a classic example nearly everyone has experienced. Car dealerships. Before you buy, it's five-star everything. Calls actually get returned. There are conversations that include "Just checking in", "Do you have any questions?", and the old faithful, "If there's anything we can do for you, please let us know". You feel important, you feel seen, you feel like you matter, and you feel that your business matters to them.

Then you sign the contract and pay for the car, and suddenly the relationship falls off a cliff. You don't get "How's the car feeling now you've had a week with it?" You don't get "Anything you're unsure about with the features?" You don't get "Let's make sure everything feels right". What you do get is a call: "Just letting you know you'll be receiving a survey about your experience. A ten would be great." Think about that. The only proactive contact after the sale isn't about you, it's about their score. It's all about how they look to their head office, not what impression and memory they could leave with you.

That's transactional thinking in its purest form. Before the sale, relationship energy, but after the sale, internal metrics. From the dealership's side, the job is complete. The car has been delivered, the paperwork has been done. From the customer's side, the relationship has just entered its most uncertain phase – they've spent a big chunk of money, they're learning the car, and they're hoping they made the right choice. And the only time the business calls is to protect a KPI. That's not support, that's optics. And customers can smell the difference.

I had the complete opposite experience with my first Harley Davidson. On the anniversary of the day I bought it, the original sales guy would call me. Every year . . . for more than ten years! Not to try and sell me something, just to ask me if I was still enjoying my Harley. He knew that the relationship doesn't stop after the purchase. Who do you think I refer people to when they are looking to buy a Harley Davidson? That one phone call each year did something no survey ever could.

AFTER THE DEAL

Here's the part most businesses miss. Customers don't consciously analyse this, they just feel the shift. They go from feeling looked after to feeling processed. And when customers feel processed, they behave transactionally in return. They shop around next time. They don't default to you, and they definitely don't refer with confidence. Not because the product was bad, but because the relationship stopped the moment the transaction did. That's how relationships quietly die.

Transactional thinking treats service as something that helps close the deal. Relational thinking treats service as the environment the deal lives inside. The difference is where attention goes after the exchange. This is the moment where most loyalty is either built or lost. The second a customer commits, their brain flips into a quiet loop: "Did I just make a smart decision?" You don't hear it, but it's running around in their heads.

Relational businesses know this and step in quickly. "Here's exactly what happens next", "Here's who looks after you", "Here's when you'll hear from us", and "If anything feels unclear, call me".

Transactional businesses disappear into process. Silence gets filled by doubt and doubt makes people watch more closely. Watching then turns into managing. Managing something quickly kills ease. And ease is one of the strongest drivers of loyalty in business.

In a transactional mindset, once the payment is made or the agreement is signed, the focus turns inwards: delivery schedules, internal coordination, operational efficiency. All important, but the customer is now one step removed from the centre.

In a relational mindset, the moment after commitment is when reassurance matters most because that is when the customer is most emotionally exposed. They've committed, so their money, time, or reputation is now tied to the decision. That's when the quiet question starts running in their head: Did I make the right choice? If the business disappears into process at that moment, uncertainty grows. If the business stays present, clarifies next steps, and checks that the customer feels confident, trust deepens. Transactional thinking doesn't see that moment as critical. It sees it as the start of the job. Relational thinking sees it as the start of the relationship.

This applies whether the transaction is a retail purchase, a service engagement, a long-term contract, or a public-service interaction. The structure changes, but the psychology is the same. The exchange is not the emotional finish line for the customer. It is the point where their need for certainty often increases.

When businesses treat that point as the end of the emotional effort, the experience starts to feel one-sided. The customer gave commitment, but the business shifted focus. Over time, this creates a pattern where customers feel valued when they are buying and managed when they are owned. That shift might not be obvious in any single interaction, but across the journey it changes the tone of the relationship. And tone is what drives loyalty.

A SINGLE EVENT OR AN ONGOING STORY?

When a business operates with a transactional mindset, it starts measuring success in closed loops rather than ongoing confidence. A deal is won, a job is completed, a case is resolved, and those outcomes get ticked off as proof that things are working. What doesn't get measured is how the customer felt in the space between those points. That space is where loyalty either grows or weakens.

Customers don't experience their relationship with a business as isolated events. They experience it as a continuous experience. When that flow feels like a set of separate transactions, each with its own start and finish, the relationship feels shallow. When the flow feels continuous, with the business present throughout, the relationship feels stronger than any individual exchange.

Transactional thinking goes all in on the deal . . . then mentally moves on the second the invoice is paid. Relational thinking keeps attention on how the customer is travelling through the journey, even when nothing urgent is happening. This is why customers often describe certain businesses as “being there” for them. They don’t necessarily mean constant contact. They mean the business feels present and engaged beyond the specific moments of buying or problem-solving. They feel remembered, not just recorded.

Transactional environments struggle with that because their internal systems are built around events: a sale triggers activity, a complaint triggers activity, a renewal triggers activity. In between those triggers, the relationship can go quiet. From the business side, that quiet feels efficient, but from the customer’s side, it can feel like absence, and absence creates space for doubt. And doubt is expensive – not emotionally, but commercially. When doubt creeps in, three things happen: customers start double-checking you, then they start comparing you, then they stop referring to you. They may not leave, but they stop growing with you. This is where businesses say “Customers just aren’t loyal anymore”. No . . . Customers are loyal where they feel safe.

Transactional thinking makes customers feel served, whereas relational thinking makes customers feel supported. There’s a huge difference between those two. This is particularly visible in long-term service relationships. A client might sign a contract, receive the agreed delivery, and have no major issues. Yet if communication between milestones is thin and largely reactive, the client can feel disconnected from the provider. The relationship becomes something that exists on paper rather than something they feel in practice.

CONTACT WITHOUT SELLING

Here's a simple test to see if your business has slipped into transactional mode. Ask this question: If we stopped actively selling for the next 30 days, would our customers still hear from us? If the answer is no, you're operating transactionally.

Relational businesses don't only contact customers when money is due, renewal is close, or something went wrong. They stay visible between events. Not with spam, but with presence – a check-in call not tied to a sale, a "just letting you know" update, a reminder before the customer needs to remember, or sharing something useful with no invoice attached. These are not marketing moves. They are reassurance signals, and reassurance is the emotional glue in relationships.

When a competitor shows up with a more proactive style, even if the offering is similar, the contrast is powerful. The client suddenly experiences what it feels like to be actively looked after rather than simply served. That contrast exposes how transactional the previous relationship had become.

In retail and direct service environments the same pattern plays out on a shorter timeline. A customer receives friendly attention when purchasing, but once the sale is complete, follow-up, support, or post-purchase communication feels minimal. The business may believe it delivered exactly what was promised. The customer feels like the energy was tied to the transaction, not to them.

Over time, customers learn to treat transactional businesses transactionally in return. They shop around more often, they negotiate harder, and they feel less obligation to stay. The relationship becomes purely economic because the emotional layer that creates attachment was never consistently built. There is no emotional attachment anymore.

Relational thinking changes where effort is invested. In a wolf pack, protection doesn't stop once the hunt is done. The pack doesn't say "Food delivered, job over". Formation holds before, during, and after the hunt. They move together. That's relational thinking.

Transactional businesses think the job is done when the product is delivered. Relational businesses think the job is done when the customer feels confident. That's not soft, that's behavioural discipline. It means you don't end communication at delivery, you transition it. You don't say "All good", you say "Here's what happens now." That small change keeps the emotional thread alive. It recognises that trust is built in the periods where nothing dramatic is happening. It shows up in check-ins that are not tied to selling, in updates that are not triggered by complaints, and in communication that keeps the customer feeling oriented even when things are running smoothly. It doesn't mean constant contact, it means having visible continuity.

When customers feel that continuity, they stop experiencing each interaction as a separate transaction and start seeing the business as a steady presence. Transactional thinking focuses on exchange, where relational thinking focuses on experience. And in markets where options are plentiful, experience is what makes customers stay beyond the next transaction. This is where the cost of transactional thinking becomes properly visible because it doesn't just affect how customers feel, it changes how the business grows.

BUSINESS GROWTH

When the relationship is treated as a series of exchanges, the business becomes dependent on creating new transactions to maintain momentum. Sales activity has to stay high because the emotional attachment that drives repeat behaviour and referrals has not been consistently built. Customers come, buy, and move on without much friction, but also without much loyalty, creating a constant need to replace customers rather than deepen relationships.

From the inside, this gets blamed on the market, competition being strong, customers being price sensitive, or loyalty being low. All of those statements can be true, but they are often symptoms of a transactional environment rather than unchangeable conditions. When customers don't feel a relational connection, their decisions naturally default to the most obvious variables, which are price, convenience, and speed. Without the relational layer, there is nothing else to anchor the decision.

This is where businesses start feeling like they are working harder for the same results. Marketing spend increases to keep the pipeline full, and sales pressure rises to convert quickly. Margins get squeezed because price becomes the main lever available. The business might be busy, but it doesn't feel stable, which is often a sign that the emotional side of the relationship has been underinvested.

Relational thinking shifts the focus from individual transactions to the health of the relationship over time. It recognises that every interaction either strengthens or weakens the customer's confidence in continuing the journey. When the experience consistently reduces uncertainty and shows visible care, customers begin to see the business as a safe default rather than just one option among many. That safety changes the customers' behaviour, and they don't compare as aggressively, don't delay decisions as often, and are more willing to refer because their reputation feels protected. They give the business more room when small issues occur because the relationship has depth. There's that buffer again. None of this comes from grand gestures. It comes from how the business behaves after the transaction, not just during it.

This is also where Service Rebellion connects directly to growth. Rebellion in this context means refusing to treat the exchange as the finish line. It means recognising that the moment after commitment is when the relationship actually begins to take shape. And it means keeping emotional presence in the journey even when the operational work is underway. The specific actions vary by industry, but the principle is the same: the business stays visible as a partner in the experience, not just a provider of a product or service.

When that becomes the norm, you stop chasing transactions and start building a base of customers who feel connected, not just served. That base stabilises revenue and reduces the need to constantly chase new business. Transactional thinking is a treadmill. Relational thinking is leverage.

And the commercial reality?

- Transactional growth – sell, deliver, move on, repeat.
- Relational growth – sell, support, deepen, expand, refer, repeat.

One depends on constant acquisition. The other multiplies what you already have.

DIFFERENT WAYS OF THINKING

Here's where this becomes practical because relational thinking is not about being "nice" or adding endless extra touches. It's about changing what the business treats as a continuation point instead of an endpoint. Most transactional businesses unconsciously treat these moments as the finish line: sale made, job delivered, invoice sent, problem resolved. Relational businesses treat those same moments as transition points. Instead of thinking "Done", they think, "What does the customer need to feel confident from here?" That question changes behaviour immediately.

- After a job is delivered, the transactional mindset says "Great, that's complete". The relational mindset says "Do they know what happens next, what to expect, and what to watch for?"
- After an issue is resolved, the transactional mindset says "Ticket closed". The relational mindset says "Do they feel reassured, or just processed?"
- After a purchase, the transactional mindset says "They've bought". The relational mindset says "They've trusted us. Have we made that feel safe?"
- This is not about more work. It's about finishing differently. A relational finish always includes one of three things: clarity, continuity, or confidence.
- Clarity is explaining what happens next before the customer has to ask.
- Continuity is showing that the relationship is still active, not paused until the next transaction.
- Confidence is checking that they feel steady, not just informed.

If you want to see whether your business operates transactionally or relationally, listen to how things end. Transactional endings sound like: "All good", "That's sorted", "Let us know if you need anything". Relational endings sound like: "Here's what happens from here", "I'll check back in next week once you've had time with it", "If anything feels unclear, call me straight away". Same job. Different experience.

And this is where most leaders get it wrong. They try to improve service at the *start* of the journey . . . better sales process, better onboarding, better scripts. All good things. But loyalty is not built at the start. It's built in the handovers, the quiet periods, and the way things are finished. Transactional thinking focuses on how things begin, whereas relational thinking protects how things continue. That's the difference between customers who buy again and customers who stay.

And here's what a lot of people miss. Relational growth reduces chaos. Confident customers ask fewer reactive questions, panic less, need less reassurance, and stay longer.

It feels like more work to care, but it's actually less work over time. And in a world where customers have endless choices, building trust over time beats chasing one more transaction. You just need to make sure you and your staff are the customer's reason for choice, not their reason for change.

This chapter isn't saying transactions are bad. After all, every business has them. What kills loyalty is when the transaction becomes the ceiling instead of the starting point. The sale is not the relationship, the payment is not the finish line, and the delivery is not the end. That's the beginning.

Service Rebellion is the refusal to treat the moment money changes hands as the moment care changes direction. The businesses that win long term are not the ones that close the most deals. They're the ones that keep the relationship alive long after the deal is done.

That's not premium service. That's baseline discipline.

Chapter summary

- One of the quietest but most damaging shifts in modern business is the move from relationships to transactions.
- Transactional thinking feels efficient to the business, but it feels like abandonment to the customer.
- If you reduce the relationship to a transaction, don't be surprised when the customer reduces you to a price.
- Transactional thinking treats service as something that helps close the deal – relational thinking treats service as the environment the deal lives inside.
- In a transactional mindset, once the payment is made or the agreement is signed, the focus turns inwards.
- In a relational mindset, the moment after commitment is when reassurance matters most because that is when the customer is most emotionally exposed.
- Transactional thinking makes customers feel served, whereas relational thinking makes customers feel supported.
- Transactional businesses think the job is done when the product is delivered – relational businesses think the job is done when the customer feels confident.
- When the relationship is treated as a series of exchanges, the business becomes dependent on creating new transactions to maintain momentum.
- Relational thinking shifts the focus from individual transactions to the health of the relationship over time.
- A relational finish always includes one of three things: clarity, continuity, or confidence.

Chapter 9

LOOKED AFTER, NOT MANAGED

There's a big difference between managing customers and looking after them. Most businesses think they're doing the second one when in reality they are doing the first.

Let me give you an example because nearly everyone has felt this. You call a company because something hasn't gone right. Not a major drama, just something off. The person you get on the phone is polite. They're following the script, they log the issue, give you a reference number, explain the steps, and tell you someone will contact you within 48 hours. Technically, that's good service, but how did it feel? It felt like you were entered into a system. You weren't reassured, you were recorded. You weren't looked after, you were processed. You didn't hang up thinking "I'm in good hands". You hung up thinking "I hope this doesn't get lost". That's the difference between a system working and a person caring.

BEING MANAGED VS BEING LOOKED AFTER

In a wolf pack, no one gets "logged". The pack closes ranks. The job is to protect the member, not process the problem. Managing customers makes them feel like a number, but looking after customers makes them feel like a person. People relax with people, but they stay alert with systems.

From the customer side, being managed can feel like being handled. No one says that out loud, but people feel it. They feel when they are being moved through a system versus being guided through an experience. The two can look similar operationally, but emotionally they are worlds apart. Management keeps the business comfortable, but looking after people is what makes the customer feel safe.

In a managed experience, communication often sounds like instructions. Fill this out, wait for that, we'll contact you if needed and so on. It's efficient, but it can feel impersonal. In a looked-after experience, communication sounds more like guidance. Here's what happens next, this is what you can expect, if anything changes, we'll let you know. The information might be similar, but the emotional tone is different. And that difference is massive. Tone is what tells customers whether they are in safe hands or just in a system.

Most businesses drift towards management because systems scale more easily than emotional awareness. Processes can be documented, workflows can be optimised, and software can track progress.

Looking after people, however, requires consistent human behaviours layered over those systems. That part is harder to standardise, so it often becomes secondary – or sometimes non-existent.

But customers don't separate the two. They don't think "The process is efficient, but the experience is cold". They simply feel whether the interaction reduced uncertainty or added to it. When people feel managed, they stay alert. They watch for mistakes and they double-check everything. They feel like they need to stay on top of things, just in case. When people feel looked after, they relax, and they trust that someone is thinking ahead for them. Relaxation is a sign of trust.

Looking after the customer, not managing them, shows up everywhere.

In retail, a managed customer is directed to aisles, pointed to policies, and left to scan their own items while a machine thanks them for shopping. A looked-after customer is noticed, guided, reassured, and served by a real person.

In professional services, a managed client receives structured updates and formal communication. A looked-after client feels someone is personally invested in their confidence, not just the deliverables.

In government and large organisations, management dominates through forms, queues, and procedures. Some of that is necessary. But without visible care, it doesn't feel like support, it feels like red tape.

WHEN CUSTOMERS FEEL MANAGED

Customers understand that businesses need systems. But what they are looking for is a sense that the system is there to support them, not control them. And that feeling is created through behaviour, not process.

When customers feel managed rather than looked after, their behaviour changes in ways businesses often misinterpret. You know that feeling when you're on hold and the automated voice says "Your call is important to us"? Nobody has ever heard that and thought "Ah good, I feel valued now". Your instant thought is "Right. I'm in the queue". That's management language. And while you sit there listening to the same music on loop, being reminded every two minutes that your call is apparently "really important", the only thing going through your head is "If my call is that important, maybe answer it!"

Looking-after language sounds different. It sounds like someone taking responsibility, not deflecting it. One says "You're in the system". The other says "I've got you". Same organisation but completely different emotional experience.

Your customers or clients become more cautious, not because they don't trust the organisation entirely, but because they don't feel fully supported by it. They read the fine print more closely, and they ask more questions. They hesitate before committing. From the business side, this can look like customers being difficult or overly demanding. In reality, it's just a response to uncertainty. Because people manage risk when they don't feel cared for.

Looking after someone, on the other hand, reduces that perceived risk. When customers feel like someone is actively thinking about their experience, they don't feel the need to stay in defensive mode. They don't feel like they have to protect themselves at every step. That shift from guarded to confident changes the entire dynamic of the relationship.

This is why simply having good processes is not enough. A well-designed system can still make people feel processed if the human layer is thin. Efficiency without reassurance often feels cold, and reassurance without structure feels chaotic. Customers need both, but they feel the absence of reassurance more strongly than the absence of efficiency.

HOW TO MAKE CUSTOMERS FEEL LOOKED AFTER

So what actually creates the feeling of being looked after? It's not grand gestures, it's not freebies, and it's not being over-the-top. It's three behavioural moves.

First – tell them what's going on.

People want to know what story they are in – what happens next and where this is going? When customers don't have a narrative, they invent one, and it's usually negative. Think about ordering something online that doesn't show up when you expected. There's no update, there's no "it's delayed", there's no explanation, just silence. So what story do you write in your own head? "It's lost", "They forgot", "I'm now going to have to chase this", "This is going to be a hassle". The business might be completely on top of it behind the scenes, but because they didn't give you the narrative, you created your own. And customers are terrible authors. The story we write is almost always worse than reality.

Now flip it. "Just a heads up, your delivery is running a day behind because of the courier backlog. It's already on its way." Same delay but a completely different emotional experience. That's staying ahead of the story in their head. Without it, the customer fills the silence with doubt – with it, the customer feels oriented.

Second – stay with it.

Not "That's with another team", not "I'll escalate it", but instead "I'll stay with this and update you". Ownership lowers anxiety faster than speed. It looks something like this. You call your internet provider because your connection keeps dropping out. The first person runs a few checks then says, "Yep, I can see the issue. I need to get this to our technical team – I'll escalate it." You hang up thinking . . . great. Now I'm in the system.

Two days later, nothing. So you call back and start the story again with someone new who says, "I can see the notes here. I'll escalate it again." That's the management roundabout.

Now imagine this instead. "I can see what's going on. I'm going to stay with this until it's sorted. You don't need to repeat this to anyone else. I'll call you tomorrow afternoon with an update, even if the update is just that we're still working on it." Same fault, same internal teams, same technical process, but completely different feeling. One makes you feel like a ticket and a number, the other makes you feel like someone's responsibility. That's visible ownership. Ownership doesn't mean they fix it personally, it just means you never feel abandoned inside the process.

Third – get ahead of it.

Looking after someone means telling them things before they realise, they need to know. "You might be wondering . . .", "Just so you're aware . . .", "Heads up . . ."

You book a tradie to come fix something at your house. On the morning of the job, you get a message from them: "Hey, just a heads up, traffic's heavy so I'm running about 20 minutes late. Also, the job might be a bit noisy while I'm cutting into the wall, so if you've got calls planned you might want to step into another room. I'll explain everything before I start." You see, you hadn't even thought about any of that yet, but now you're not annoyed about the delay, you're not surprised by the noise, you're not wondering what's going on. You feel considered and informed. That's anticipation. Looking after someone creates trust before the problem even exists, whereas managing them creates frustration.

Those three things turn a process into care, but without them, even a smooth system feels cold.

WHEN PRESSURE BUILDS UP

Here's where this becomes real inside a business. No team wakes up and says "Let's manage customers today instead of looking after them". That's not how it goes. In reality it creeps in quietly. Pressure builds, work piles up, the inbox gets stupidly full, the phone doesn't stop, and without anyone deciding it, the goal quietly shifts from *how this feels* to *how much we can move*. You start hearing things like "Let's clear this queue", "Just close those off", or "We need to get through these before lunch".

None of those sentences sound terrible, but they tell you exactly what the focus has become. The job is now how to move work, not how to settle people. And once that becomes normal, behaviour follows. Replies get shorter – not rude, just thin. Updates give information but not confidence. Handover happens, but the customer doesn't feel carried, they just feel passed. The work is moving, but the person inside the work isn't.

That's the shift.

You can see it in emails that technically answer the question but still leave the customer thinking "Yeah . . . but what does that mean for me?" You see it in updates that say what's happening, but not whether everything is still on track. You see it when ownership changes internally, but nobody says to the customer "I'm still across this". Nothing is "wrong", but nothing feels safe either. And customers can feel that difference faster than your metrics ever will.

No one decided to lower the care. But over time it got squeezed out by pace. That's why this isn't a "be nicer" conversation, it's a standards conversation. Looking after customers has to be treated as part of the job, not an optional layer you add when you have time, otherwise, the system will always win. Because systems are loud and care is quiet. And quiet things disappear first when pressure rises.

This is where Service Rebellion draws the line in concrete. The job isn't to move customers through the process, it's to carry them through it, so they don't feel like they have to carry it themselves. Uncertainty isn't logical, it's emotional, and if you ignore that, it leaks into everything.

A FEELINGS FAILURE

You can always tell when a business has slipped into management mode by what customers say afterwards. They don't complain about the job being wrong. They say things like "I had to chase them", or "I never really knew what was going on", or "I felt like just another number".

That's not a systems failure, it's a feeling failure because the work might have been completed, the issue resolved, the box ticked, but if the customer felt like they had to stay on top of it the whole way, like nobody was clearly carrying it for them, then the experience has landed flat, no matter how technically correct it was. And when that happens, they don't usually walk away angry, they walk away detached. Not because something exploded, but because after everything they went through it felt like they were the ones managing you.

Customers don't leave businesses because they were "managed badly". They leave because they never felt looked after in the first place. When the experience feels like a process instead of a partnership, your business becomes functional rather than relational, and functional gets swapped out quickly in a market full of options. Care creates resistance to that swap because when people feel looked after they don't rush to compare. Without the protective layer of care, you're always one better offer away from being replaced.

This is particularly visible when things don't go perfectly, which is inevitable in any organisation. In a managed environment, problems are handled according to process: tickets are logged, steps are followed, policies are applied. In a looked-after environment, those same steps happen, but with visible ownership and reassurance layered over them.

The difference isn't in what gets done – because the steps are often identical – it's in how it feels while it's being done, and in the end that emotional imprint wins every time. When customers feel looked after during an issue, trust often increases. Think about two ways a problem gets handled.

Version one: "We've logged your issue. Someone will contact you."

Version two: "I'm sorry this happened. I'm going to stay with this until it's sorted, and I'll call you tomorrow, even if there's no update yet."

Same issue. Same solution path, but a completely different trust outcome. One manages the problem while the other looks after the person, and when things aren't perfect, which they rarely are, you can probably guess which one gets forgiven.

ON THE CUSTOMER'S SIDE

Here's something most business owners and management know, even if they don't frame it this way: the businesses that cop the least heat from customers aren't the ones that never make mistakes, they're the ones where customers feel someone is actually on their side when something goes wrong.

When people feel managed during a problem, they think, "I have to stay on top of this." When they feel looked after, they think, "They've got this." That difference determines whether a small issue becomes a complaint, an escalation, or just a bump in the road, and this is where staff need to understand something important. Looking after customers is not about being emotional, it's about removing emotional load from the customer, and it's about making them feel like they don't have to manage the relationship themselves. That might be as simple as saying "I'll stay with this and update you" instead of "You'll hear from us". One keeps the responsibility with the business, but the other hands the emotional burden back to the customer.

Customers don't get tired of problems as much as they get tired of having to manage the people who are supposed to be solving them. When they stop feeling looked after, they don't always explode, they just quietly detach, they become more formal, less forgiving, and more open to alternatives. That's why *looking after* is not a "service style", it's relationship insurance. When customers feel managed through an issue, trust weakens, even if the resolution is technically correct. The emotional memory of the experience shapes how they talk about the business later.

Looking after customers does not mean abandoning structure, it means using structure to create confidence rather than simply control. It means recognising that people are not just moving through a system, they are having an experience inside it. Experiences are judged on how safe they feel, not just how efficient they are.

This is where you realise this isn't about service technique. It's about what kind of culture you've actually built. When management becomes the default, people stop owning the experience. They move things along, close items, and stay within process.

Control replaces care. Nothing breaks . . . but nothing feels owned either. Looking after customers requires a different standard. And leadership either sets it . . . or suffocates it.

If your staff are measured purely on speed, closure rates, ticket times, and how many things they can get off their desk in a day, then don't be surprised when that's exactly what they focus on. All their focus will be about how to move more work, not how to settle people. If leaders only talk about efficiency, the culture becomes management heavy.

If leaders talk about how customers feel at the end of interactions, behaviour shifts. What gets spoken about gets repeated, which in turn plays out in actions and creeps into the culture of that business. If "Did the customer feel steady?" becomes as normal a question as "Was it completed?", then looking after stops being personality and starts being standard.

That's how the Wolf Pack Standard works. Not by hoping people care, but by making care a shared behavioural expectation. It means people are not only aware of what needs to be done, but also how it feels to be on the receiving end of what they are doing. That awareness changes small behaviours in powerful ways: explanations become clearer, transitions become smoother, and ownership becomes more visible.

The work may be the same, but the emotional tone of the journey shifts, and customers pick up on that tone very quickly. When they sense they are being looked after, they don't just see the business as a provider of a product or service. They start to see it as a partner in their situation and that sense of partnership is what creates resilience in the relationship.

When small issues occur, customers who feel looked after are more patient. They assume positive intent, and they believe the business will sort it out. Customers who feel managed, however, don't give that benefit of the doubt as easily. This is where the commercial impact becomes obvious. If a relationship is built purely on management, it only holds while everything runs perfectly. The second something slips, there's no buffer. But when it's built on care, trust absorbs the bumps, and that buffer is what keeps customers from jumping ship the moment a cheaper or easier option appears. All of that comes from making sure your customers feel like they are being looked after.

THE STANDARD FOR LOOKING AFTER CUSTOMERS

You don't get a "looked-after" culture by telling staff to care more. You get it by making reassurance part of the job, not something you hope certain people are naturally good at. If care only lives in "the good staff", then you're running a lottery because the experience depends on who the customer happens to get. But when care lives inside the standard itself it becomes culture, and customers can feel that difference in the first 30 seconds without anyone needing to explain it.

Looking after customers does not require dramatic gestures. It requires:

- consistency in behaviours that signal attention
- clear communication about what happens next
- proactive updates when things change
- a sense that someone owns the journey, not just the task.

These behaviours tell customers they are not alone inside the system. When those signals are steady, customers relax, but when they're inconsistent, customers stay slightly alert, and alert customers compare while relaxed customers commit, which is why this isn't a soft concept, it's a commercial one.

That difference is at the heart of Service Rebellion. It is not about rejecting systems or structure. It is about refusing to let the system become the dominant experience because the system should support the journey, not replace the human side of it. Systems move work and care moves people, and while you absolutely need both, only one of them creates loyalty that actually lasts.

Customers understand they are part of a process, but what they are quietly asking is "Am I just in your system, or am I in your care?" The answer to that question determines whether they stay when things get hard, forgive when things wobble, and refer when someone asks.

And that is why Service Rebellion is not about removing structure, it's about making sure structure never replaces the human aspect. When businesses get this balance right, customers don't feel like they're being pushed through a process, they feel carried through it. They understand there's a system – of course there is – but they don't feel like they're navigating it alone or bracing for what might fall through the cracks. What they're really asking, quietly and constantly, is whether they are just another entry inside your workflow or someone genuinely held in your care. When that question is answered through behaviour – not slogans – people relax, they stay longer, they forgive more easily, and they refer with confidence because their reputation feels safe with you. When it isn't, they don't usually complain or create drama, they simply lean back emotionally, become more cautious, and start keeping their options open. And once a customer stops leaning in, the relationship is already weaker than your reports will ever show.

Chapter summary

- Managing customers makes them feel like a number, but looking after customers makes them feel like a person.
- Most businesses drift towards management because systems scale more easily than emotional awareness.
- A looked-after client feels like someone is personally invested in their confidence, not just their deliverables.
- Managing language says "You're in the system", looking-after language says "I've got you".
- No team wakes up and says "Let's manage customers today instead of looking after them" – in reality it creeps in quietly.
- Looking after customers has to be treated as part of the job, not an optional layer you add when you have time.
- Service Rebellion draws the line in concrete here – the job isn't to move customers through the process, it's to carry them through it, so they don't feel like they have to carry it themselves.
- In a managed environment, problems are handled according to process.
- In a looked-after environment, those same steps happen, but with visible ownership and reassurance layered over them.
- When people feel managed during a problem, they think, "I have to stay on top of this." When they feel looked after, they think, "They've got this."
- Looking after customers requires:
  - consistency in behaviours that signal attention
  - clear communication about what happens next
  - proactive updates when things change
  - a sense that someone owns the journey, not just the task.

Chapter 10

REBELLION ISN'T SCRIPTED

Customers don't switch off because of the wrong words. They switch off because they can feel they're being processed.

This chapter is personal for me because nothing switches me off faster than feeling like I'm being run through a script instead of spoken to like a human being. You can feel it instantly. The words are right, but the person isn't there. You're not being helped, you're being handled. It feels managed and clinical, and that moment isn't a people problem, it's a culture problem.

BIG AND SMALL BUSINESSES USE SCRIPTS

Whenever businesses realise service has slipped, the first thing they reach for is scripts. It feels logical. Except they tighten the language, control the wording, and start managing the conversation instead of the experience. Scripts don't create care, they create coverage, and those two things are not the same. Coverage means you technically said what you were supposed to say, but care means the customer actually felt reassured. You can deliver one perfectly without delivering the other.

You've probably seen this when you are a customer or client. You ask a question, and the staff member gives you a perfect answer – to a different question. You say, "I'm worried about the delivery date," and they reply, "Your order has been processed successfully." Technically that is correct, but for the customer or client hearing that, it is emotionally useless. The script satisfied the process, but it didn't answer the person.

What you really want to hear is "I can understand why that would worry you. Let me check the delivery date properly and get you a clear answer". It's the same meaning but a completely different presence, and in turn, a completely different outcome.

This isn't just a big business problem. Small businesses script service all the time, they just don't call it that. "Tell them we're flat out", "Say we'll call back", "Tell them to email instead", "Just apologise and move on". That's still scripting because it swaps thinking for phrases, and while everything technically gets said, the customer walks away feeling handled instead of helped. And in small businesses, scripts often hide behind the word "experience".

Most small businesses don't write scripts. They repeat habits, and repeated habits become invisible scripts. You can give two people the exact same words and create completely different feelings. One interaction feels human and calming, the other feels like someone reading instructions off a laminated card. They are both the same words. However, how they were delivered creates a totally different experience.

SCRIPTS AND CULTURE

Here's the unintended lesson scripts often teach: they quietly tell staff that the job is to avoid saying the wrong thing instead of making the customer feel right. So people play it safe. They stick to the wording, they avoid ownership, and they don't go beyond the line because the line starts to feel like the boundary. You end up with technically correct yet emotionally absent service at the same time. No one gets in trouble, but no one builds trust either.

Culture works differently. It doesn't hand people a script and tell them what to say. Culture shapes how they think about the person in front of them and what matters most in that moment. Instead of focusing on wording, it focuses on responsibility, reducing uncertainty, taking ownership, and protecting the experience.

That's the Wolf Pack Standard in action. A pack doesn't move because someone hands them a script. They move because everyone understands the job is to protect the experience, to protect certainty, and to protect trust, and when that responsibility is clear, behaviour adjusts naturally without anyone needing lines.

That's culture: shared instinct, not memorised lines. In a strong service culture, people know the goal isn't just to move the task forward, it's to reduce uncertainty for the customer. They understand that clarity matters, that follow-up matters, and that ownership matters. So even if the words vary, the experience feels consistent because the intention behind the behaviour is aligned. That's why some organisations with almost no scripting still create brilliant experiences, while others with scripts for everything still feel robotic. One environment is built around standards. The other is built around compliance. And compliance makes people careful. It doesn't make them caring.

Scripts are often a response to symptoms. Leaders hear complaints about communication, so they tighten the language. They see inconsistency, so they standardise phrases. What actually needs to be standardised is the behaviour underneath. Do we clarify next steps clearly? Do we take ownership instead of passing things around? Do we follow up when we say we will? Those things shape experience far more than exact wording ever will.

Culture is what makes those behaviours non-negotiable. It tells people "This is how we operate here", and not "This is a nice extra if we remember". Culture spreads through what leaders reinforce, what people model around them, and what gets corrected early before it becomes normal. Sure, scripts can support culture, but they cannot and should not replace it.

When scripts become the main tool, service starts to feel staged. Customers hear the right phrases, but something feels off because it's delivered like a performance instead of a conversation. The words are there, but the person isn't fully there. And that's the difference. Trust isn't built by wording alone. It's built by presence, and presence doesn't come from a template. Culture gives people permission to be human while still holding the standard. It keeps the focus on the person in front of them, not just the process they're following.

That's why culture wins in the long run. It creates consistent human behaviour, not just consistent wording. Customers don't stay because you used the right sentence. They stay because of how the experience felt. They don't remember your phrasing. They remember whether they felt steadied or handled. It's the difference between someone having a conversation with you and someone waiting for you to stop talking so they can say the next line. Even if the line is technically correct, the experience feels thinner. When attention shifts to saying it right, presence drops. When presence drops, reassurance drops. When reassurance drops, certainty drops. And when certainty drops, trust starts to erode.

Culture doesn't compete for attention in the same way. Culture shapes the natural response from your team. When standards are embedded in the business, people don't have to consciously remember to be clear, to follow up, to take ownership. Those behaviours become the natural way things are done. That's what makes culture scalable because it lives in habits, not just in documents.

This is also where scripts can accidentally send the wrong message internally. When leadership puts heavy emphasis on wording, staff can assume that the appearance of service matters more than the substance of it. Saying the right thing starts to feel more important than doing the right thing. Over time, this creates a culture of performance rather than care. People learn how to sound helpful without necessarily being helpful. They learn the tone, the phrases, the structure.

From the outside this can look polished, but from the customer's side, it can feel like they are being handled rather than genuinely supported. You don't lose customers in one bad scripted interaction. You lose them in the slow build-up of moments where they felt handled instead of helped. That gap between sounding caring and being caring is where trust erodes quietly. Trust never disappears loudly. It erodes quietly in tone, in patience, in how quickly someone looks elsewhere next time. That's why this isn't about language, it's about loyalty.

Service Rebellion is the refusal to let service become surface-level. When the focus shifts to saying the right thing instead of reducing doubt, customers feel it. The job isn't to perform helpfulness, it's to create certainty.

UNPREDICTABLE MOMENTS

None of this means scripts are useless. They can be valuable as support tools, especially in complex or regulated environments. The mistake is thinking they are the foundation. They're not. They can guide the conversation, but they don't create the outcome.

The structure isn't the script. It's the standard that every customer walks away more certain than when they came in. If that expectation is clear and reinforced, people naturally adjust how they speak and act to meet it. They don't need to follow a line. They follow a standard. That standard shows up in moments where scripts usually fall apart anyway. When a customer is frustrated, when something has gone wrong, when the situation doesn't fit the template, watch what happens when a conversation goes off script. Silence . . . panic . . . "Let me check that for you."

Scripts handle the expected, but culture handles reality. Customers don't judge you on the smooth interactions, they judge you on the messy ones, and messy moments don't follow templates. In those moments, people fall back on culture, not wording. If the culture values process and compliance, people hide behind the script. If the culture values ownership and reassurance, those behaviours appear. One guides behaviour when things are predictable where the other guides behaviour when things aren't. A customer can tell which one they are dealing with.

It's the unpredictable moments that define how customers remember you, and this is where businesses often get stuck in a loop without realising it. Service feels inconsistent, so they add more scripts. Interactions start feeling robotic, so customers become less engaged. Staff feel like they're performing rather than helping, so their presence in the moment drops even further. The experience becomes more controlled on the surface and less human underneath. The problem wasn't a lack of words. It was a lack of shared understanding about what the words were meant to achieve.

THINK OF THE DESIRED OUTCOME

Culture fixes that because culture operates underneath the language. It answers the question people are really asking in the middle of an interaction: "What matters most here?" If the answer is "Stay within the script", behaviour narrows. But if the answer is "Make sure the customer feels confident and looked after", behaviour expands in the right direction. That's the key difference. Scripts tell people what to say, but culture tells people what outcome they are responsible for.

Here's what that looks like in the real world.

Script mindset: "Your request has been escalated."

Culture mindset: "I've got this. You don't need to chase. I'll update you tomorrow."

Script mindset: "That's our policy."

Culture mindset: "Here's why that rule exists and what we can still do for you."

Same organisation, same rules, but different emotional outcome. One protects the system, where the other protects the customer's certainty.

When outcome is clear, people adapt naturally, and they use different language with different customers. Instead of teaching staff what to say, teach them what to listen for: confusion, hesitation, frustration, and doubt. Those are all cues. Culture-trained staff respond to cues. Script-trained staff respond to lines. Only one of those feels human.

Culture-trained staff adjust tone based on the situation. They slow down when reassurance is needed and move faster when clarity is already there. The experience feels personal without being chaotic because the intention behind it is consistent. This is where leadership influence becomes critical. Culture doesn't form from posters or handbooks. It forms from what gets noticed, reinforced, and corrected in everyday work. If someone communicates clearly and takes ownership, is that recognised? If someone hides behind process and leaves the customer uncertain, is that addressed? Those signals tell people what really matters.

If your coaching conversations with staff are about wording, you build performers. If your feedback sounds like "Make sure you say . . .", "Next time include . . .", "Don't forget to mention . . ." then you're building script compliance.

If your feedback sounds like "Did they feel reassured?", "Did you remove their doubt?", "Did they need any more information?" then you're building service culture. What you coach and train becomes what people focus on and in turn deliver to your customers or clients.

BUILDING THE RIGHT CULTURE

A huge number of businesses – from small operators right through to large organisations – don't consistently train staff about customer experience at all. They might train on systems, on compliance, on product knowledge, but not on how the customer should *feel* at the end of an interaction. Nothing structured, nothing ongoing, nothing reinforced.

When culture doesn't get built, it gets left to personality, and personality is random. Your culture cannot be left to whatever is happening on the day. It needs to be set and lived. Some staff naturally reassure, some don't. Some take ownership, some pass things on. Some think ahead, and others just follow the steps. From the inside, it feels like "We have good people", and from the outside, it feels like roulette. One interaction feels great, but the next feels cold. The customer never knows which version they're going to get. It's a lucky dip, where you just hope there's a good outcome, but you never know. That's not a people problem. That's a standards problem.

Culture isn't created by hiring nice humans. It's created by repeatedly teaching, modelling, and reinforcing what "looked after" actually means in behaviour. If you don't train the standard you want, you don't get the standard you deserve. And when there's no shared standard, scripts become the desperate backup plan. That's the difference between compliance and culture.

Over time, those signals become habits, and habits become the environment. In that environment, service doesn't depend on remembering lines. It depends on people understanding that the emotional side of the experience is part of their job, not a separate function. That's when interactions feel natural and consistent at the same time. The words might differ, but the customer leaves with the same sense of certainty. Customers don't stay because the phrasing was consistent. They stay because the feeling was.

When businesses understand this, scripts move back to where they belong – as support tools, not the foundation. They provide structure, but they don't carry the experience because the experience is carried by people who understand the standard and have permission to meet it in a human way. Scripts are training wheels where culture is the balance. Training wheels stop you from falling. But it's the balance that lets you move naturally without thinking about every turn.

Businesses that never move past scripts create staff who sound safe but don't feel safe to customers. Businesses that build culture create staff who may use different words but always deliver the same outcome: certainty, reassurance, and ownership.

That's the Wolf Pack Standard. It's not about memorising lines, it is all about protecting the experience. If protection is real, you can see it in behaviour: how clearly the next step is explained when things are uncertain, whether someone takes ownership when something slips, and whether follow-up happens without being chased.

Culture means nothing if you can't see it in action. If it doesn't change how people respond when something goes wrong, it's just language. If protection is the standard, then it has to show up when it matters. When something slips, when someone's frustrated, and especially when the script doesn't fit the moment. Because this isn't about polishing language and being slick. It's about building a business where customers feel certain and seen, even when things go wrong. It's where ownership is obvious, where follow-up doesn't need chasing, and where reassurance isn't left to personality.

That doesn't happen by accident. It happens when the standard is clear enough to guide behaviour and strong enough to hold under pressure. Protection is not something you talk about. It's something you build. And once you understand how to build it, you stop hoping your culture is strong. You start knowing where it is strong, and where it isn't.

That's what we build next.

Chapter summary

- Customers don't switch off because of the wrong words – they switch off because they can feel they're being processed.
- Whenever businesses realise service has slipped, the first thing they reach for is scripts.
- Most small businesses don't write scripts – they repeat habits, and repeated habits become invisible scripts.
- The unintended lesson scripts often teach is that they quietly tell staff that the job is to avoid saying the wrong thing instead of making the customer feel right.
- In a strong service culture, people know the goal is to reduce uncertainty for the customer – they know clarity, follow-up, and ownership matter.
- Service Rebellion is the refusal to let service become surface-level.
- Scripts handle the expected, but culture handles reality.
- Scripts tell people what to say, but culture tells people what outcome they are responsible for.
- Instead of teaching staff what to say, teach them what to listen for: confusion, hesitation, frustration, and doubt.
- If you don't train the standard you want, you don't get the standard you deserve.

— PART 3 —

THE LEVELS THAT BUILD LOYALTY

Chapter 11

THE LEVEL OF IMPORTANCE

Up to now we've been talking about what customers feel and why businesses drift away from it. From here, we stop talking about feelings in theory and start looking at the things that actually drive them: the real behaviours, the small moments, and the signals customers react to without even knowing they are.

This isn't guesswork. There's a pattern to how people decide whether they trust you or not, and it starts with one simple question running in their head. Before customers judge your price, your product, your systems, or your expertise, they make a much faster decision, and it happens emotionally before they even realise, they've made it: Do I matter here?

Your customer or client sends you an email and hears nothing. They follow up and still hear nothing, and then three days later they receive a casual "Sorry, just saw this" message. In that moment they don't assume you're busy. Instead what lands is the feeling that they simply weren't important enough to notice.

You've probably felt this yourself. You walk into a place and no one looks up. Not because they're rude but because they're busy. In that moment, you don't feel like a customer, you feel like background noise and an interruption to their day. But what if in that exact same environment, with the same workload and the same pressure, someone looks up, makes eye contact, and says, "Hey, we'll be with you in a minute." You haven't moved up the queue, but emotionally you have because that simple acknowledgement changes everything. That's importance shown in real action.

That judgement takes seconds, and once it's formed, everything else you do gets filtered through it. You can be technically brilliant, competitively priced, and operationally efficient, but if the customer feels like they are low on the list of priorities, the emotional tone of the relationship starts in the wrong place. Customers do not expect to be the centre of the universe. They understand businesses are busy, but what they are looking for is not exclusivity, it is significance. They want to feel like when they are dealing with you, they are not an interruption to something more important.

THE LEVEL OF IMPORTANCE IN ACTION

The Level of Importance is about whether the customer feels like a priority in the moment they are interacting with your business.

That signal is rarely sent through grand gestures. It comes from small behaviours that most organisations overlook because they seem too simple to matter – how quickly someone acknowledges a message, whether the response sounds present or distracted, whether a conversation feels like it has your attention or is happening while three other things are being juggled. Customers feel the difference instantly.

From inside the business, everyone might be working flat out. Emails are flying, phones are ringing, systems are beeping, and people are under pressure. From the team's perspective, they are doing their best to keep up. From the customer's perspective, the only thing that exists is the interaction they are in right now.

Effort that isn't felt does not build loyalty because customers can't reward effort they can't see. You don't get credit for being busy. You get judged on whether someone felt seen. This is where businesses get caught out. They believe they care – and they do. They believe they are trying – and they are. But if the customer does not feel that care through the interaction, the emotional conclusion is different. The customer does not think "They must be busy", they think "I don't feel very important right now". Those feelings change behaviour. This is not about perfection. It is all about presence.

In professional services, this level shows up in communication patterns. Does the client receive a prompt acknowledgement when they send something through, or does silence stretch out with no context? Even if the work is progressing behind the scenes, lack of visible attention creates uncertainty, and uncertainty lowers perceived importance.

In trades or service businesses, this level shows up in reliability and updates. A customer who has to chase for confirmation of timing or status starts feeling like they are managing the relationship. A customer who receives proactive confirmation feels like they are being looked after. That difference has nothing to do with skill. It has everything to do with the signal of importance.

Large organisations struggle here because scale creates distance. People become case numbers, job numbers, ticket numbers. Systems track progress, but customers don't feel seen inside those systems. When someone feels like an entry in a queue rather than a person with a situation, their sense of importance drops, even if the process is efficient. Efficiency without significance feels cold.

THE FOUNDATION LAYER

This level also influences how customers interpret everything that follows. When someone feels important early, they assume positive intent later. Delays feel understandable, and issues feel like problems to solve together. But when someone feels unimportant early, the same events feel like confirmation that the business is disorganised or doesn't care. Businesses often try to fix later stages of the journey without realising the emotional baseline was set in the first few interactions. If those early signals were weak, everything that follows has to work much harder to rebuild confidence.

This is why the Level of Importance is the first structural layer of trust. If this layer cracks, everything built on top of it becomes unstable. When people feel important, they believe someone is paying attention. When they believe someone is paying attention, they worry less. When they worry less, the experience feels lighter. Light experiences build attachment. Heavy experiences create distance, and distance is where customers start drifting.

This is exactly where the Wolf Pack Standard starts. In a pack, no member feels like a spare part. In a real pack, awareness is constant, they don't ignore signals, and they don't leave one member unsure where they stand. That's how packs survive and that's how teams build trust. And that's how customers decide if they're safe with you or not. Every movement signals awareness, it signals position, and it signals attention. No wolf is wondering if they matter to the group.

Service Rebellion at this level is simple: it refuses to let customers feel like background tasks. It says presence is not a personality trait, it's a behavioural standard. It cannot rely on the naturally warm staff member who remembers everyone's name. It has to be built into the environment. Acknowledgements are not optional. Updates are not occasional. Presence is not a bonus.

So what does "importance" look like in behaviour? It's not grand gestures. It's this: acknowledgement within minutes, not hours, updates before customers wonder, transitions where context moves with the person, and ending conversations with "Here's what happens next". None of these take long, but all of them tell the customer one thing: you matter enough for us to think ahead. These behaviours become part of how work is done.

When that happens, customers feel like their time and situation are respected. Respect is one of the earliest building blocks of trust. Without it, the relationship starts on unstable ground. Once customers feel like they do not matter, every other level in this system has to work twice as hard to compensate.

AFFECTING THE FUTURE RELATIONSHIP

Once the Level of Importance is set, it starts influencing how customers interpret everything else that happens. It becomes the emotional baseline they carry into the relationship. When someone feels important, they give you the benefit of the doubt. When they don't, they look for confirmation that they were right not to trust too much. That's why this level affects tolerance more than most businesses realise. A delay, a small mistake, or a bit of confusion feels very different depending on whether the customer believes they matter. If they feel valued, they assume there's a reason and that someone is on top of it. If they feel like a number, the same situation feels like neglect. Nothing about the event changes, the emotional interpretation does.

When customers don't feel important, they start managing the relationship themselves – following up sooner, double-checking information, asking for confirmation of things that should already be clear, becoming alert to gaps. That's chasing behaviour. From inside the business customers can appear demanding. In reality, it's customers trying to reduce uncertainty because they don't feel confident that someone else is fully across it. That extra communication creates more workload for the team, which often leads to shorter responses and more rushed interactions. That, in turn, lowers the customer's sense of importance even further.

Now you have a loop. Lower perceived importance leads to more chasing, and more chasing creates pressure. Pressure thins communication, and thin communication lowers perceived importance even further. Businesses end up working harder while customers feel less looked after and trust weakens. This is the irony most leaders miss: when customers don't feel important, they create more work, but when customers feel important, they relax. Relaxed customers reduce operational load.

Importance isn't soft, it's an efficiency strategy. Businesses think attention slows them down, but the opposite is actually true. When customers feel ignored, they create work, but when customers feel seen, they remove work.

OPERATIONAL IMPACTS

This is why the Level of Importance has a direct operational impact, not just an emotional one. Relaxed customers don't chase as much because they trust that things are being handled. That trust reduces unnecessary communication and friction. It also affects how customers speak to your team. When someone feels important, they are generally more patient and respectful. When they feel ignored or low priority, their tone shifts. They become sharper, more direct, sometimes more aggressive. The team then feels under attack, which can make interactions more defensive. The cycle unfortunately feeds itself.

You can see this in environments where response times are inconsistent. A customer sends something in and hears nothing for days. Eventually, they follow up, not because they want to be difficult, but because silence feels like neglect. By the time the reply arrives, their emotional state has already shifted from calm to concerned or annoyed. From the business side, the work may have been progressing the whole time. From the customer's side, the emotional experience was waiting in the dark. And dark creates stories and those stories are rarely positive.

This level also shows up in handovers. When a customer is moved from one person or department to another, how that transition is handled tells them how important they are. If they have to re-explain everything, it feels like no one cared enough to pass on context. If the next person is already across the situation, the customer feels continuity and attention. Continuity reinforces importance, which is why customers relax when context moves with them instead of resetting every time.

In larger organisations, continuity with handovers becomes one of the biggest gaps. Work moves efficiently through internal systems, but customers feel like they are starting again each time they interact with someone new. That repeated reset lowers their sense of significance. It's not dramatic, it's cumulative.

Over time, these small signals shape the emotional story the customer tells themselves about the business. "They're always busy", "I have to chase them", "You don't really get much attention unless you push". None of these statements sound like disasters, but they quietly weaken attachment. And when attachment weakens, loyalty becomes conditional. Customers who feel important stay through small inconveniences. Customers who don't feel important leave when a slightly easier option appears. That's the commercial difference.

Importance also drives referral confidence. When someone feels genuinely valued, they assume others will be treated the same way. They feel safer putting their name behind the business. When they feel like they were just another case in the system, they hesitate to refer because they can't predict the experience. Nobody risks their reputation referring a business that made them feel like a number. Referrals don't come from satisfaction alone. They come from emotional certainty.

THE CULTURAL SIGNAL

The Level of Importance is not a "nice to have". It is one of the early levels that determines whether customers behave like partners or like temporary users. Partners stick around. Temporary users shop. The signal that drives that behaviour is often as simple as whether the customer felt like someone was properly present with them. This is where the Level of Importance stops being an individual behaviour and becomes a cultural signal.

In some organisations importance is accidental, depending on who the customer happens to deal with. One person is naturally attentive, another is more task focused. The experience varies not because of intention but because there is no shared standard about how customers should feel during interactions. In other organisations, importance is built into how the business operates. Acknowledging people promptly is normal. Context is passed on during handovers, and conversations are not ended abruptly. These things aren't treated as extras, they are part of the job.

That difference comes from what leadership reinforces. If speed and output are the only things recognised, people will prioritise those. If clarity, follow-up, and presence are also noticed and valued, people build them into how they work. Culture forms around what gets attention internally.

When leaders consistently model and reinforce behaviours that signal importance, teams pick up the cue. They see that how the customer feels is not separate from performance, it is all part of it. When leaders ignore those behaviours, staff quickly learn that getting the task done matters more than how the journey felt. Customers feel that gap, even if they never see the leadership decisions behind it.

This is also where price sensitivity connects back to emotion. When customers feel important, price becomes part of the decision, but when they don't, price *is* the decision. Price becomes an issue to your customers and clients when they cannot see value. Without emotional significance, you are just a provider, and providers are replaceable. Importance builds loyalty buffers, and without that buffer, every decision becomes a transaction. With it, the relationship has depth, and depth is what keeps customers from leaving at the first sign of a cheaper option.

SERVICE REBELLION AND IMPORTANCE

Service Rebellion at this level means refusing to let customers feel like interruptions. It means protecting presence even when pressure is high. It means understanding that attention is not a courtesy, it is part of the product or service.

When customers consistently feel like they matter, the relationship becomes more stable. They are more patient when things are not perfect, and they are more open to communication. They are more willing to refer because they believe others will be treated with the same care. That stability reduces the constant need to chase new business just to replace what quietly leaks out the back.

The Level of Importance, then, is not about being overly attentive or dramatic. It is about making sure that in every interaction, the customer feels seen, acknowledged, and respected. Those signals form the emotional ground the rest of the experience stands on. If that ground is solid, everything else is easier. If it's weak, every other level in this system has to work twice as hard to compensate, and even then, the relationship often feels more fragile than it should.

THE FIVE SIGNALS THAT TELL A CUSTOMER THEY MATTER

If you want to train this, train these five behaviours because if importance is not observable, it is not real. And if it is not real, it is not a standard. It's just a story you tell yourself. These behaviours are observable, they're coachable, but more importantly, they're repeatable.

Importance isn't a feeling you *hope* customers get. It's a set of signals you either send . . . or you don't.

Here's what importance looks like in behaviour:

1. **Fast acknowledgement**
   Not a full answer, just recognition. "Got this", "Seen it", and "We're onto it".
   Silence = low importance.
2. **Visible attention**
   No multitasking tone, and no half-presence – customers can hear distraction.
   Attention is felt, not declared.
3. **Forward clarity**
   Every interaction ends with "Here's what happens next . . ."
   Unclear next steps = emotional drop.
4. **Proactive updates**
   Customers shouldn't have to chase movement because chasing = "I'm not a priority."
5. **Continuity in handovers**
   If a customer has to repeat themselves, importance drops instantly and you dropped the ball.

None of these are big. But together, they answer the question customers are silently asking: "Do I matter here?"

If your team can't explain these five signals without reading them, you don't have a service standard, you have individual personalities doing their best. That's not culture, that's luck. And luck is not a strategy. Your standards should be that this is the line, the non-negotiable way we treat every customer, every time. Anything less and you're not building loyalty, you're hoping for it.

Loyalty does not begin after you prove yourself. It begins the moment someone feels like they matter. And it all comes back to that first silent question customers ask in their own head. Do I matter here? If the answer consistently feels like yes, you are building the kind of trust that holds relationships steady, even when the market gets noisy.

Most businesses think loyalty is earned through performance. It's not. Loyalty starts before performance is ever judged. It starts with importance.

Before customers judge your expertise, your pricing, or your results, they decide whether they matter. If that answer feels uncertain, every other level in this system is working uphill. Get this level right, and everything that follows becomes easier, but get it wrong, and nothing fully stabilises.

This is where the practical work begins.

Chapter summary

- Before customers judge your price, your product, your systems, or your expertise, they make a much faster emotional decision: Do I matter here?
- Customers do not expect to be the centre of the universe, but want to feel like they are not an interruption to something more important.
- The Level of Importance is about whether the customer feels like a priority in the moment they are interacting with your business.
- Once customers feel like they do not matter, every other level in this system has to work twice as hard to compensate.
- When someone feels important early, they assume positive intent later.
- Service Rebellion at this level is simple: it refuses to let customers feel like background tasks.
- Importance looks like: acknowledgement within minutes, not hours, updates before customers wonder, transitions where context moves with the person, and ending conversations with "Here's what happens next".
- When customers don't feel important, they start managing the relationship themselves.
- Customers who feel important stay through small inconveniences – customers who don't feel important leave when a slightly easier option appears.
- When leaders consistently model and reinforce behaviours that signal importance, teams pick up the cue.
- Service Rebellion at this level means refusing to let customers feel like interruptions.

- The five signals that tell a customer they matter:
  - fast acknowledgement
  - visible attention
  - forward clarity
  - proactive updates
  - continuity in handovers.

Chapter 12

THE LEVEL OF UNDERSTANDING

Most people think they are good listeners, though some customers would argue otherwise. There's a massive difference between hearing words and actually understanding what someone is trying to solve, and that gap shows up in almost every industry.

Conversations happen, information gets exchanged, notes get taken, and systems get updated. From the inside, it looks like communication has occurred, but from the customer's side, it can feel like they had to say the same thing three different ways just to be properly understood.

Here's where businesses trip up all the time. Just because you or your staff understand the situation doesn't mean the customer does. Internal knowledge is invisible. You know the process, you know the system, you know the constraints, and you know the terminology. The customer knows none of that. So when communication skips steps, jumps language, or assumes shared context, customers feel lost, not supported. They don't think "That makes sense internally". What they do think is "I don't really get what's happening". Understanding isn't proven by what you say, it's proven by what the customer can confidently repeat back. If they can't explain what's happening in simple terms, you haven't finished the job yet.

That is the Level of Understanding.

UNDERSTANDING MAKES EVERYTHING SMOOTHER

Customers don't just want answers. They want to feel like someone truly gets their situation – not just the surface request, but the context, the concern, and the outcome they're hoping for. When that happens, the interaction feels easy, but when it doesn't, the experience feels heavier than it should. Understanding reduces effort, and effort is one of the biggest silent drivers of loyalty or drift.

Here's the issue: in busy environments, listening often turns into waiting to reply. People hear enough to form a response, then move on. They fill gaps with assumptions because they've heard similar situations before. It feels efficient but too often it isn't. Customers feel the moment someone has jumped to a conclusion. You can see it when someone explains their situation and the response is technically correct but not quite right. The solution addresses part of the issue but misses what actually matters most. Now the customer has to correct the conversation, restate the priority, or explain again. None of this feels dramatic, it just feels like work – work the customer didn't expect to do.

That extra effort builds friction, and friction is rarely blamed directly. Customers don't walk away saying "They didn't understand me". They say "It was a bit of a process", or "I had to explain things a few times", or "In the end it was fine". Fine is often the emotional label for unnecessary effort.

Understanding is what makes interactions feel smooth. When someone truly listens, they clarify before acting. They check assumptions, they reflect back key points, so alignment is clear. These behaviours don't make conversations longer. They make them more accurate. And accuracy early prevents frustration later.

If you want this level trained, not hoped for, it comes down to three observable behaviours.

1. **Reflect back**
   "So what I'm hearing is . . ."
   Not to be polite, but to check alignment before action.
2. **Clarify priorities**
   "Out of all that, what matters most to get right?"
   Because customers often share multiple things, but one carries the emotional weight.
3. **Check understanding before closing**
   "Does that make sense?"
   "Have I missed anything important?"

None of these make conversations longer. They make mistakes shorter because understanding is built through confirmation, not assumption.

REMOVING STRESS

The Level of Understanding matters because customers often approach businesses in situations where something already matters to them. They might be making a financial decision, dealing with a problem, navigating something unfamiliar, or trying to avoid a mistake. In those moments, they are not just looking for information, they are looking for confidence that the person on the other end understands what this actually means for them.

When they feel understood, stress drops. When they don't, stress rises, even if the information provided is technically correct. This is why the Level of Understanding has such a strong emotional impact. It tells customers whether they can relax into the interaction or whether they need to keep managing the conversation themselves. And managing the conversation is tiring.

You can see this across different environments. In retail, it's the difference between someone asking what you're looking for and actually listening versus pointing you towards a generic option. In professional services, it's the difference between advice shaped around your priorities and advice based on a template or a generic answer. In corporate relationships, it's the difference between a partner who understands your pressures and one who just sticks to the brief. The outcome might still be delivered, but the experience feels completely different.

ALIGNMENT

The Level of Understanding also influences how much trust customers will place in future interactions. If they felt understood the first time, they assume the next conversation will be aligned. If they felt misunderstood, they approach the next interaction with caution. They explain more, they repeat themselves, and they check things more often. That caution adds weight to the relationship.

This isn't about being polite, it's about being aligned. When everyone's aligned, you don't have to redo things, chase things, or explain things twice. Confusion drops, tension drops, and customers feel like the business actually knows what it's doing.

This is where the Wolf Pack Standard becomes obvious. In a pack, members don't just hear signals, they read them. Body position, pace, energy, and direction. A wolf doesn't think "I heard a noise". It thinks "What does that mean for the group?" That's understanding. It's not just about the message. It's about sensing the pressure and the situation behind it. That's why packs move smoothly. They don't keep bumping into each other, repeating signals, or correcting direction. They adjust early because they understood the signal properly the first time.

Businesses that operate like packs don't just process requests, they read what the customer is actually dealing with. They don't move until the signal is clear. They don't assume direction. They read it properly, adjust early, and align before they act. Is this urgent? Are they stressed? Are they unsure? Is there risk here? That awareness changes how the response is delivered. Without that awareness, teams operate like individuals sharing noise, but with it, they operate like a coordinated group protecting the outcome.

Understanding isn't passive, it's paying attention to what's really going on. That's why this level isn't about being polite. It's about being aligned. Because customers don't just want someone who can do the job. They want someone who understands what the job means to them. That's the difference between being served and being supported. When understanding is strong, customers feel like they don't have to fight to be clear. But when it's weak, they feel like they need to constantly steer the interaction to keep it on track. And when customers feel like they are doing the steering, the relationship never quite feels safe.

Misunderstanding does more damage than most businesses realise. It doesn't just create errors, it creates emotional friction. Customers start wondering whether they will have to keep correcting things, repeating themselves, or watching closely to make sure nothing important is missed. You can deliver the right result in the end, but if the path involved the customer constantly steering the conversation back on track, the experience feels heavier than it should. People remember that weight. They remember having to say "No, that's not quite what I meant", or "Let me explain again", or "That's not really my concern". Customers don't use the word misalignment. They just know when it feels off, and when it feels off, confidence drops.

LISTENING TO UNDERSTAND

When someone feels understood, they don't have to monitor the conversation. They don't have to pre-empt being misread. They can focus on the outcome rather than managing how well they are being heard. This is especially critical in situations where customers are already under pressure. They might be making a financial commitment, trying to solve a problem quickly, or navigating something unfamiliar. In those moments, the last thing they want is to feel like they also have to manage the quality of listening. Good listening reduces stress, but poor listening increases it, even if everything else is polite and efficient.

Poor listening can lead to assumptions, which quietly mess things up. Staff often believe they understand because they have seen similar cases before, and they respond based on patterns rather than the specifics of this person's situation. From the inside, it feels experienced, but from the customer's or client's perspective, it can feel like being treated as a type instead of a person. And being treated like a type feels impersonal.

Customers don't want to be slotted into a category. They want their situation to be understood in its own context.

Listening to understand doesn't mean every interaction needs to be long. It just means key details are clarified rather than guessed. Assumptions save seconds but cost trust, yet most businesses don't realise they're doing it. You can see this in environments where questions are answered quickly but not precisely. The customer walks away with an answer but still feels unsure because the response didn't address what mattered most to them. That lingering doubt becomes part of the emotional memory.

INTERNAL LANGUAGE CAN CONFUSE

Understanding is also visible in the questions businesses ask. Are they surface questions to move the process forward, or clarifying questions that show someone is trying to get the full picture?

Here's a rule most businesses break without even realising they're doing it: just because the sentence makes sense internally doesn't mean it makes sense to the customer. Internal language is efficient for staff, but it's often confusing for the person on the other end. You say, "Your request has been escalated," and to you that's clear. To the customer, however, it raises five new questions:

- To whom?
- What does that actually mean?
- When will I hear something?
- Is anything happening yet? Do I need to do anything?

Nothing about that sentence made them feel more certain, it just shifted the confusion.

Customer language sounds different. It sounds like "Here's who is handling this . . . here's what they're doing . . . you'll hear from us by tomorrow, and you don't need to do anything right now". Same situation, same process, completely different emotional load. Internal language creates effort while customer language creates clarity. When customers have to translate your language, effort goes up. When they understand instantly, effort drops. Good understanding means the customer doesn't have to do mental gymnastics after you explain something.

When customers sense genuine curiosity, they feel supported, but when questions feel like boxes being ticked, the experience feels procedural and transactional. Procedural might feel efficient internally, but it rarely feels supportive externally.

The Level of Understanding has operational consequences too. When the initial understanding is weak, mistakes and rework increase. Teams end up fixing issues that could have been avoided with clearer listening at the start. Handovers to another department or staff member become messy because the original context wasn't captured properly, and internal pressure rises because people are solving the same problem twice.

Poor understanding wastes time on both sides, but good understanding creates flow. Misunderstanding is very expensive. It creates corrections, escalations, remakes, frustration, and follow-up calls that should never have existed. Good understanding is not a soft skill, it's cost control.

Businesses think listening slows things down, but poor listening is what actually destroys efficiency. And yet most leaders still reward speed over clarity by praising fast responses and celebrating quick turnarounds while rarely measuring whether the customer actually felt understood. Behaviour that gets rewarded is behaviour that gets repeated.

UNDERSTANDING AND POSITIVE RELATIONSHIPS

Understanding also affects how customers describe the business later. When they felt understood, they say things like "They really got what we needed", or "I didn't have to over-explain". That language signals emotional ease. When they didn't feel understood, the story sounds different. "It took a bit to get there", or "I had to clarify a few things". Those comments don't sound like disasters, but they carry a sense of friction, and friction weakens referrals. People are more likely to recommend businesses that made their life easier, not just delivered the end result. Understanding is one of the main ways for businesses to reduce invisible effort for customers. When customers don't have to fight to be clear, the relationship feels lighter. Light relationships grow. Heavy ones stall.

This is where the Level of Understanding connects directly to trust, loyalty, and referrals because people don't just remember what you did, they remember whether you got them. When someone feels understood, they don't need to work hard to explain your business to others. They say things like "They really listened" or "They just understood what we needed". That language is powerful because it speaks to emotional alignment, not just technical competence. When someone doesn't feel understood, the story changes. While phrases like "I had to explain it a few times" or "In the end it was fine, but it took a bit to get there" might not sound like a complaint, they carry a sense of effort. Effort reduces enthusiasm, and reduced enthusiasm weakens referrals.

Understanding builds confidence that the business can handle complexity. Customers assume that if they were heard properly, their situation will be addressed properly. Even if small issues arise later, that early sense of alignment makes them more patient. They believe the business is working with them, not just working on their case.

That belief changes behaviour. Customers who feel understood are more open, more cooperative, and more willing to share information that helps you serve them better. Customers who feel misunderstood hold back. They become cautious about how much they rely on the business. They double-check more, repeat themselves more, and keep emotional distance. That distance weakens loyalty.

The Level of Understanding also has strong internal benefits. When teams build the habit of truly understanding customers, fewer mistakes happen, fewer corrections are needed, and handovers are clearer because context has been captured properly. Time that would have been spent fixing misunderstandings gets used for forward progress.

Understanding improves performance as well as experience. It means valuing clarity over speed when the two compete. It means recognising that the time spent truly understanding the customer is not a delay, it is an investment in getting the experience right the first time. Customers feel the difference immediately. One experience feels like they were processed through to a set solution, where the other feels like the solution was shaped around them. Only one of those builds the kind of trust that holds relationships steady when alternatives appear.

Service Rebellion at this level refuses to confuse speed with competence. It refuses to let teams hide behind quick answers that miss the real issue. It insists that alignment comes before action because action without understanding isn't service. It's movement. And movement without alignment creates friction.

When customers don't feel understood, they start protecting themselves, but when they do, they start trusting you. And trust is what keeps them when options appear.

Customers don't remember every detail of what you said. What they remember is whether they felt heard, whether they had to fight to be clear, whether dealing with you felt easy or like hard work. When people feel understood, they relax, and when they relax, they trust. And when they trust, they stay.

But when they don't feel understood, they start protecting themselves. They double-check, they repeat things, they hold back a bit, and people don't stay loyal in places where they feel like they have to guard the conversation.

Understanding is where trust actually starts. If customers don't feel heard, every other level has to work twice as hard to compensate. You can't build loyalty on top of misalignment.

Chapter summary

- There's a massive difference between hearing words and actually understanding what someone is trying to solve.
- Understanding isn't proven by what you say, it's proven by what the customer can confidently repeat back – if they can't explain what's happening in simple terms, you haven't finished the job yet.
- Training for this level comes down to three observable behaviours:
  - reflect back
  - clarify priorities
  - check understanding before closing.
- When customers feel understood, stress drops – when they don't, stress rises, even if the information provided is technically correct.
- If customers feel understood, they assume the next conversation will be aligned.
- Understanding isn't passive – it's paying attention to what's really going on.
- Good listening reduces stress, but poor listening increases it, even if everything else is polite and efficient.
- Internal language is efficient for staff, but it's often confusing for the person on the other end.
- Poor understanding wastes time on both sides, but good understanding creates flow.
- When someone feels understood, they don't need to work hard to explain your business to others.
- Service Rebellion refuses to confuse speed with competence.

Chapter 13

THE LEVEL OF EMOTION

Let's talk about the thing most businesses avoid because it feels awkward and because the moment you say the word out loud, someone in the room will roll their eyes and say, "Here we go, fluffy stuff!" . . . Emotion.

But in reality, it's not fluffy, it's not soft, and it's not optional. It's happening whether you like it or not, and customers are making decisions based on it every single day. The only question is whether you are deliberately shaping it or accidentally leaving it to chance.

Here's the part that trips up logical, process-driven organisations. Customers don't decide with logic. They justify with logic, they decide with emotion, then they go looking for reasons to make it sound sensible. So they'll tell you it was price, or convenience, or timing, or the package, or the tender process, or the purchasing process, or the new budget, or the restructure. All of those might be part of the story, but underneath it, what actually tipped them was how dealing with you felt.

Now, before anyone says "But we're not in the feelings business", yes, you are! Every organisation, small or large, that deals with a human is in the feelings business whether it sells coffee, cars, consulting, construction, software, healthcare, or government services. You might not sell feelings, but you absolutely create them. Every interaction leaves a feeling behind, and feelings drive behaviour.

Here's what businesses forget. This job you do every day, this claim, this project, this order, this sale, it's one of a hundred on your to-do list. But for the customer, it might be their savings, their house, their business, their health, their time, or their reputation. You're managing a process, but they're carrying emotional weight. That mismatch is where most emotional friction is born.

When staff forget what it all means to the person on the other end, interactions become transactional. And transactions don't build loyalty, emotional investment does. Loyalty is not built in the transaction, it's built in the emotional state surrounding the transaction.

If you want a simple way to understand the Level of Emotion, it comes down to this. When a customer interacts with you, do they leave feeling calmer and more certain, or do they leave feeling like they need to keep an eye on things? That's it. That's the whole thing. Customers might not be able to articulate it, but their body knows. Their shoulders drop or they don't . . . they relax or they stay tense. They trust the journey or they prepare to chase the journey. When they stay tense, loyalty becomes fragile, and this is where a lot of businesses are about to make a massive mistake.

TECHNOLOGY AND EMOTION

A lot of businesses right now are trying to replace human reassurance with automation – AI replies, chatbots, auto-updates, ticket numbers. Look, I'm not anti-technology. Efficiency matters, removing friction matters, but there's something people are missing: efficiency removes friction, but humans remove fear. AI can answer a question. It can give you a status update, and it can send a notification at exactly the right time. What it can't do is sense tension in someone's voice, pick up that hesitation before a question, or recognise that someone is worried but doesn't quite know how to say it. Technology is brilliant for process. It just isn't built for emotional safety. That part is still human work.

When businesses automate the emotional layer out of an interaction, customers don't relax. They stay in watch mode. They keep checking. They screenshot confirmations. They double-read emails. And when a customer feels like they have to monitor everything, loyalty quietly starts to erode.

On the weekend, right in the middle of writing this chapter, we were at a casual BBQ. Someone asked what I'd been up to lately. I mentioned some coming speaking engagements, and then said I was writing this book. The response was immediate: "No one's going to read that. AI will replace all customer interaction soon anyway." It wasn't said aggressively. It was just matter of fact, like it was obvious. But that comment sums up exactly why this chapter matters.

Technology will keep advancing. It should. It should assist, it should streamline, and it should make things faster and clearer. But it won't replace the human need underneath it. Customers don't just want information delivered efficiently. They want to feel understood. They want to feel safe. They want to feel like someone is actually across their situation. You can automate updates. You can automate reminders. You can automate answers. But you can't automate the feeling that someone genuinely has your back.

The businesses that mistake speed for safety will strip out the very thing that builds loyalty. The businesses that understand that technology supports connection rather than replaces it are the ones that will quietly pull ahead. This is why you can have a business that is technically excellent and still lose customers. Because technical excellence can still be delivered in a way that feels cold, rushed, or dismissive. You can fix the issue, deliver the service, meet the requirements, and still leave the customer thinking "I'm glad that's done" instead of "I'm glad it was them". The first one is relief that the task is over, the second one is confidence in the relationship. And confidence is what creates repeat behaviour.

SAFETY NOT STRESS

Here's what businesses often get wrong. They think emotion is about friendliness, so they tell staff to smile more, be more upbeat, use the customer's name, add a bit of enthusiasm. None of those hurt, but they miss the point. Customers don't just want friendliness. They want emotional safety, they want certainty, they want to feel respected, and they want to feel like the person on the other side is actually paying attention and has their back.

You can be friendly but still feel unreliable. Unreliable doesn't mean incompetent. It means the customer feels like they might have to manage you. It means chasing updates, repeating themselves, double-checking details, and staying alert instead of relaxing. That's emotional stress.

A lot of businesses accidentally create stress while trying to be efficient. They send short messages, provide minimal updates, assume no news is good news, or fire off an SMS saying "I'll call you in 10 minutes" and then never do. None of that feels dramatic in isolation, but it creates a quiet layer of tension. They move customers through processes quickly without taking the time to settle them into what is happening. Internally, that feels productive, but from the customer's or client's perspective, it can feel like being pushed through a system with no reassurance. The process might work, but you don't relax inside it. You stay alert, you keep checking, you prepare for the next frustration before it even happens. That's emotional memory in action.

Now let's make this practical across different environments because the whole point of this book is that it applies anywhere humans deal with humans.

In retail, the Level of Emotion shows up in whether the customer feels welcome or tolerated. You don't need a staff member doing cartwheels at the entrance, you just need the customer to feel noticed and not like a nuisance. That feeling changes everything – whether they browse or rush, whether they ask for help or avoid it, and whether they come back or simply go to the place that feels easier next time.

In trades and services, emotion shows up in communication and reliability. A customer doesn't just want the job done, they want to feel like you're on top of it. When there's silence, vague messages, or missed calls, they don't just think you're busy, they start creating stories. Maybe they forgot, maybe they're disorganised, maybe the quote will blow out, or maybe they'll turn up late. That uncertainty becomes stress, and stress makes customers look elsewhere, even if you're good at what you do.

In professional services, emotion shows up in whether the client feels guided or left to figure it out. You can deliver great advice and still make the client feel dumb, rushed, or like they're asking too many questions. The client might still proceed, but the emotional memory becomes "I had to push to get clarity" rather than "They made it easy". And again, it affects referrals. People don't refer someone who makes them feel uneasy, even if they're competent.

In corporate and B2B relationships, emotion shows up in the difference between proactive reassurance and reactive updates. When a client has to chase for status, the relationship becomes stressful. When updates are given before the client asks, the relationship becomes calm. Stressed clients are always one good pitch away from switching, but calm clients stay longer and are harder to steal.

In government and large systems, emotion shows up in whether people feel helped or handled. People don't expect luxury from public service. They expect to feel respected and guided. When the system makes them repeat themselves, sit on hold, get transferred, or feel like they're bothering someone, the emotional memory becomes frustration. That frustration doesn't just affect that one interaction, it becomes a story they tell about the entire organisation. Unfortunately, government departments make this harder than it needs to be because of transactional thinking and processes. There are too many processes that are there just because they are.

Customers who don't feel safe behave like referees. Customers who feel emotionally safe behave like partners. When they don't feel safe, they watch you. When they do, they work with you. Referees don't relax. Referees watch for mistakes, and referees blow the whistle.

TRAINING FOR THE LEVEL OF EMOTION

Think about this. You can't control how customers feel in the sense of forcing a reaction, but you can absolutely control the behaviours that create the conditions for certain feelings. That's what these levels are. They are the actions that decide how customers walk away feeling. When people feel important, understood, and reassured, emotion rises in the right direction. When they feel ignored, misunderstood, or left guessing, emotion turns negative. It's not complicated, it's just rarely managed properly. The Level of Emotion is not about asking your team to be more emotional.

So if emotion isn't personality, what is it? It's behaviour, and it's trainable like this.

1. **Call out the situation**
   "I know this is stressful."
   "That's a lot to deal with."
   "That's frustrating."
   The moment it's recognised, the pressure eases.
2. **Show you've got it**
   "Here's what we're doing."
   "Here's what happens next."
   Control creates reassurance.
3. **Don't leave them guessing**
   Even if the answer is "We don't know yet".
   Bad news is easier to handle than silence.
4. **Don't rush them**
   Don't rush past emotion to the solution.
   People calm down when they feel heard, not when they feel fixed.
   Be present in the conversation or communication.
5. **Make sure they are okay**
   "Does that help?"
   "Are you feeling clearer now?"
   Make sure the tension has actually dropped.

That's emotional skill in business, and it's totally trainable. It's about building behaviours that reduce stress and increase confidence. It's about acknowledging that every interaction carries a tone and that tone is either strengthening trust or weakening it.

FIXING THE PROBLEMS

If you get the emotional level right, customers feel calmer, safer, and more confident dealing with you, and that confidence becomes sticky. If you get it wrong, customers might still buy, but they won't attach. And if they don't attach, you end up back on the treadmill, chasing new transactions because the old ones don't turn into long-term loyalty or the customer has raved to others about your business or staff. That treadmill is expensive, and unnecessary.

If the customer already feels safe and confident with you, they give you room. If they already feel uncertain, every small issue becomes proof that their doubt was justified. That's why emotion acts like a multiplier. Positive emotional experience softens problems, and negative emotional experience amplifies them.

You see this all the time in businesses that say, "We fixed the issue, but they were still unhappy." Of course they were. You solved the technical problem, but the emotional experience leading up to it made them feel stressed, ignored, or unsure. By the time the solution arrived, the emotional account was already overdrawn. Emotion builds up across moments. It's shaped by how someone is greeted, how clearly things are explained, how confident the communication sounds, how issues are handled, and whether the customer feels like they're dealing with people who are on their side or people who are simply managing a process. Each moment either adds emotional credit or emotional debt. When customers have emotional credit with you, they're more patient. When they have emotional debt, they're quicker to react.

This is especially visible when things go wrong, which they always will at some point. No system is perfect, no team is flawless, and no process runs without hiccups. The real test isn't whether problems occur. It's the emotional state the customer is in when they do. If they feel supported, a problem becomes a situation to solve together. If they feel processed, the same problem becomes evidence that the business doesn't really care. That interpretation changes everything.

Emotion is also heavily influenced by how uncertainty is handled. Customers can tolerate complexity, they can tolerate delays, they can tolerate bad news. What they struggle with is not knowing where they stand. Silence, vague responses, or unclear next steps create emotional tension. People fill that gap with their own assumptions, and those assumptions are rarely generous. Clear communication reduces that emotional load.

You don't have to have all the answers immediately. You just have to show that someone is paying attention and steering the situation. Even a simple update that says "Here's where we're at and here's what happens next" can drop a customer's stress level dramatically. Without that, they stay in watch mode, waiting for something to go wrong, and watch mode is not a relaxed place to build loyalty from.

TONE AND EMOTION

Another thing businesses underestimate is how tone affects emotion – not what is said, but how it is delivered. A short, clipped message might be efficient, but it can feel dismissive. A slightly warmer explanation might take the same amount of time but leave the customer feeling reassured. These nuances don't show up on reports, but they shape the emotional memory of the interaction, and that memory is what customers carry forward.

Businesses often miss the positive effects of tone because they are measuring outcomes, not feelings. The job was delivered, the invoice was paid, and the case was closed. From the inside, everything looks successful. From the customer's side, the journey might have felt heavier than it needed to be, and heavy experiences don't create attachment. This is why emotion is such a critical level in the behavioural system. It is the layer that sits over all the others: importance, understanding, expectation, effort, certainty, personalisation, consistency. All of those behaviours feed into how the customer feels. Emotion is the result.

When the emotional result is positive, customers feel like they are in safe hands. When it's neutral or negative, they feel like they are in a system they need to monitor. Monitoring is tiring, and tired customers don't become advocates. This is where the Level of Emotion connects directly to loyalty and referrals because emotion is what customers remember long after the details fade.

EMOTIONAL MEMORY

Ask someone about a business they dealt with six months ago and they probably won't remember the exact timeline, the precise steps, or the specific information they were given. What they will remember is how it felt. Whether it felt easy or hard, calm or stressful, supportive or cold. That emotional summary becomes the shortcut their brain uses the next time they have to choose. If the emotional memory is positive, returning feels safe. If it's neutral, returning feels optional. If it's negative, returning feels risky.

Emotional memory explains why two businesses can deliver the same technical outcome and end up with completely different levels of loyalty. One leaves customers feeling confident and looked after, whereas the other leaves customers feeling like they got through it. Those are very different emotional memories, and they drive very different behaviours.

This is also where emotion becomes critical in referral behaviour. When someone refers you, they are putting their own reputation alongside your service. They don't just think about whether the job was done, they think about how the person they refer will feel during the journey. If their own experience felt supportive and reassuring, referring feels safe. If it felt tense, uncertain, or emotionally flat, they hesitate, and that hesitation is expensive. You can ask for referrals all day, but if the emotional experience hasn't built confidence, people won't risk their name. Referrals are trust transfers, and trust is emotional before it is logical. Someone referring for you is putting their reputation on the line before your reputation kicks in. Read that last sentence and let that sink in.

CONNECTION AND EMOTION

Emotion explains why how problems are handled often matters more than the problems themselves. When something goes wrong and the customer feels heard, respected, and supported, the emotional bond can actually strengthen. They feel like the business has their back when it matters. If the same issue is handled in a way that feels defensive or procedural, trust weakens, even if the technical solution is identical. It's never just about the fixing of an issue. It's the feeling around the process of the fix.

Service Rebellion at this level means drawing a line when service starts to feel cold instead of connected. It means recognising that every conversation, every message, every update carries an emotional tone whether you intend it to or not. You don't need drama, and you don't need forced friendliness. What customers need is emotional safety, and that comes from clarity, patience, and visible care.

When teams understand this, behaviour shifts in subtle but powerful ways. Explanations include reassurance, not just facts. Delays are acknowledged rather than left in silence. Questions are welcomed instead of rushed past. And tone matters as much as the message.

These shifts don't slow the business down, they reduce friction because customers feel less need to chase, clarify, or worry. Their mental load drops, and when mental load drops, loyalty rises.

This is where it hits your business. Customers who feel emotionally safe decide faster, complain less, stay longer, and refer more. Customers who don't feel safe compare more, question more, and leave more easily. The difference between those two groups is not product alone. It is the emotional experience layered over the journey. Without it, transactions stay separate and shallow. With it, relationships become stable and resilient.

This is exactly how packs operate. A wolf doesn't just react to movement, it reads energy, tension, fear, and alertness. If one member is tense, the pack adjusts. Businesses that operate like packs don't ignore emotional signals. They respond to them early. That's why packs move smoothly under pressure, and they regulate emotion as much as they regulate action.

Businesses think customers leave because of price, but customers leave because it stopped feeling good to deal with you, and most businesses never even realise that's what changed.

The Level of Emotion isn't a soft extra. It's one of the forces shaping customer behaviour whether you manage it or not. Every interaction either strengthens the emotional foundation of the relationship or weakens it slightly. Most of those shifts happen in moments so small they barely register internally. But they are felt. Every time.

Chapter summary

- Customers decide with emotion then justify with logic.
- You might not sell feelings, but you absolutely create them – every interaction leaves a feeling behind, and feelings drive behaviour.
- Customers should leave interactions feeling calmer and more certain, not like they need to keep an eye on things.
- Technology is brilliant for process – it just isn't built for emotional safety.
- Businesses that understand that technology supports connection rather than replaces it are the ones that will quietly pull ahead.
- Customers don't just want friendliness – they want emotional safety, certainty, to feel respected, and to feel like you are paying attention and have their back.
- Train the Level of Emotion with these points:
    - call out the situation
    - show you've got it
    - don't leave them guessing
    - don't rush them
    - make sure they are okay.
- Emotion builds up across moments, either adding emotional credit or debt.
- Tone affects emotion – not what is said, but how it is delivered.
- The emotional summary of last time a customer dealt with you becomes the shortcut their brain uses the next time they have to choose.
- Service Rebellion at this level means drawing a line when service starts to feel cold instead of connected.

Chapter 14

THE LEVEL OF EXPECTATION

Expectations are where a lot of businesses quietly shoot themselves in the foot while thinking they're being smart. You've heard it a thousand times: under-promise and over-deliver. Sounds like wisdom, it sounds safe, and it sounds like something you'd hear at a conference right after someone tells you to "work on your mindset" and then sells you a course.

Here's the problem though. Customers do not want to be surprised as much as businesses think they do. They want to be certain. A surprise is nice occasionally, but certainty is what builds trust. If I buy something and it arrives earlier than expected, great. I'll smile. I might even mention it. But what makes me come back to your business is knowing the next time I buy it will arrive when you said it would. What makes me come back isn't that you surprised me. It's that I know exactly what I'm going to get next time. That's the Level of Expectation.

Service Rebellion at this level starts here. It refuses to let expectation be something that just "happens". It treats clarity as a behavioural standard, not a communication preference. This level is about how clearly and realistically the journey is set up in the customer's mind. Not just what you deliver, but what they think will happen, how it will happen, when it will happen, who is responsible for what, how communication will work, and what "normal" looks like. Customers don't judge you against what you did, they judge you against what they expected. If expectations are wrong, good work still feels bad.

Who sets the expectations?

Here's where businesses get this badly wrong. They think expectations are something they get to set. They design a process, they build a timeline that works for them, they decide how communication happens, then they expect the customer to just slot into that structure and behave. That's not expectation management, that's making the customer adapt to you.

Customers already have a picture in their head when they walk in, before you even open your mouth – how long this will take, how often they'll hear from you, what good service looks like, and what "normal" should feel like. If you don't find out what that picture is, and ask questions, you are working blind. And when reality clashes with their mental picture, they don't think misalignment, they think, "This feels off." If expectation and reality line up, the experience feels smooth. But if they don't, even good delivery can feel disappointing, and disappointment has a longer memory than delight.

This is why you can have a business that is genuinely good, with hard-working staff and solid capability, and still have customers quietly drifting away. Not because you failed them dramatically, but because the experience didn't match the picture they had in their head. And the moment a customer feels like they have to manage you, the relationship changes. It becomes heavier, less relaxed, more transactional, less referable, and more likely to be compared on price. Your customers and clients will question price when they don't see or feel value. Meeting their expectations is value for them.

ACCURATE AND CONSISTENT

Now, before we go any further, let's get clear on something. This isn't about lowering the bar so you can step over it and celebrate. It's about being accurate and consistent. Accurate expectations create calm customers, and calm customers are loyal customers. Loyal customers are cheaper to keep than constantly replacing people who leave because they were fed a vague, optimistic story at the start before reality showed up like a wet blanket.

Most expectation failures start the same way. You say things you can't pin down, you promise things you can't control, and you hope the customer won't notice the cracks.

Let's start with vague language because it's the silent killer. Soon . . . shortly . . . as soon as possible . . . we'll try . . . we'll get back to you . . . it should be fine . . . we're onto it . . . we're looking into it. Those phrases sound harmless. They're polite, they keep your options open, but they also create uncertainty because they don't anchor the customer to anything real. Soon means different things to different people. To your team, soon might mean in a couple of days, but to the customer, soon might mean today. When you respond two days later, your team thinks nothing is wrong. However, the customer thinks they've been ignored. No one lied. You just left the customer in a grey zone, and grey zones are where frustration grows.

Service Rebellion removes grey zones. It doesn't hide behind "soon" or "we'll try". It names timeframes. It names responsibility. It names next steps. Clarity prevents more conflict than capability ever will.

ALIGNING EXPECTATIONS

And here's the part most businesses skip completely. You don't just tell customers what to expect, you need to ask them what they expect. "What does a good outcome look like for you?", "How often would you like updates?", "What are you most worried about in this process?" Those questions change everything. Because now you're not just setting expectations, you're aligning expectations. That's the difference between running a process and leading a customer through a journey.

Certainty is not created by good intentions. It's created by clear commitments. If you say "You'll hear from us by Thursday afternoon", the customer relaxes. They now have a timeline, and their brain has something to hold onto. They don't have to keep checking their phone, they don't have to wonder if they should follow up, they don't have to create stories. And if Thursday passes with no contact, the gap is obvious and fixable. Without clarity, the customer is stuck deciding when it's reasonable to chase, and nobody wants to chase. People chase when they feel like they have to, and the moment they start chasing, the emotional tone drops.

OVER-PROMISING DOESN'T WIN THE RACE

Now let's talk about optimism disguised as service. A lot of businesses over-promise because they want to win. They want the customer to feel excited and confident, so they paint an attractive picture – short timelines, simple processes, easy outcomes, smooth onboarding, and quick results. And to be fair, sometimes it can go that way. But the customer isn't judging you by "sometimes". They are judging you by what happens with their own experience with you.

Customers don't get upset about delays. They get upset about being told something that wasn't true. If you say two weeks and it takes four, the customer doesn't think, "That's okay, things happen." They think, "Why did you tell me two?" A small delay is forgivable, but a broken expectation isn't. Delays can be understood, but being misled, even unintentionally, is harder to forgive. It creates suspicion, and it makes customers watch you more closely. It makes them question your competence or your honesty. The moment they feel like they need to supervise you, the relationship changes. Supervised businesses don't get referred. They get compared.

This is what that happens when the business has no consistent way of setting expectations because internally everything is changing daily. Staff turnover, workload spikes, unclear handovers, overloaded managers, broken systems, too many priorities . . . Customers don't see any of that, but they absolutely feel it through inconsistent expectations. One staff member tells them one thing, then another tells them something else. Customers don't need perfection. They need to feel safe. And safety comes from knowing what's going on and knowing it won't keep shifting. When expectations are steady, customers lean in. When they're inconsistent, customers lean back. This is why managing expectation isn't a communication trick. It's where trust either starts or quietly breaks.

EXPECTATIONS AFTER THE SALE IS MADE

Now, here's the part most businesses unfortunately miss. Expectation management doesn't stop once the customer has paid. In fact, after the customer commits is where expectations matter more because the customer is still in decision mode after they buy. They're still evaluating whether they made the right choice, and they're emotionally exposed. Their money, time, reputation, or internal standing is now tied to the outcome. That's when the little voice starts asking "Did I make the right call here?" If the business goes quiet after the sale, the customer doesn't think, "They must be working." They think, "Have they moved on now that they've got my money?" You may not intend that, but intention doesn't matter because interpretation now becomes truth.

This is why onboarding and early communication are so important. Customers need to feel oriented. They need to know what happens next, who is doing what, when they'll hear from you, and what silence means. If three days of quiet is normal, say that, or if weekly updates are normal, say that. When people know what's normal, they stop guessing.

PACK EXPECTATIONS

So what does setting expectations properly actually look like in the real world?

- You give timeframes that are specific where possible and honest where they can't be.
- You don't use vague filler words to avoid commitment – you give the customer something they can rely on.
- You explain the process in plain language, not internal jargon.
- You tell customers what you need from them and what happens if you don't get it.
- You set communication expectations, so they know when they'll hear from you.
- When something changes, you update them before they have to ask.

That last one alone is a gamechanger. A customer who has to chase for updates feels like they're carrying the relationship, but a customer who receives proactive updates feels like you're in control and they're in safe hands. Same work but different feeling. Packs don't move because one wolf decides the pace, they move because everyone reads the situation first – distance, terrain, risk, energy – then they adjust.

That's the Wolf Pack Standard in business. Before they move, they check the terrain. Before they run, they know where they're heading. Packs don't run because they're excited. They run because they're clear. Businesses that charge ahead without checking expectations are like a pack that runs ahead before checking where the rest are. That's how your customers and clients get lost, and that's how trust breaks. Expectation clarity is pack behaviour because everyone knows the direction before the run starts.

EXPECTATIONS IN YOUR BUSINESS

Let's apply this across different environments. The psychology is the same even when the process isn't.

In retail, expectations show up in simple things like availability, timing, and returns. If a staff member says "It'll be here next week", and the customer organises their week around that, next week becomes a commitment. If the item arrives the week after and nobody updates them, the customer feels messed around. They don't say, "The supply chain is complex." They say, "They told me next week." That's an expectation gap.

In direct service businesses, expectations are everything. Hair, beauty, health, trades, mechanics . . . people want to know what's happening, how long it will take, what it will cost, and what they need to do. If you don't set expectations clearly, you create stress. If you do set them clearly, customers relax and trust you.

In professional services, expectations are often the main product. Clients are paying for expertise, but they're also paying for clarity. They want to understand the timeline, milestones, what information you need, what the next steps are, and what outcomes are realistic. When expectations are vague, clients feel like they're in the dark. When expectations are clear, clients feel guided, and guided clients stay longer.

In corporate and B2B relationships, expectations aren't just about customer satisfaction, they're about internal credibility. Your contact person often has their reputation tied to your delivery. If you make them look good, you become hard to replace. If you make them look unsure in front of their leadership, you become risky. And people do not keep risky suppliers. This is why expectation management in corporate environments has a multiplier effect. You're not just setting expectations for a customer, you're helping them set expectations internally. When you give them clear timelines, clear milestones, clear communication, they can go to their leadership and sound confident, and that confidence makes them loyal.

In government services, expectations are often the main source of frustration. People can tolerate procedure if they understand it. They lose their mind when they don't know what's happening, how long it will take, what they need to do, or what the outcome will be. The frustration isn't always the policy: it's the uncertainty, and uncertainty is what makes people angry.

WHERE DOES IT ALL GO WRONG?

So let's talk about where businesses mess this up most commonly.

They over-promise to win, they avoid committing when it matters, and they go quiet when things get busy and assume effort is an excuse. Then they're shocked when customers say, "It was fine, but . . ." That phrase is a warning sign. It means the outcome might have been acceptable, but the journey felt heavier than it should, and most churn – customer turnover – is hidden inside "fine".

Now, here's the thing about under-promise and over-deliver. The original intention behind that phrase was to stop businesses making promises they can't keep, and it was meant to promote realism. The way it's often applied now is more like a performance tactic. Set low expectations so you can exceed them and look great. That in itself creates its own problem.

If your expectations are always low, customers don't know what to rely on. One time you do it fast, then another time you do it slow.

One time you over-deliver, then another time you just meet the basics. Customers can't predict the experience, and unpredictable is not impressive. It's exhausting. Customers would rather have a consistent expectation that is met every time than occasional pleasant surprises that make the journey feel like a roll of the dice. Consistency is what builds confidence, and confidence is what builds loyalty.

This is why the Level of Expectation is closely tied to the Level of Certainty later in the book. Expectations are how you create certainty before anything has even happened. They are the roadmap. A roadmap doesn't guarantee the trip will have no traffic, it just means you know where you are going and what the route looks like.

THE COST OF UNREALISTIC EXPECTATIONS

Now, let's bring in the commercial side properly because this is where businesses underestimate what expectation gaps cost.

When expectations are unclear or unrealistic, customers chase more. That increases workload. Staff become more reactive, replies become shorter, tone becomes more procedural, the customer feels less looked after, and they have to chase more.

Now you've got a loop. Vague expectations create chasing, and chasing creates pressure. Pressure creates thinner communication, then thinner communication creates more uncertainty. In turn, more uncertainty creates more chasing. And all of this is happening while the business thinks it's just "busy". Being busy is not the issue, being unclear is the issue. Most "difficult" customers are just people standing in expectation fog.

This loop increases costs in ways businesses rarely calculate: time spent responding to chasing emails, calming customers down, handling escalations that were preventable, re-explaining, and fixing trust. Rebuilding trust is expensive, but setting expectations properly costs nothing.

Expectation gaps also increase price sensitivity. When customers feel uncertain, they default to comparing, but when they feel confident, they commit. So if your expectation management is sloppy, you might still win customers, but you'll win the kind who negotiate harder, churn faster, and refer less. That's not a customer problem, that's an experience problem.

LEADING EXPECTATION

Now, let's talk about the leadership angle. Expectation management is not something you leave to individual staff to "figure out". Leaders don't just set internal standards. They have to build a culture where staff are allowed and expected to ask customers about their expectations. Not assume, not guess, not project . . . Ask! Because when staff are scared to have that conversation, they blur the edges instead of being clear. Blurry communication creates unsafe experiences. It needs to be designed.

Leaders have to decide what realistic timelines are. Leaders have to decide what updates customers should receive and when. If you are a business owner, regardless of whether you have no staff, ten staff, or you are a CEO with hundreds of staff, you are a leader. *You* set the tone and *you* set the benchmark. Leaders have to decide what is acceptable communication, and what is not. Leaders have to remove vague language from the business by setting standards.

Service Rebellion makes expectation clarity non-negotiable. Not personality-driven. Not optional. It's not a document. It's how you operate. Because if you don't, expectation setting becomes a personality contest. One staff member is confident and specific, but another is vague and cautious. One gives proactive updates, yet another goes quiet. One explains the process clearly, and another assumes the customer knows. The customer experiences inconsistency, and inconsistency creates uncertainty.

This is why the Level of Expectation is one of the easiest places to build trust quickly, if you treat it seriously. Customers don't need you to be perfect, they need you to be clear. Clear expectations are a form of respect, but confusion feels like carelessness. Clear expectations respect the customer's time, planning, and emotional need for certainty. When you set expectations clearly and meet them consistently, customers feel safe. They stop watching you, they stop chasing, they stop comparing, and they start trusting. And trust is what turns a one-off customer into a long-term customer.

HOW SERVICE REBELLION FITS INTO THIS LEVEL

At this level, Service Rebellion is simply this: no hiding behind "soon" and "we'll see". It refuses to say what sounds good if it won't hold up. It chooses clarity, even when clarity feels uncomfortable, because clarity builds trust faster than charm ever will. So the rebellious move is clarity. Not performance, not buzzwords, not under-promise and over-deliver theatre. Clarity!

This is also why setting expectations accurately is one of the strongest ways to differentiate in a market where everyone's offering looks similar.

Two businesses can deliver similar capability. One creates a calm journey through clear expectations yet the other creates a stressful journey through vague promises and inconsistent updates. Customers will always choose calm. And they'll pay more for it too, even if they don't say that out loud. They may call it professionalism, or reliability, or being organised, but what they're really buying is emotional safety.

Chapter summary

- You can't protect the customer if you don't understand what matters to them.
- Service Rebellion at this level is about understanding more, it's about having the ability to say "Before we start, let's make sure we see this the same way".
- The Level of Expectation is not all about fancy service gestures – it's about setting the customer up to feel oriented, informed, and confident.
- When expectations and reality line up, the experience feels trustworthy.
- But when they don't, even good work can feel like a hassle, and no one refers hassle.
- Customers refer certainty, calm, and businesses that make the journey feel easy because the customer always knows where they stand.
- Certainty is not boring. Certainty is power. That's what this level is about.

Chapter 15

THE LEVEL OF EFFORT

Here's something businesses hate hearing because it sounds too simple to be powerful. And if you really think about it, most of the time simplicity is what most businesses miss and overlook. Customers don't usually leave because you're bad. They leave because dealing with you feels like work. Not dramatically hard. Not "I'm storming out" hard. Just that low-level, ongoing friction where dealing with you feels like more effort than it should.

Effort is one of the biggest silent killers of loyalty, and most businesses don't see it because nothing explodes. There's no big complaint, there's no blow-up email, and there's no one slamming the phone down. Customers just start choosing easier options when they appear.

WHO IS DOING THE WORK?

The Level of Effort is about how much work the customer has to do to deal with you. Not how hard your team works, not how complex your systems are, not even how many moving parts you're juggling. The only thing that matters is how heavy it feels from the outside. Because customers don't experience your internal effort, they experience their own.

Service Rebellion doesn't let customers do unpaid work. If someone has to chase you, translate you, repeat themselves, or babysit the process, that's not "how it works", that's you pushing your workload onto them. And that's where loyalty starts to leak.

This is where businesses get it backwards. They think, "We're working hard, so the customer should understand." Customers are not meant to understand your workload. They are meant to feel the absence of it. The effort belongs to the business. If the customer is carrying it, something's off. You can be working flat out behind the scenes, solving problems, coordinating people, juggling deadlines, putting out fires. But if the customer still has to chase updates, repeat information, fill in the same details twice, navigate confusing processes, or guess what's happening next, the experience feels heavy.

Let's be honest. Most businesses don't lose customers in big dramatic moments. They lose them in small, repeated moments of unnecessary effort: having to call twice, explain again, log in through a clunky system, wait on hold for ages, and follow up on something that should have been automatic. None of these alone feels like a dealbreaker. But together they tell the customer "This takes energy". And energy is limited.

Customers are not just comparing your product or price. They are comparing how easy it feels to deal with you versus the alternative. If another business makes the same outcome feel smoother, that's often enough, and ease is competitive advantage. The tricky part is that businesses often confuse internal efficiency with customer ease. A process might be efficient for the team, structured around internal systems, approvals, or reporting, but if that process requires the customer to adapt to your structure rather than the other way around, the effort lands on them.

Customers don't care how your system works. They just care how easy their part is. You see this in forms that ask for information the business already has. In handovers where customers have to repeat their story. In support interactions where the person on the other end can't see previous notes. In appointment systems that are rigid. And in communication that requires the customer to interpret what's going on. Each of these is a small tax on the customer's time and attention. One tax doesn't matter much, but a dozen of them does.

REMOVING THE MENTAL LOAD

Now, here's where businesses get defensive. They say "But our industry is complex", or "There are regulations", or "That's just how it works", or "We have to follow procedure". All of that might be true, but complexity is not the enemy, unnecessary customer effort is. And this is where the excuses usually show up. "That's just how our company works", "We have to follow process", "It's compliance", "That's our platform", or my personal favourite, "The system won't allow that". All of those might be true, but they are still not the customer's problem. Customers didn't design your system, so they shouldn't be paying for its weaknesses with their time and energy.

Customers can handle complexity if they feel guided through it because guidance reduces perceived effort. They struggle when they feel like they are navigating it alone. A pack doesn't make one member work twice as hard just to keep up. They close the gap. They adjust.

They carry the load so the group stays smooth. That's the Wolf Pack Standard in business. The customer shouldn't have to fight the terrain you built.

In high-functioning teams, the strong carry more so the group moves smoothly. In strong businesses, the systems carry more so the customer moves easily. When the customer has to carry the weight, the pack is failing.

This is why the Level of Effort is not just about removing steps. It's about reducing the mental and emotional load on the customer. Even when a process has to be detailed, how it is explained and supported makes a massive difference. If a customer knows exactly what to do, why they're doing it, and what happens next, the effort feels manageable. If they are left guessing, the same process feels like a chore. And chores don't create loyalty.

You can see this in everyday life. Think about a place you deal with that just feels easy. You don't have to chase, and you don't have to explain things repeatedly. Things happen when they say they will. If there's a delay, you're told. If something is needed from you, it's clear.

Now think about the opposite. Places where you have to keep following up. Where you never quite know what's happening, and where you have to remember details because they don't. You don't look forward to dealing with them. So you stop choosing them, and when a better option shows up, you move.

This is why effort is such a big driver of drift. Customers don't always leave because they're unhappy. They leave because something else feels easier.

Effort also affects referrals. People don't just refer based on quality, they refer based on how safe it feels to send someone else into that experience. If the journey felt like work, they hesitate. If it felt smooth, they feel confident recommending. Referrals follow ease.

WHO ARE WE MAKING IT EASIER FOR?

Now, here's the part that's a bit uncomfortable. A lot of customer effort is invisible internally because teams get used to their own processes. They know the shortcuts, and they understand the jargon. They know which forms matter and which don't, they know who to talk to, and they know what delays are normal. Customers don't live in your environment, they visit it. What feels normal to you can feel like a maze to them.

This is why effort drift happens slowly. Each small step makes sense internally. Each extra field on a form, each new approval layer, and each additional email chain. Over time, the journey gets heavier, but no single change feels dramatic enough to question. Until customers start quietly leaving. And by then, businesses blame price, competition, the market, or customer behaviour instead of looking at how much effort they've been asking people to carry.

The Level of Effort is about constantly asking one question: Are we making this easier for the customer, or just easier for ourselves? When that question is ignored, effort creeps up. When it's taken seriously, loyalty becomes easier to build. Customers don't stay where they have to work hard.

Effort doesn't just show up in big obvious steps. Most of the time it's invisible, and that's what makes it dangerous. Customers rarely sit there thinking, "This business requires too much effort." What they feel is a slow build-up of tiny drains. Having to log in again, having to repeat a detail, having to wait without context, or having to send a follow-up because something didn't happen when it was meant to. Each one is small, but together they create emotional fatigue.

Fatigue is different to frustration. Frustration is sharp, it gets attention. Fatigue is dull, it doesn't make noise. It just slowly reduces how much energy a customer wants to put into the relationship. And when energy drops, attachment drops. This is where businesses get blindsided. Customers haven't complained, they haven't left angry. They've just become less engaged. They respond slower, and they stop asking questions. They stop exploring additional services, and they don't refer. Then one day they're gone. From the inside, it feels like they disappeared. From the outside, they were drifting for months under the weight of effort. And effort compounds over time.

The first time a customer has to chase something, it's fine. The second time, they notice. The third time, it becomes a pattern. Now they are emotionally preparing for more work every time they deal with you. That preparation changes behaviour. They keep backups, they double-check, they hold off on committing fully, they compare more, and they may become price sensitive because the emotional value of the relationship has dropped. Heavy relationships get reduced to numbers.

Effort also links directly to trust. When customers have to do work that should have been handled by the business, confidence drops. They start wondering what else might be missed. That uncertainty creates tension, and tension makes interactions feel harder than they need to be. This is why two businesses with similar outcomes can have completely different loyalty levels. One makes the journey feel smooth, where the other makes the customer feel like they have to stay switched on. Switched-on customers are not relaxed customers. They are always on alert waiting to manage something.

You see this in environments where internal processes are king. The system says the customer has to fill in this, upload that, confirm this, wait for approval, then move to the next stage. Internally, it's organised, but externally, it can feel like navigating a maze.

If no one is guiding the customer through the maze, the effort becomes their problem.

THROUGH THE MAZE TO LOYALTY

Guidance is one of the biggest effort reducers. A clear explanation, a simple checklist, a proactive update, or someone saying "Here's what happens next and I'll let you know when we reach the next step", removes a huge amount of mental load.

Mental load is effort, and mental load turns into emotional weight, which is why effort and emotion are always linked. And when effort rises, emotion drops. When mental load is low, the experience feels easy, even if the process is detailed. When mental load is high, the experience feels heavy, even if the process is short. This is why effort is not just about steps. It's about clarity, communication, and ownership.

Ownership is huge here. When customers feel like they are carrying responsibility for making sure things happen, the effort feels unfair. When they feel like the business is carrying that responsibility, the effort feels shared and manageable. Shared effort builds partnership, and one-sided effort builds resentment.

Effort also affects how customers talk about you. Businesses that feel easy get described as "great to deal with" and "smooth" – "They just handle it". Businesses that feel heavy get described as "Fine, but . . ." or

"You have to stay on top of them", or "It works, but it's a process". That "but" is where referrals go to die. Because when someone recommends a business, they are not just recommending the outcome, they are recommending the journey. If the journey felt like work, they hesitate to put someone else through it. Effort doesn't just influence satisfaction, it influences advocacy, and advocacy is where real growth happens.

This is where the Level of Effort becomes a loyalty issue, not just a convenience issue. Customers don't leave only because something goes wrong. They leave because dealing with you takes more energy than it should. When the emotional and mental load of the relationship keeps creeping up, the customer slowly shifts from engaged to tolerant. And tolerant customers are already halfway out the door. Tolerance is not loyalty. Tolerance is "I'll stay as long as nothing better comes along". Loyalty is "I'd rather deal with them". The difference between those two states is often effort.

LOYALTY LOOP

Effort also creates what you could call loyalty loops. If the experience is smooth, customers engage more. They ask questions, they explore additional services, and they respond quickly. The relationship deepens. That makes future interactions even easier because both sides understand each other better. Easy experience, more engagement, stronger relationship, even easier experience. That's a positive loop.

Heavy experience creates the opposite as customers engage less. They only interact when they have to, and they keep things transactional. That makes interactions feel less connected and more procedural. Which makes them feel heavier again. Heavy experience lowers engagement, lower engagement weakens the relationship, and weaker relationships don't survive competition. That's the loop that leads to quiet churn.

This loop is why effort is one of the biggest predictors of whether a customer is easy to lose. A customer who feels like they have to work to deal with you is already open to alternatives. The moment someone else offers a similar outcome with less friction, they move. Not out of anger, but out of relief. Businesses often misread this and blame price or competition. They say "We were cheaper" or "Our product was better". None of that matters if the journey felt like effort. People will happily pay more for ease and less for hassle, as ease is value.

LEADERSHIP AND EFFORT

Now, here's where leadership comes in because most effort is not created by frontline staff. It's created by systems, processes, and decisions made higher up. It's extra approval layers, complicated forms, disconnected systems, poor handover structures, and overloaded teams. All of these add effort somewhere.

If your systems make customers work harder than they should, that is not a frontline issue. That is leadership design. Friction is rarely created at the counter. It's created in decisions made months earlier in meeting rooms.

If leaders don't regularly ask "Where is the customer doing work that we could remove?" effort drifts upward over time. Every internal change that makes life easier for the business can accidentally make life harder for the customer, and customers don't care why it's harder.

This is why reducing effort is not about telling staff to "try harder". It's about designing experiences that are simpler, clearer, and more supportive. It's about removing unnecessary steps. It's about making sure customers don't have to repeat information. It's about proactive communication that removes guesswork.

It's also about ownership. When someone takes responsibility for guiding the customer, the effort feels shared. When responsibility is unclear, the customer ends up carrying more than they should.

Service Rebellion at this level is simple. Stop making customers do your job. Every extra step is a withdrawal. Every removed step is a deposit. And the Wolf Pack Standard is this: the pack carries the load, so the customer never has to.

Chapter summary

- If your customer is carrying the mental load of the process they will recognise it as taking too much effort.
- Question processes that create work for customers – the process should make it easier for the customer, not the business.
- Recognise that every unnecessary step is a small withdrawal from the relationship because that's what effort does, it drains goodwill.
- When goodwill is high, customers are forgiving, but when it's low, they are critical.
- The positive loyalty loop – easy experience, more engagement, stronger relationship, even easier experience. That's a positive loop.
- The negative loyalty loop – heavy experience lowers engagement, lower engagement weakens the relationship, and weaker relationships don't survive competition.
- Most effort is created by systems, processes, and decisions made higher up.

Chapter 16

THE LEVEL OF CERTAINTY

If importance makes customers feel seen, and understanding makes them feel heard, certainty is what makes them feel safe. Safety is not a dramatic word here – it doesn't mean physical danger, it means emotional and decision safety. It means the customer feels confident they've chosen right, that things are under control, and that nothing is about to surprise them.

Certainty is one of the strongest drivers of loyalty and one of the biggest reasons customers leave when it's missing. People can handle complexity, delays, and even problems, but the moment they don't know where they stand, stress kicks in and stress changes behaviour.

The Level of Certainty is about how confident the customer feels during the journey, not just about the outcome at the end. You can deliver a good result and still leave the customer feeling uneasy if the path there was full of guesswork. Silence, vague updates, unclear responsibilities, shifting information . . . all of these create uncertainty, even if nothing actually goes wrong. And when customers feel uncertain, they start protecting themselves.

You see this behaviour all the time: customers start following up more, asking more questions, double-checking details, looking for reassurance elsewhere, comparing options, pulling other people into decisions, and dragging their feet on committing. None of this is because they want to be difficult. It's because uncertainty triggers caution and puts them into protection mode. Cautious customers are slower, less loyal, and less likely to refer.

Certainty, on the other hand, creates momentum because when customers feel confident, they decide faster, engage more openly, and stop feeling the need to monitor what's happening. They lean in instead of hovering. They trust the process and the people. That trust reduces friction across the whole relationship.

CREATING CERTAINTY

Certainty is built through visible control. Not control over the customer, but control over the situation. When someone explains clearly what's happening, what comes next, and how changes will be handled, the customer relaxes. They feel like they are in capable hands. You don't have to remove every unknown, you just have to remove the feeling that things are drifting. Certainty isn't personality and it isn't a confident tone of voice either, it's a pattern of behaviour customers learn they can rely on, and the real test is whether it shows up before they even start wondering if something's off.

Uncertain businesses are reactive while certain businesses anticipate, and you can hear the difference because reactive communication says, "Sorry for the delay," while certain communication says, "You'll hear from us Thursday." and instead of waiting for the question to come, answers it before it even forms.

You don't build certainty by being impressive, you build it by being predictably reliable in the moments that usually create doubt. Customers feel certain when updates arrive as promised, when timelines are realistic and explained, when changes are acknowledged early, when ownership is visible instead of hidden behind "the team", and when silence never lasts long enough for doubt to grow.

COMMUNICATING CERTAINTY

Most businesses think certainty comes from expertise, but expertise without communication still feels risky because knowing what you're doing doesn't calm the customer if they can't see that you're in control. Clear communication with visible ownership feels safe, even when the situation is complex. That's why a junior staff member who communicates clearly can create more certainty than a senior expert who disappears into silence. Certainty is felt through consistency, not hierarchy. Certainty isn't about job titles. It's about consistency.

It's also not about sounding confident. It's about setting the next step before the current one finishes, defining what "normal" looks like, explaining what might change, addressing delays before they're felt, and naming who owns what. Certainty grows when customers know three things at all times. Miss one of those, uncertainty creeps in.

1. Where we are.
2. What happens next.
3. Who is responsible.

This is why communication is such a big part of certainty. It's not about flooding customers with information. It's about reducing doubt. A short update that says "Here's where we are and here's what happens next" can do more for certainty than a long technical explanation that doesn't answer the real concern. Your customers and clients want to know that someone is steering the ship.

You can see this in everyday life. Think about being on a flight with turbulence. If the pilot says nothing, anxiety rises. If the pilot comes on and calmly explains what's happening and that its normal, people settle. Nothing changed about the turbulence, but the explanation changes how safe it feels, and that's what certainty really is.

Packs don't go quiet when conditions change. They increase communication. If the terrain shifts, the pack adjusts formation. If risk increases, signals increase. Wolves communicate more when uncertainty rises, not less. That's the pack standard. Silence in a pack creates danger, and silence in a business creates doubt. Doubt slows movement. And slow movement costs momentum.

SILENCE IS NOT GOLDEN

High-functioning teams increase communication when variables increase. Low-functioning ones go quiet because they're overwhelmed. Customers don't know which one you are, they just judge by what they hear. No signal equals no control.

The same thing happens in business interactions. When something changes and no one addresses it, customers start creating stories. Maybe something is wrong, maybe the team is behind, or maybe there's a problem no one is telling them about. Stories fill the gap where certainty should be. We've all done it. You order something online. There's no update, no tracking, and no message. Day three you're checking emails like a detective. Day five you're convinced it's lost in a warehouse fire in another country, and then on day six, it turns up perfectly fine. Nothing was actually wrong with the delivery, but certainty went missing, and that's what created the stress.

Businesses think problems damage trust, but uncertainty damages it faster. This is why silence is one of the biggest certainty killers. Internally, teams may think no news is good news, but externally, no news often feels like no control. Silence doesn't just create doubt, it creates imagination, and imagination is rarely generous. When customers don't hear from you, they don't think, "They must be working efficiently." They think, "Did they forget?", "Is something wrong?", or "Am I going to have to chase this?" Silence is where confidence goes to die.

Inside a business, silence often feels productive – heads down, busy getting things done. Outside the business, silence feels like drift. And drift is uncomfortable because humans are wired to look for signals of control. If no one is signalling, the brain fills the gap with risk.

That's why a simple update builds more certainty than a perfect outcome delivered in silence. You don't need big reports, you just need reassurance of motion like "We're still on track", "Nothing new yet, but still progressing", or "Next update will be on Thursday". Those lines seem small internally, but to the customer, they are emotional stabilisers. Customers don't just judge the outcome. They judge how confident the business appears while getting there. That confidence is contagious. If the business sounds unsure, customers become unsure, but if the business communicates clearly and calmly, customers mirror that confidence.

CERTAINTY AFFECTS MANY BEHAVIOURS

The Level of Certainty also links directly to trust in expertise. When a team explains decisions, trade-offs, and next steps in plain language, customers feel guided. When explanations are missing or full of jargon, customers feel like things are happening around them rather than with them. Feeling out of the loop reduces certainty.

Certainty also affects how customers react to problems. When the overall journey feels stable, issues feel like bumps, but when the journey already feels uncertain, issues feel like confirmation that something is wrong. Certainty is the emotional buffer that protects the relationship when things are not perfect. And no business is perfect.

This is why the Level of Certainty is not about guarantees. It's about clarity, communication, and visible ownership. It's about making sure the customer never feels like they are in the dark about what's going on. Because customers can tolerate a lot. What they don't tolerate well is feeling unsure about whether they should be worried. Uncertainty changes customer behaviour faster than almost anything else. When people feel unsure, their brain shifts into protection mode. They don't consciously decide to be more cautious, they just are. They hold back, they delay decisions, they ask more questions, they check alternatives, and they keep options open. From the business side, this can look like customers being slow, hesitant, or difficult, but from the customer's side, it's self-protection.

Certainty lowers the mental load of the relationship, but uncertainty raises it. Mental load is invisible work. It's the effort of thinking, worrying, monitoring, and double-checking. The more mental load a customer carries, the heavier the relationship feels, even if the technical side is fine.

Certainty is also closely tied to decision speed. Customers who feel confident about a business decide faster, as they commit more easily. They don't need endless comparisons because they feel safe enough to move forward. Customers who feel uncertain slow everything down. They ask for more information, more reassurance, more meetings. They escalate decisions internally, and they look for additional validation. From the outside, this looks like a long sales cycle or a slow client, but often it's just low certainty. Low certainty makes every decision feel riskier than it needs to be. Certainty shortens decision cycles because when certainty is high decisions move, which is why certainty isn't soft, it's progress.

This is why the Level of Certainty has direct commercial impact. It affects how quickly customers move, how comfortable they feel committing, and how likely they are to stay when competitors appear.

Certainty also reduces conflict. When customers feel confident that someone is steering the situation, they are more patient when things don't go perfectly, as they believe issues will be handled. When that confidence drops, even small problems feel bigger than they are. It's not just about the problem now, it's about how safe the journey felt before it.

This level also explains why visible ownership is so powerful. When someone says "I'm across this and I'll update you" and then follows through, certainty rises. The customer feels like there is a person accountable, not just a process running. And processes don't reassure customers, people taking ownership do. Even in highly automated or system-driven environments, the feeling of certainty comes from clear communication and visible responsibility. Without those, customers feel like they are dealing with a machine that might or might not be working properly. That feeling is exhausting.

Certainty reduces emotional fatigue because the customer doesn't have to stay alert. They don't have to monitor the situation constantly, and they trust that they will be told what they need to know. Trust reduces effort because the customer stops feeling like they have to stay switched on. And when effort and uncertainty are both low, loyalty becomes easier to build.

Certainty doesn't just affect how customers feel in the moment. It shapes whether they trust you enough to bring others into the relationship. Referrals are not just endorsements of quality. They are endorsements of safety. When someone refers you, they are putting their own reputation alongside the experience. They are putting their reputation on the line before your reputation plays out. They're saying "I believe you'll be looked after here", and that belief comes from certainty.

If their own experience felt stable, guided, and under control, referring feels safe. If their experience felt like guesswork, they hesitate. They don't want to risk someone else feeling stressed or unsure. Even if the outcome was fine, uncertainty weakens advocacy. People don't refer businesses that made them feel on edge because, as I mentioned before, their personal reputation is on the line with a referral.

This level is also a leadership issue, not just a communication skill. Certainty is built into the way the business operates. Are updates structured or left to chance? Are responsibilities clear or blurred? Are timelines realistic or optimistic? Are customers told what "normal" looks like? If business owners or management don't design certainty into the system, staff end up improvising. One person communicates clearly, but another assumes the customer knows. One provides regular updates, yet another goes quiet unless something is urgent. That inconsistency reduces certainty.

Certainty cannot rely on "good communicators". That's luck. It has to be built into the system. When certainty depends on personality, it's fragile, but when certainty is designed, it's scalable.

SERVICE REBELLION AND CERTAINTY

Service Rebellion at this level refuses to leave clarity to chance. Customers don't just experience your service. They experience whether the ride feels smooth or unpredictable. When customers know what to expect and trust that they'll be kept informed, they relax, and relaxed customers stay longer.

When customers feel certain, they don't feel the need to manage the situation themselves. That makes the relationship smoother on both sides. Your customers or clients don't need control. They need to feel like *someone* has control. When customers start chasing, micromanaging, or escalating, it's usually not because they want power. It's because certainty dropped and they're trying to rebuild it themselves. When the business leads clearly, customers stop trying to steer. Uncertainty turns customers into supervisors, whereas certainty lets them stay customers.

Service Rebellion at this level means refusing to leave customers in the dark. It means treating clarity as a standard, not an extra. It also means understanding that visible ownership and clear communication are not just courtesies. They are core parts of the product or service because what customers are really buying, alongside whatever you sell, is confidence. Confidence that someone knows what they are doing. Confidence that they will be told if something changes, and confidence that they are not about to be surprised by something avoidable. That confidence is what allows customers to commit, stay, and refer.

Service Rebellion at this level means rejecting the idea that customers should "just trust us". You can't tell customers to trust you. You have to show them why they should, with clear signals, consistent follow-through, and visible ownership. Because what customers are really buying is not just a product or service, they're buying the feeling that someone competent is steering the situation. And when that feeling is present, loyalty grows quietly.

This is why certainty is one of the most underestimated growth drivers in business. It doesn't show up in marketing. It doesn't sit on a features list. And it doesn't sound exciting in strategy meetings. But it's the reason customers stay calm when things wobble. Businesses don't just lose customers when performance drops. They lose them when confidence drops. A relationship can survive a mistake, but it will struggle to survive uncertainty. When customers feel unsure, they don't just worry about this job, this project, or this purchase. They start wondering if they chose the right business in the first place. And that doubt is expensive because once certainty breaks, every small issue feels bigger, every delay feels suspicious, and silence feels loaded. The relationship becomes heavier, not because of what happened, but because of how safe it feels.

Certainty is the emotional shock absorber in the relationship. Without it, every bump hits harder, but with it, problems feel manageable. Strong businesses don't just deliver outcomes, they manage the customer's sense of stability while getting there. And most of it comes from moments that look small internally: a clear update, a realistic timeline, an explanation before the customer even has to ask and the feeling that someone competent is steering the situation. Those moments tell the customer they are in safe hands, and customers stay where they feel safe.

Chapter summary

- The Level of Certainty is about how confident and safe the customer feels during the journey, not just about the outcome at the end.
- Certainty creates momentum.
- Uncertain businesses are reactive while certain businesses anticipate.
- Certainty is felt through consistency, a pattern of behaviour customers learn they can rely on.
- You build certainty by being predictably reliable in the moments that usually create doubt.
- Certainty grows when customers know three things at all times:
    - Where we are.
    - What happens next.
    - Who is responsible.
- Silence in a business creates doubt, which slows movement and costs momentum.
- Confidence is catching.

Chapter 17

THE LEVEL OF PERSONALISATION

There's a strange idea floating around business that personalisation means remembering someone's name, like we all get emotionally attached because an email starts with "Hi Michelle". That's not personalisation, that's basic software doing what it was built to do, and it's the business equivalent of thinking you're a great cook because you own salt. This is the part most books would call "connection", but they usually drown it in warm, fuzzy nonsense.

Connection in business is not about being everyone's best friend. It's not about forced banter, first names every second sentence, or staff being told to "build rapport" like it's a KPI you can tick off between coffee breaks. Real connection is simpler than that. It's remembering. It's the customer feeling like there's a thread running through the relationship, so they don't have to restart the conversation every time they deal with you. It's walking in and feeling like the business has memory. Not creepy memory, useful memory. The kind that says "We've got you, and we know where we left off".

When there's no memory, customers feel disconnected and they feel invisible. And when people feel invisible, they don't complain loudly, they just emotionally detach, and emotionally detached customers don't stay loyal and they definitely don't refer.

So, yes, we'll call it personalisation, but what we really mean is this . . . does your business carry people forward or do you reset them back to zero every time they interact with you? Most customers don't expect you to remember their life story. They're not looking for you to recall their anniversary or their favourite footy team. They just don't want to feel like every interaction starts at zero. They don't want to feel like they've walked into a place they've dealt with ten times before and still have to explain who they are like it's day one.

Personalisation reduces effort. When context carries forward, customers don't have to rework the same ground. The experience feels smoother, lighter, easier. That's where this level sits. In whether the relationship has memory. Because when there's no memory, there's no relationship. There's just a series of disconnected transactions pretending to be one long-term arrangement.

DOES YOUR CUSTOMER FEEL KNOWN?

You see this constantly, and businesses rarely notice it happening. A customer explains something once. Then again, then again, and sometimes again. Different person, same explanation. By the third time, they're not even annoyed about the original issue anymore. They're annoyed about having to reintroduce themselves like they've turned up to a meeting nobody prepared for. That's not a service mistake in their mind, that's a signal that says "They don't know me here". When someone feels known, leaving means going back to square one somewhere else – re-telling the story, resetting expectations, re-proving everything – and most people simply can't be bothered with that.

This shows up everywhere – in trades, healthcare, professional services, and retail. A client mentions they prefer communication a certain way. Maybe they don't want calls during work hours, or maybe they want updates by email, or maybe they've had a past issue that needs a bit of sensitivity. The first person understands, but the next person has no idea. Now the customer is back to explaining something that should already be part of the relationship. No one inside the business thinks, "We just weakened loyalty." But emotionally, that's exactly what happened. Every time someone has to repeat themselves, the relationship resets slightly towards transactional. That's the drift.

You see it clearly in healthcare. A patient fills out the same forms every visit, same history, same details. Internally, the system probably stores everything. Externally, the patient feels like they're reintroducing themselves to a new clinic each time.

Or in trades. The homeowner has already explained where the access is, what's delicate, what's been done before. A new person turns up and asks the same questions. Again, nothing catastrophic, but emotionally, the relationship just went backwards.

You don't lose loyalty in dramatic moments most of the time. You lose it through repeated small signals that say "You're not really known here". When interactions feel generic, people downgrade the relationship emotionally. It becomes functional, and functional relationships get compared on price and convenience, whereas relational ones get protected.

That's why personalisation links directly to referrals. When someone refers a business, they're putting their reputation against the experience. If they felt known, if the business demonstrated memory and continuity, recommending feels safe.

WHAT DOES PERSONALISATION LOOK LIKE?

So what does this look like in real life, without turning your business into a CRM cult or making your staff write a novel after every phone call. It comes down to one simple standard: every customer should feel like the business remembers the last conversation, even if the person they're talking to wasn't there. That's it. And you can do that in a one-person business or a multinational because it's not about size, it's about discipline.

Here's the easiest practical version I've seen work anywhere. After every meaningful interaction, capture three things:

1. What matters to them?
2. What's happened so far?
3. What happens next?

If you want a simple test that tells you instantly whether you're doing personalisation properly, it's this: when the customer calls back, do they hear "Hi, can you run me through it again", or do they hear "Yep, I can see what's happened so far, here's where we're at and here's what we're doing next". That second line is personalisation. It's also connection and certainty. It's the levels working together.

In a small business, you might use a notebook, a job card, a client card, a notes section in your invoicing software, or a single customer file in Google Drive. What you use doesn't matter. The tool isn't the point. The standard is. In an enterprise or multinational, you might design systems that store relationship information, not just transaction history. Most big organisations track orders brilliantly and relationships terribly, which is why customers feel like they're dealing with five departments, twelve tickets, and zero humans. The irony is, the bigger the business, the more personalisation matters because the customer is already fighting the machine. If you don't create continuity, the machine wins and the customer just checks out.

This is where the Wolf Pack Standard draws the line. If the whole thing only works because one person remembers everything, that's not a pack. That's a weak spot waiting to break. The pack carries the knowledge as a pack. It's embedded, it's behavioural, and it's why they move like one unit. Unfortunately, many businesses do the opposite. They rely on one great staff member who "knows all the customers", and everyone feels good about it until that staff member gets sick, takes leave, burns out, or leaves, and suddenly your best customers start feeling like strangers. We will cover this in an upcoming chapter as this is a really important issue that needs addressing.

SERVICE REBELLION AND PERSONALISATION

Service Rebellion at this level is building memory into the pack, not leaving it in someone's head. And this is the part no one talks about when the business starts expanding. More staff, more teams, more handovers, and more systems. On paper, everything looks more professional. Processes improve, tracking improves, even reporting improves. Meanwhile, the customer experience can become emotionally flatter.

Customers don't separate "the system" from "the business". They don't think, "Fair enough, that note didn't get logged." They think, "I'm not sure they really know us." That thought doesn't cause an immediate exit. It just lowers emotional weight. And lower emotional weight makes future decisions easier. Easier to compare, easier to trial someone else, and easier to move.

Personalisation stops you becoming just another option. When customers feel like just another number, you become a category. When they feel understood, you become a relationship. Categories compete on price, but relationships compete on trust, and trust is what stops price being the only conversation.

This is also where technology can accidentally make things worse. Businesses roll out portals, apps, automation, chatbots . . . all in the name of efficiency. And, yes, those things can make processes smoother, but efficiency without recognition feels cold. A slick digital system that still makes someone feel anonymous doesn't build loyalty. It builds convenience, and convenience is fragile. Someone else can build a slightly better interface and suddenly your advantage disappears. Being known adds emotional weight that technology alone can't create.

The slow emotional drift shows up later as "They've been with us for years and suddenly left", or "They went with a competitor who was more expensive", or "They didn't even give us a chance to quote". It looks like a market issue, but it's often a memory issue, and most businesses never even think to look there.

EMOTIONAL DETACHMENT

So here's the part not to miss. If customers have to repeat themselves with you, you're not just annoying them, you're training them to emotionally detach. Because repetition sends a message, even if you don't mean it to. It says "We don't hold onto you". It says "We don't have a thread". And it says "You're not important enough for your context to survive". Now, no business owner says that out loud, but customers don't listen to your intention, they listen to the feeling. And feelings sound louder than words. Once a customer feels interchangeable, your business becomes interchangeable, and interchangeable businesses get shopped.

That's when the dangerous stuff starts because customers stop telling you the full story, they stop giving you chances when something goes wrong, they stop asking about other services, they stop referring, and when a competitor pops up, even if they're more expensive, the customer tries them because it feels like a fresh start. That's why you get blindsided by "they left after years". They didn't leave after years. They left after the tenth time they had to reintroduce themselves.

I've seen this firsthand with an airline I used to use a lot. Because I'm constantly asked to speak at conferences, I was on their top-tier frequent flyer level. They called it "exclusive", special status, priority everything. Except when you rang them. Every call felt like I was interrupting their day. No recognition and no sense of "this person's been loyal for years". I had to prove who I was, explain my history, and justify my request like I was brand new. There was nothing exclusive about the experience, just a label.

And that's the point. Loyalty badges don't create loyalty, recognition does. Because the moment a loyal customer feels like a stranger, the emotional contract breaks. Not loudly . . . quietly. Once someone stops feeling known, they start wondering what else out there might feel easier. And that's exactly what I did. I went to their competitor. Not because the planes were different. Not because the price was wildly better. Because I was tired of feeling like I had to reintroduce myself to a business that claimed I was one of their most "valued" customers. Years of flying. Gone. Not over a crisis, just over repetition.

In B2B environments this is even more commercial. If a supplier understands your business model, your constraints, your internal politics, your history, you don't have to keep re-educating them. That saves time and mental energy, and it makes them easier to work with. And ease builds loyalty. Not because it's fluffy, but because it reduces the mental load. Mental load is effort, and effort erodes attachment.

Leadership plays a role here whether you realise it or not. Personalisation doesn't usually disappear because frontline staff suddenly stop caring. It disappears in process design, in handovers that don't include context, and in systems that track transactions but not relationships. In KPIs that measure speed but not continuity. What gets measured gets protected. If no one is accountable for carrying context forward, it won't happen consistently. And inconsistency is the enemy of trust. Customers don't judge you by your best interaction. They judge you by the repeated experience. If sometimes they feel known and sometimes they don't, the overall feeling becomes uncertainty, and uncertainty weakens loyalty.

Another subtle sign this is happening is when customers stop offering information voluntarily. Early in a relationship, people explain background, preferences, details. When they don't feel known, they stop bothering. Conversations get shorter, more transactional and less open. That's not because they're difficult. It's because they've learned the information doesn't carry forward anyway. When customers stop sharing, relationships stop deepening. And when relationships don't deepen, they don't strengthen. They just sit there, exposed to anyone who comes along and simply demonstrates understanding.

This is why personalisation is not a "nice touch" or a "customer experience extra". It's structural. It's what stops relationships flattening into transactions over time.

PERSONALISATION BRINGS EMOTIONAL SAFETY

When customers feel known, the relationship has history. It has depth. It feels like there's something there beyond the current job, order, or issue. That feeling creates emotional safety. Emotional safety makes people more comfortable staying, expanding, and referring because referring a business where you feel known feels safe. You're not just saying the outcome was good, you're saying "They'll actually look after you". That's a much bigger endorsement.

If your experience feels generic, you hesitate. Not because the service was terrible, but because you don't have confidence in how the next person will feel. There's no emotional certainty in it. So referrals don't just follow quality, they follow recognition.

You can also see how this links to the earlier levels. When someone feels known, effort drops. They don't have to repeat themselves, and they don't have to manage the relationship as much. Certainty rises because they feel understood, and importance rises because the business demonstrates memory.

CREATING PERSONALISATION

Businesses don't lose personalisation on purpose. It slips as they grow. There are more staff, more layers, and more handovers. And somewhere in that expansion, the customer starts feeling like a file instead of a person. Over time, the experience becomes smoother on paper but flatter in reality. Flat experiences don't offend, but they don't excite either. They just sit in the middle, and the middle is where loyalty quietly fades.

If you want an easy, repeatable way for staff to create personalisation in one sentence, here it is: "Before we go further, can I just check I've got this right? Last time we did *X*, your main concern was *Y*, and today we're trying to get to *Z*."

That line does three things:

1. It proves memory.
2. It proves listening.
3. It proves direction.

And it makes the customer feel known without the staff member needing to be a charismatic people person.

Another one that works brilliantly in any industry is "Anything from last time you don't want repeated this time?" This isn't about friendliness, it's about rebellion against forgettable service. This is where Service Rebellion shows up at this level. It's pushing back against the drift towards treating everyone the same in the name of efficiency. Standard processes are necessary. However, standardised experiences are not. Efficiency is not an excuse for being forgettable.

Customers don't need you to be wildly different every time. They just need you to remember them, to pick up where things left off, and to show that the relationship has a thread running through it. That thread is what turns repeat business into loyalty. Without it, you're always starting again, and that's exhausting for customers *and* businesses. It means you're constantly re-selling, re-proving, and re-establishing. That's expensive. In the end, customers stay where they feel known, and they drift where they feel interchangeable, and the brutal part is they rarely tell you when this is happening because it doesn't feel like a complaint, it feels like a conclusion.

The pack standard is simple: carry the context, protect the thread, make people feel recognised. In a world full of options, good isn't rare. Being remembered is!

Chapter summary

- Real connection is simple: it's remembering.
- When there's no memory, customers feel disconnected and invisible – they don't complain loudly, they just emotionally detach.
- One simple standard: every customer should feel like the business remembers the last conversation, even if the person they're talking to wasn't there – they should feel known.
- After every meaningful interaction, capture three things:
  - What matters to them?
  - What's happened so far?
  - What happens next?
- The bigger the business, the more personalisation matters because the customer is already fighting the machine.
- If customers have to repeat themselves with you, you're not just annoying them, you're training them to emotionally detach.
- When customers stop sharing, relationships stop deepening, stop strengthening.
- To create personalisation, prove memory, listening and direction.
- Standard processes are necessary. However, standardised experiences are not.

Chapter 18

THE LEVEL OF CONSISTENCY

There's a belief sitting quietly inside a lot of businesses that causes more damage than people realise, and the annoying part is it sounds completely reasonable when people say it. "We're good most of the time", which sounds fair, honest, and in someone's head even feels like a compliment. But customers don't experience your business as an average score at the end of the month, they experience it as a run of moments. Loyalty isn't built on your best moments, it's built on what people learn to expect every single time they deal with you. That's what consistency is, the difference between a business that's good and a business that's safe to stay with. Consistency turns a good experience into a reliable one, and reliability is what trust is built on. Without consistency, every interaction feels like a roll of the dice, and no one stays loyal to a dice roll.

CONSISTENTLY GOOD – OR BAD

Think about a restaurant that is fantastic three out of four times. The food is great, the staff are great, the vibe is great, and then every fourth visit something just feels off. Maybe the service is slow, maybe the meal is average, maybe the staff look like they've been personally offended by your existence. It's still "mostly good", but how does it feel walking in? You don't relax into it, you don't assume it'll be great, you kind of hope it will, and hope is not the same thing as trust.

We lived this recently. My wife and I took some friends to a restaurant near where we live. It is marketed as a bit up-market, the kind of place you'd take people to have a nice night out – you know, those places that all the "cool" people hang out. We arrived, got shown to our table, sat down, and then nothing. No menus, no water, no hello, no "I'll be looking after you tonight", none of the normal set-up that tells you how the night is going to run and what you can expect.

After a fair while of being completely invisible, I had to call our waitress over just to ask for menus, and while I was at it, see if we could order drinks too. Another ten minutes passed before the menus arrived, and she dropped them on the table and walked off again without a word. At that point you are not thinking about service standards, you are wondering if you somehow offended someone by existing. So I got up and went to the bar myself to ask if I could at least get some drinks happening because our waitress had vanished. The drinks eventually arrived, and for a moment you think, "Okay, maybe they're just busy, maybe it'll settle."

About 45 minutes later, still no one had come back. No check-in, no "can I take your order?" Nothing. I got up again, tracked down our waitress, and told her we'd like to order some food. We ordered for the whole table and settled back in, assuming things were finally moving. Sixty minutes later . . . still no food. I called over a different staff member this time, and she went to check what was happening. She came back looking sheepish and told us our original server had forgotten to put the order into the system. Forgotten! I mean, that's the job!

Frustrated with this now new outcome I asked if the kitchen could rush it through. We were then told that the kitchen was closing, so there was no way we'd be getting any food at all. We'd been sitting there for the better part of two hours. I spoke to the manager, explained the whole situation, and to her credit she apologised and gave us a discount voucher for our next visit.

And here's where consistency really matters. My wife still wanted to try the food, and as we all know, happy wife, happy life, so a few weeks later we booked again, giving them another chance. But this time they forgot our drinks order. That's when it clicked. They weren't having a bad night the first time, they had a pattern. They were consistent – consistently bad.

And that's the point. One bad experience can be forgiven. Two experiences that feel the same stop being an "off day" and start becoming your reputation. We didn't get angry and make a scene. We just quietly stopped going, and we stopped trusting their marketing. Not because of one disaster, but because the experience had a pattern, and the pattern didn't feel reliable.

ALERT CUSTOMERS DON'T STAY

That's how inconsistency kills loyalty, not with drama, but with doubt. Customers don't leave because of one bad moment. They leave when bad moments start to feel familiar. Once an experience has a pattern, people stop hoping it will be better next time and start assuming it won't. That shift, from hope to expectation, is where loyalty quietly dies because trust isn't built on your good days, it's built on whether people feel safe betting on your normal ones.

Customers do this every day with businesses. If the experience changes depending on who they get, what day it is, or how busy you are, they stay slightly alert, and alert customers don't attach deeply, they keep options open, they compare, and they stay ready to move, even if they're smiling to your face while they do it.

From inside the business, inconsistency usually comes from pressure. Workloads fluctuate, staff vary in style and experience, systems get stretched. None of it is malicious. From the customer's side though, inconsistency feels personal because one day they feel looked after and the next day they feel like a number, one interaction is smooth and the next feels clunky. The message they receive isn't "We're under pressure", the message is "You might matter, or you might not". It's like a lucky dip, and that uncertainty erodes trust even if nobody has done anything technically wrong.

CUSTOMERS DON'T JUDGE YOU ON THE HIGHS

This is where businesses confuse themselves because they love pointing at their best examples like a proud parent holding up a crayon drawing. The great review, the amazing job, the staff member who went above and beyond, and the big win. But customers don't judge you by your peak, they judge you by the weakest experience they regularly encounter. If someone has one outstanding interaction and two average ones, the business feels average because consistency sets your real standard, not your highlights. Customers don't live in your highlight reel – they live in the pattern.

There's an ego trap though. Business owners remember the day they nailed it and the glowing feedback and the big moment where the customer raved, but customers remember last Tuesday – that average day, the normal interaction, and the moment where nothing special happened but nothing went wrong either. Because your reputation is built on your "Tuesdays", the normal days, not your highlight reel, and most businesses don't design Tuesdays, they leave them to chance, then act shocked when loyalty doesn't stick.

The hidden cost of "good enough most of the time" rarely shows up as dramatic complaints, it shows up as emotional downgrades. Customers become less enthusiastic, less open, less willing to refer, and they stop talking about you positively. Not because you're bad, but because they're not confident about what others will experience. Referrals follow confidence, and when someone isn't sure what their friend will get, they hesitate. That hesitation is lost growth, and it happens quietly.

THE COST OF INCONSISTENCY

Inconsistency also increases effort. Customers can't rely on your rhythm, so they manage the relationship more, they double-check, they follow up, they clarify, and that extra effort makes the experience feel heavier, and heavy experiences weaken attachment. That's why inconsistency links back to effort, certainty, and importance. When things are consistent, customers relax, and when they're not, customers stay alert, and alert relationships don't feel safe. People don't settle where they don't feel safe, they stay ready to leave.

The frustrating thing is inconsistency usually doesn't start with a big failure. It starts with standards getting vague: "Be professional", "Look after the customer", or "Do your best". They sound good, but they don't create consistent behaviour because everyone does "good" differently, and different versions of good create inconsistent experiences. From inside the business, everyone thinks they're doing a decent job. From outside, the experience varies, and variation feels like risk.

Here's the thing that will really hurt you in the long run if you don't make consistency a priority. Businesses don't lose customers because they're bad, they lose them because they're unpredictable because unpredictable experiences don't build trust, they build caution, and customers stay where they know what they're going to get, not because it's exciting, but because it feels safe.

CONSISTENCY CHANGES INTERPRETATIONS

Consistency also shapes how customers interpret problems when they happen, and this is where a lot of businesses get surprised because when a company is consistent, a mistake feels like an exception, but when a company is inconsistent, a mistake feels like confirmation. The exact same issue lands completely differently depending on the pattern that came before it, which is why consistency doesn't just improve good experiences, it protects you when things wobble because it gives you the benefit of the doubt.

That's why customers forgive big mistakes in businesses they trust and leave over small frustrations in businesses they don't. It's not about the size of the issue, it's about the pattern because patterns shape interpretation, and interpretation shapes loyalty. If the overall experience has been steady, the relationship has weight, but if it's been patchy, there's no emotional reserve to draw from, so the first wobble becomes the last straw.

You see this in professional services all the time. One client feels their adviser, broker, agent, is always on top of things, communicates clearly, follows through, and that client will tolerate the occasional delay because the pattern tells them the relationship is solid. Meanwhile another client who has experienced mixed communication and uneven responsiveness reads that same delay as a warning sign. Nothing dramatic has changed, but the meaning of the event is completely different. And consistency shapes meaning.

There's also an internal effect businesses rarely consider: inconsistent environments are harder for staff too. When expectations shift depending on the day, manager, or workload, people operate reactively. They make judgement calls in the moment rather than working from a clear baseline, increasing mental load and variation even further, which is why consistency isn't just for customers. It stabilises the working environment as well. When standards are clear and reinforced, staff don't have to guess as much, and that steadiness shows up on the outside.

THE SLOW DRIFT INTO INCONSISTENCY

Customers don't see flexibility because unfortunately, all they see is unpredictability. The drift into inconsistency happens in small allowances that feel reasonable in isolation. A follow-up gets skipped because it's busy, an update gets vague because there wasn't time, a handover gets rushed because the day got away, and none of those moments feel like "culture", but over time they form a pattern, and customers experience the pattern, not your reasons behind it.

They don't see the workload, they just feel whether the experience is stable or shaky, which is why businesses often misread their own performance. Sales might still be happening, complaints might be low, and everything looks functional. Meanwhile, loyalty is thinning because customers aren't necessarily unhappy, they're just not anchored. They're still in the relationship – well, sort of – but they're not committed to it, and the next competitor who shows up with a steadier, more reliable experience looks appealing, not because they're dramatically better, but because they feel safer to deal with.

Consistency also shapes how valued customers feel because when treatment varies, people don't know where they stand, and one interaction feels attentive, another feels rushed, one staff member seems engaged, another seems distracted, and that variation sends a subtle message that care is conditional, even if that's not true. Reliable care builds loyalty, where conditional care builds caution.

And here's where consistency gets sneaky because most businesses don't lose it when they're struggling, they lose it when they're busy – because busy feels like success. With everyone trying to keep up, "good enough is good enough for now" becomes normal.

Customers don't experience "temporary" though. They experience pattern, and once they feel that wobble, the relationship changes tone. They don't pull away dramatically, they just tighten and become alert. That is emotional fatigue right there, and emotional fatigue is one of the quiet killers of loyalty because when a relationship feels steady people relax into it, but when it feels inconsistent they stay alert. Staying alert is work, and the more work a relationship feels like, the less attachment it builds, not because the service collapsed, but because the customer never fully settles. Consistency is what allows people to exhale because when the experience is steady, the customer's system stops bracing for the next wobble.

HOW TO BUILD CONSISTENCY

Here's how you build consistency without turning your team into robots. If you want consistency, you need non-negotiables, not scripts, not robotic behaviour . . . non-negotiables. The fundamentals that must show up every single time, no matter who the customer gets, no matter how busy it is, and no matter what mood the staff member is in.

These following examples work in a one-person business or a multinational. They are the ones that matter because they create stability without killing personality.

- Every customer leaves the interaction knowing the next step and not guessing.
- Every customer gets a timeframe that's realistic, not optimistic.
- Every customer knows who actually owns it, not "the team".
- Every customer gets an update rhythm when things take longer than a day, so silence never grows doubt.
- Every customer gets a response that doesn't make them feel like a burden for asking.

Notice what I didn't list? I didn't list "be friendly", or "smile more", or "build rapport" because consistency isn't personality, it's behaviour. Personality can vary and style can vary, but clarity, ownership, follow-through, and communication need to be steady because that steadiness is what allows customers to relax into the relationship.

And this is where the Wolf Pack Standard fits perfectly because packs survive through coordinated behaviour, not because individuals occasionally perform brilliantly. A pack doesn't win because one wolf has a great day, a pack wins because the pack moves like one unit. That's consistency. Not a hero moment. A repeatable standard.

One great staff member can create a great moment, but a consistent team creates a reputation, a standard, a culture, and customers don't stay because you impressed them once, they stay because dealing with you feels safe over and over, and that safety is what turns transactions into relationships. Without consistency you're always re-earning trust, but with it trust compounds, and compounding trust is where retention, referrals, and margin live.

So, yes, consistency is what makes everything else believable because you can say you care about customers, but if the experience swings depending on who they get or how busy it is, the message doesn't land. You can have strong moments of service, but if they aren't repeatable, they don't build trust. Trust doesn't come from your best day, it comes from your normal ones. Inconsistent businesses always feel like they're trying, while consistent businesses feel like they're in control. Trying earns sympathy but control earns. Customers don't stay because they see effort, they stay because they feel steadiness.

CONSISTENCY AFTER THE SALE

There's another layer to consistency that businesses don't like talking about. Anyone can perform while they're chasing the deal. Consistency after the deal is character. Most businesses are incredibly consistent while they're trying to win you: calls get returned fast, emails are detailed, follow-ups are sharp. Everyone's responsive, attentive, and helpful. Then the moment you become a customer, the tempo changes. Replies slow down, ownership gets blurrier, and you start getting passed around. The energy that existed before the contract or sale feels like it quietly left the room, and customers feel that instantly. Nothing dramatic was said, but the message lands loud. You mattered most before you purchased.

That's one of the fastest ways to damage trust because it tells people the relationship had a sales phase and now it has a service phase, and the two don't match. Real consistency means the standard doesn't drop once money changes hands – it increases! In fact, the post-sale experience carries more emotional weight because now customers aren't judging your promise, they're judging your character. Consistency after the deal is what tells people who you really are. This is where loyalty is actually decided.

When post-sale consistency is strong, customers relax deeper into the relationship. They stop wondering whether they made the right decision because they feel reassured. Reassured customers stay longer, buy more, and refer with confidence. When post-sale consistency drops, customers don't always complain. They just recalibrate their expectations downward. They become more transactional. Less emotionally invested. Easier to lose.

And here's the irony. Businesses obsess over marketing consistency, brand colours, messaging, campaigns, followers (oh, please!), but the consistency customers remember most is behavioural. Did the care stay the same once they were no longer a prospect? Customers don't judge you by how well you sell, they judge you by how steady you stay after the sale. Effort impresses, but being steady reassures, and reassurance is what people build loyalty on.

If your business feels inconsistent, unpredictable, or patchy, it's not a marketing problem, it's not a pricing problem, and it's not even a competition problem. It's a standards problem. And standards are a choice. These levels aren't theory. They aren't something to nod at and move on from. When effort drops, certainty rises. When customers feel known, they stop bracing. When the experience is steady, they relax. And when people relax into a relationship, they stay longer, buy more, and refer without hesitation.

This is what Service Rebellion is really about. Not hype. Not slogans. Not "great service" on your best day. It's the decision to make these levels non-negotiable. To stop leaving loyalty to chance. To stop hoping customers will understand when things wobble. To build a business that feels reliable even when it's busy, even when it's under pressure, even on a random Tuesday. Because reliable businesses grow. Not because they're flashy, not because they're loud, but because they're safe to stay with.

And in a market full of noise, safe wins.

Chapter summary

- Loyalty isn't built on your best moments – it's built on what people learn to expect every single time they deal with you.
- Inconsistency kills loyalty, not with drama but with doubt – customers don't leave because of one bad moment, they leave when bad moments start to feel familiar.
- Inconsistency feels personal because one day the customer feels looked after and the next day they feel like a number.
- Customers don't judge you by your peak, they judge you by the weakest experience they regularly encounter.
- Inconsistency increases effort – customers can't rely on your rhythm, so they manage the relationship more.
- Businesses don't lose customers because they're bad, they lose them because they're unpredictable – unpredictable experiences don't build trust, they build caution.
- Reliable care builds loyalty, whereas conditional care builds caution.
- Personality can vary and style can vary, but clarity, ownership, follow-through, and communication need to be steady – steadiness is what allows customers to relax into the relationship.
- Real consistency means the standard doesn't drop once money changes hands – it increases!

PART 4

WHERE STANDARDS LIVE OR DIE

Chapter 19

IT ONLY WORKS WHEN YOU ARE WATCHING

Every business thinks it has a culture, but most of the time what people really mean is what they *say* they stand for, not what actually happens once the day gets busy and everyone just gets on with it.

Culture sounds like a big word, but it doesn't show up in big ways, it shows up in small moments that repeat. It's not the values on the wall – it's the follow-up that didn't happen, the handover that was rushed, or the update that was vague and no one corrected. None of those moments feel important when you're inside the business. When you're outside it, they start forming a pattern.

Patterns are what customers and clients feel, not intentions. And the brutal part is intentions don't scale, but patterns do. No customer ever says, "I know they meant well." They just feel the experience that repeats. If the pattern is clarity, ownership, and follow-through, the business feels reliable. But if the pattern is drift, excuses, and small misses, the business feels like work.

Culture decides which pattern wins long before strategy ever gets a vote. Business owners and leaders inside businesses often believe culture is something they communicate. It's not. It's something people observe. They watch what gets challenged and what slides. They watch how problems are handled when they pop up. They watch what someone can get away with without consequence. That's where the real rules sit.

CULTURE IS LEARNED FROM LEADERSHIP

You see culture most clearly when something goes slightly wrong. Not a disaster, just a wobble. Does the team lean in and sort it, or do they lean back and explain? Do they take ownership or start passing it around like a hot potato no one wants to hold? Those reactions aren't random, they've been learned. And that learning didn't come from a training session. It came from watching leadership behaviour, watching what the business owner does day after day. If the business owner or management get defensive, staff get defensive. If the owner or management stay calm and focus on solutions, that becomes normal. If the business owner ignores small standards because there are "bigger things going on", everyone else learns those standards weren't that important to begin with.

Culture spreads through what's tolerated, not what's written down. And this is where everything you've read so far either holds together or falls apart. Importance, understanding, emotion, expectation, effort, certainty, personalisation and consistency, they don't live in frameworks or chapters, they live in behaviour. They either show up repeatedly when things are busy, or they quietly disappear. Culture is what decides whether those levels survive pressure or collapse under it.

I see this all the time in mentoring. I'll spend a day with a business owner, and we'll go deep. We'll unpack ownership, tone, follow-through, clarity, sales, service, the whole thing. They leave fired up because they see it, and they get it. You can almost feel the shift in how they're thinking. But here's what happens next more often than most people would admit.

They go back into the business and assume the culture will just absorb what they now understand. They have the insight, they've had the breakthrough, they're clearer, they're sharper, but the team hasn't moved. No one has reset the standards. No one has translated the thinking into behaviour. And no one has said, "This is how we now handle follow-up, this is how we now handle tone, this is how we now handle ownership when something wobbles." So nothing changes, and if nothing changes . . . nothing changes!

The owner is operating at a new level, but the business is still operating at the old one. And within weeks the insight fades because culture pulls behaviour back to whatever was normal before. That's when they call me and say, "It was powerful, but it didn't stick." Of course it didn't stick. It's because culture wasn't shifted. You cannot upgrade thinking in isolation and expect behaviour to follow automatically. Culture is not wi-fi. It doesn't update and spread because you've had a good conversation. It updates and spreads because behaviour is reinforced consistently enough that the old way feels uncomfortable. And that right there is the difference between inspiration and culture.

This is where business owners and management get blindsided. Culture doesn't change in meetings, it changes in moments, and most of those moments don't look important at the time. Someone makes a sarcastic comment about a customer, and it gets a laugh instead of a correction. A follow-up doesn't happen and the excuse sounds reasonable, so no one circles back. Or a rushed handover becomes normal because everyone's under pressure and "we'll tighten it up next week", but next week never comes. None of those things feel like leadership decisions. Culture isn't shaped by big speeches, it's shaped by repeated allowances, and every allowance teaches the pack how loose the standard really is. From the inside, every small behaviour has a reason. From the outside, it just feels inconsistent. That inconsistency is how your culture is experienced.

This is why two businesses in the same industry, offering similar things, can feel completely different to deal with. One feels steady, organised, predictable, while the other feels reactive, slightly chaotic, dependent on which person you happen to get. That difference rarely comes from systems alone. It comes from behavioural norms. And norms become invisible internally. "That's just how we do things." But to customers and clients, that's the experience.

STANDARDS OR SUPERVISION?

Business owners and managers sometimes think stepping back shows trust, and it does, but it also exposes the culture. If standards only hold when the boss is present, there aren't really standards, there's supervision. Real culture is what holds when nobody is checking.

You've probably felt this yourself. You walk into a business and within seconds you know the owner isn't there or the manager is off that day. No one thing is technically wrong, but nothing is quite on point either. The greeting's flat, the attention is sort of there, and the urgency feels optional. Everything works, but only just. You can feel that experience improve the moment someone senior steps back into the room. Things tighten, attention lifts, and standards suddenly matter again.

If a business only performs well when someone is watching, the culture isn't embedded, it's being policed. And customers feel that instantly.

They don't think, "Management must be away today." They just feel a drop in confidence, a slight wobble, and a sense that the experience depends on who's around, not on how the business actually operates. That's when the experience becomes like tofu. I've never really understood tofu. It's there, but you're never quite sure why. It fills space, but it doesn't add anything. Nothing tastes bad, nothing stands out, and nothing fails hard enough to complain about, but nothing makes you want to come back either. That's what culture looks like when it only works under supervision: present, functional, technically fine, but completely forgettable. And forgettable experiences don't build loyalty. They just pass through people's lives without leaving a mark.

A real wolf pack doesn't need the lead wolf watching to move as one. The behaviour is embedded. If one drifts, the others correct it instantly, not because of hierarchy, but because survival depends on coordination. In business, survival depends on the same thing, but we tolerate drift because no one wants to be the person who pulls someone up on the small stuff. Except the small stuff *is* the stuff. It's the difference between a pack that moves together and one that quietly drifts apart.

In a pack, the small signals are survival signals. A missed cue means someone doesn't eat. In business, the consequences are slower, but just as real. Missed cues become missed follow-ups, then missed follow-ups become frustrated customers, and frustrated customers quietly exit. The pack doesn't fall apart in one dramatic moment, it loosens one behaviour at a time, and leaders don't notice because each moment looks minor. Culture doesn't collapse loudly. It erodes politely.

This is where Service Rebellion moves out of theory and into leadership behaviour. It's the refusal to let small drifts slide because everyone's busy. It's correcting early, not when patterns have already formed. And it's understanding that every tolerated behaviour becomes a signal, and signals shape the environment people operate in. That environment then shapes how customers and clients experience the business, without anyone ever talking about culture at all.

Which means culture is not an internal topic, it's a commercial one. Culture decides whether customers feel safe or cautious, whether staff take ownership or pass things sideways, and whether problems get solved or explained. Every one of those behaviours affects loyalty, referrals, retention, and growth, but we keep talking about culture like it's about how people feel at work, instead of what customers actually experience when things get busy. People don't walk away saying "Their internal behavioural norms were inconsistent". They say "They're easy to work with" or "They're a bit hard to deal with". That's culture translated.

Business owners and management think they are building culture when they communicate it, but people don't follow what leaders say, they follow what leaders allow. What gets laughed at becomes normal, what gets ignored becomes acceptable, and what gets rewarded becomes the real priority. No one needs a memo to understand culture. They read it in reactions, in tone, and in where attention goes. Business owners and leaders don't scale customer experience by adding more policies. They scale it by shaping the environment where behaviour becomes predictable. Because behaviour repeated becomes culture, and culture repeated becomes experience, and experience is what people remember long after they've forgotten what your values and mission statement said.

CULTURE IS ABSORBED

What makes this tricky for business owners or management is that culture doesn't feel like a decision, it feels like momentum. Things don't suddenly change, they slowly settle. A slightly rushed tone becomes normal, a bit of internal sarcasm about customers becomes humour, a loose handover of a customer to another department becomes "that's just how that department works". Nobody announces the shift. It just happens through repetition. Once something repeats enough, it stops looking like behaviour and starts looking like reality.

That's when drift becomes dangerous because no one inside the system sees it as drift anymore. They see it as normal. New staff absorb it within weeks without needing training on it. They just mirror what they see. That's how culture spreads faster than strategy. Because behaviour is visible. Visible behaviour beats invisible values every time. You can print "integrity" on a wall in vinyl letters three feet high, but if people watch leaders dodge hard conversations or tolerate sloppy standards, that sign might as well say "optional".

Culture doesn't listen to words, it listens to reactions. That's why staff copy tone faster than policy, and why one eye roll from a leader can undo an hour of training. You can also see culture in how people talk when customers or clients aren't present. The tone matters. Are they spoken about with respect or as interruptions? Are problems framed as things to solve or annoying problems to manage? That language shapes mindset long before any policy does. Customers never hear those conversations directly, but they do feel the outcome of them. The difference between being treated like a person with a situation versus being treated like another task in a queue often starts with internal language.

CULTURE AND BUSYNESS

Calm days make most businesses look good. Culture shows up when deadlines stack, when the team is stretched, when something goes wrong and someone has to choose between the easy way and the right way. If standards disappear under pressure, they weren't standards, they were preferences. Customers don't live in your calm-day culture. They live in your pressure-day culture.

Pressure doesn't create culture, it reveals it. When time is tight, people fall back on what's normal, not what's written. If normal is ownership, they lean in. If normal is excuse, they lean out. Business owners and management think they see culture in meetings, but in reality customers feel it when deadlines hit. If standards only apply when it's convenient, they aren't standards, they're preferences.

This is why owners and leaders can be genuinely surprised by feedback. From their perspective, the business stands for certain values. From the customer's perspective, the experience feels inconsistent. The gap isn't dishonesty, it's visibility. Leaders often see the intended culture, but customers feel the lived one. And the lived one is built from the behaviours that repeat under pressure.

This leadership trap for business owners and managers feels reasonable but causes damage: business leaders often prioritise fixing big issues and let small ones slide. It makes sense at the time. There's always something urgent. But small behaviours compound – the missed follow-up here, the vague update there, the shrug when a standard isn't met. None of them are catastrophic alone, but together, they form the behavioural climate. And that daily rhythm shapes the experience more than any big event ever will.

CULTURE AFFECTS BUSINESSES BIG AND SMALL

Here's where small business owners think, "Yeah but this is more for bigger companies." It's not! Culture actually shows up faster in a business with three people than in one with three hundred because there's nowhere to hide. If you run a small team, your reactions are the culture, and your tone is the culture. What you laugh at, ignore, rush past, or let slide becomes the rulebook, even if you never meant it to be. If you say "Just do your best" when something drops, your team hears "standards are flexible". If you constantly step in to fix things but never reset the expectation afterwards, your team doesn't learn standards, they learn dependence. If you let your own stuff slide but pull them up on theirs, don't be surprised when the standard collapses. In a small business, culture is not set by a department. It's set by the owner's daily habits because in a small pack the lead wolf's behaviour spreads instantly.

In larger organisations people assume culture sits in HR. It doesn't. It shows up in how managers react to problems and how senior leaders respond to bad news. The reaction chain becomes the culture chain. It lives in what happens when pressure hits and someone decides whether to fix or deflect. A frontline team member watches how their manager responds to a mistake. That manager watches how senior leaders respond to bad news. The chain of reaction becomes the chain of culture. It cascades, whether you mean it to or not.

And here's the uncomfortable bit. Culture does not reflect your intentions. It reflects your patterns. You might care deeply about customers, and you might talk about standards constantly. But if the lived rhythm inside the business is rushed, reactive, or inconsistent, that is the culture customers experience.

That's why two businesses with the same values on paper feel completely different. One feels calm, clear, steady, while the other feels like you're interrupting them just by being there. That difference isn't strategy. It's the gap between what the business says and what actually happens.

CULTURE IS DRIVEN BY BEHAVIOUR

The way things feel day to day always traces back to whoever sets the tone, whether you are the owner with two staff or the executive team in a corporation. Culture follows the loudest behaviour in the room – and that's usually leadership. You don't build culture in workshops. You build it in Tuesdays – just a normal day – and in the way issues are handled when nobody's watching and nobody's filming a LinkedIn video about it.

One big initiative can impress people once, but the day-to-day experience decides how it actually feels to deal with you. Daily feeling is what builds or weakens loyalty. You don't lose customers because of one bad project if the climate feels steady. You lose them when the climate feels messy, reactive, or emotionally heavy. That's culture, not service technique. You can launch a big customer initiative, a new program, a big announcement about raising standards, but if everyday behaviour doesn't shift, the culture doesn't move. Staff take their cues from what happens after the meeting, not during it.

That's why culture change is slow when it's driven by communication alone, and fast when it's driven by behaviour. The moment leaders start noticing, addressing, and reinforcing the small stuff, the environment shifts. What used to slide now gets noticed. That recalibration is uncomfortable at first, but it's the point where culture actually starts to change.

Here is where the Wolf Pack Standard matters more than ever because a pack survives through shared behaviour, not personality. No wolf says "That's not my section of the hunt". No wolf says "I thought someone else would cover that". The pack succeeds because responsibility is collective, not convenient. In business, drift happens when responsibility becomes situational. "That's not my job." "I didn't know." "I thought someone else was doing it." Those are not communication issues, they are culture signals. They show people what level of ownership is normal.

If you want to shift culture, stop talking about values and start reinforcing behaviours that protect the pack:

- Who owns the next step?
- Who follows through?
- Who updates before being chased?
- Who fixes before explaining?

When those behaviours are noticed and reinforced, culture shifts. When they are ignored, drift wins. Small business owners often think culture change means being stricter. It doesn't. It just means being clearer. Clear expectations reduce stress because people know what "good" looks like. Vagueness creates anxiety, and anxious teams create messy experiences. Consistent standards create confidence, and confident teams create calm experiences. In larger organisations, leaders often hide behind process because they think the system will hold culture. Systems help, but systems don't correct tone, ownership, or attitude. Only people do that. Culture is built in the moments where someone could let it slide and chooses not to.

And here's how it will hit your business. When culture stabilises, your customers and clients feel it before you measure it. Communication smooths out, there are fewer surprises, and there is less chasing and emotional friction. Loyalty grows not because you ran a campaign, but because the experience stopped feeling like work.

That's why culture isn't soft. It decides whether customers feel safe or cautious, whether ownership holds or gets passed sideways. When leaders aren't in the room, their culture is. It speaks in tone, in ownership, in whether someone says "I'll sort it" or "That's not my area". Customers don't judge leadership by speeches. They judge it by how the pack moves when no one's watching.

If the levels you've just read about only hold when you're present, they were never fixed in place. They were supervised. Service Rebellion isn't about inspiring people in meetings. It's about building standards that survive without you. Because when you leave the room, your culture either carries the pack or it collapses without you.

Chapter summary

- If standards disappear under pressure, they weren't standards, they were preferences.
- Culture is what actually happens once the day gets busy and everyone just gets on with it.
- Customers read culture in reactions, in tone, and in where attention goes.
- Customers and clients feel patterns, not intentions.
- If you run a small team, your reactions are the culture, and your tone is the culture.
- In larger organisations culture shows up in how managers react to problems and how senior leaders respond to bad news.
- Culture spreads through what's tolerated, not what's written down.
- Culture updates and spreads because behaviour is reinforced consistently enough that the old way feels uncomfortable.
- Culture change is slow when it's driven by communication alone, and fast when it's driven by behaviour.

Chapter 20

THE LESSONS YOUR BUSINESS LEARNS FROM YOU

There is a strange myth in business that teaching only happens when someone stands at the front of a room and says "Here is what we believe" or "Here is how we operate". That formal version of teaching looks organised and deliberate, and it makes people feel like they have experienced leadership.

But if you have ever run a business for more than five minutes you know that the real shaping of behaviour rarely happens in those tidy moments. It happens on the Tuesday when something is late, when a customer is irritated, when a team member drops the ball, when you are already stretched. And it happens when you are tired, when the week has run long, when something is inconvenient and you have to decide, in real time, how much something actually matters. That decision is a lesson. And this is what Service Rebellion is really about. Not the poster version of standards, the pressure version.

If you own a business, whether you see yourself as a leader or not, people are learning from you constantly – from your tone when something escalates, from what makes you tense and what barely gets a reaction, from the speed at which you move towards revenue problems versus the speed at which you move towards customer friction, and from what you fix quietly yourself and what you reset clearly with everyone watching. You do not need to announce the lesson because they feel it.

Most business owners do not think of themselves as teachers. They think of themselves as operators, problem-solvers, builders, and fighters . . . people who are just trying to make it all work. Your reactions are setting the weight of the business. Where your energy spikes, people know that matters. Where you barely react, they assume it doesn't. And over time, that energy determines what holds under pressure and what bends.

The complicated part is that you can care deeply about customers and still accidentally train your business to treat friction as optional. You can speak passionately about standards, and still, without meaning to, you teach that standards relax when things get busy. You can preach ownership to your staff all you want, but if you keep rescuing them instead of resetting the standard, you're not leading. You're parenting. Caring is not the same as backing it up, and culture is built in what you back up when it costs you something.

ACCESS HIDES FRICTION

There is another layer to this that most people do not consider until it is pointed out to them. As your business grows, or even just as you become more experienced inside it, your experience of your own operation changes. You stop moving through it the way your customers do. You already know how things work, you already know who to call, you already know the backdoor when the front door feels slow. From your perspective, the system mostly works. But you are not using the same version of the system your customers are.

If you run a café, you do not experience the uncertainty of standing in front of your menu trying to understand what something means. Because you wrote it. If you run a trade business, you do not experience the quiet anxiety of wondering when someone will arrive. Because you can see the schedule. If you run a larger organisation, you do not sit on hold navigating layers of process when something goes wrong. You message someone directly and it moves. Your path through the business is smoother. That is not manipulation, it is access, but access hides friction. And when you do not feel friction, urgency dulls.

You see this in big organisations all the time. A telco CEO for example has an issue with their own personal service. They don't sit on hold for an eternity, they don't navigate automated menus, they don't repeat their story three times to three different departments and have to provide their identity details every time for "privacy and security reasons". They don't get told "I can't see that on my system". They message their PA, who messages the technical director's PA, and within minutes the issue disappears.

From their perspective, the system works. It's responsive and it's efficient, so it's fine. But they have never actually walked the customer journey. They have never felt the hold music looping for 55 minutes, hearing every 30 seconds "Your call is important to us". They have never felt the small frustration of explaining the same issue again because the notes weren't passed on, and they have never felt the subtle doubt creep in when no one can clearly tell them what happens next.

So for those at the top the system looks smooth, but from the customer side, it can feel heavy and painful. When you don't feel the heaviness, you don't feel the urgency to remove it. This is why it is so important, no matter how big or small your business is, to do a customer journey stocktake regularly, so you can understand the processes your customers and clients go through just to do business with you.

VISIBLE LEADERSHIP

You might still believe experience, clarity, and certainty matter. But the emotional charge inside you shifts towards the things you actually *feel* – revenue, targets, deadlines, visibility, or whatever's making your day harder. Your team watches where that charge lives. If revenue drops, energy spikes. If a customer describes confusion, does the energy spike in the same way? If a target is missed or a customer had to repeat their story three times, does attention sharpen immediately? They feel that difference, so they do not need to analyse it. They adjust to it.

You do not get the culture you describe. You get the culture your reactions build, and that culture becomes the lived experience your customers move through every single day. If the strongest emotional reaction in your business shows up around money, your customers will feel pressure before they feel care. If it shows up around broken promises, they will feel reliability. If it shows up around internal inconvenience, they will feel that blame travels faster than ownership. If it shows up around customer friction, they will feel protection.

Culture is not internal, it leaks outward. A wolf pack doesn't run on quarterly values meetings. It learns by watching the lead wolf move. Whatever the lead wolf lets slide becomes normal. Whatever gets corrected early becomes instinct. That's the pack. And that's your business. In a small business, this is magnified. There is department or distance to hide behind. If you say follow-up matters but consistently step in and fix missed follow-ups yourself without resetting expectations, you have just trained dependence. If you say clarity matters but quietly fix vague communication instead of addressing it, you have just protected the moment and weakened the standard. If you say pace is important and constantly move fast under pressure without protecting clarity, you have just trained speed over certainty.

Standards do not collapse in explosions. They soften gradually and settle. And once they settle, they become normal. Normal is what customers experience. They don't experience your intentions, they experience your defaults, and your defaults are built from whatever you repeatedly reinforced when it would have been easier not to.

You can have frameworks, values on the wall, beautifully articulated standards, and your mission statement plastered everywhere, but sitting in a parked car does not get you to your destination. The vehicle can be immaculate, the fuel tank full, the map clear, but unless you turn the key and drive, nothing changes. Without backing it up in behaviour, everything looks impressive in the driveway but goes nowhere.

What makes this even more confronting is that most business owners genuinely believe they are reinforcing standards simply because they care about them. But caring is internal, and reinforcement is visible. Your team cannot feel your internal standards. They can only feel your external reactions. If something goes wrong and you tighten your jaw but say nothing, they don't experience your disappointment. They only experience your silence, and silence, over time, becomes permission.

SIGNALLING BEHAVIOUR

This is where businesses slowly drift into something they never consciously chose. Not because anyone lowered the bar intentionally, but because the bar was not lifted often enough when it mattered. You do not wake up one day and decide that clarity is optional or that ownership is flexible. You simply fail to correct it often enough when it is inconvenient, and slowly the baseline moves. The team adapts to what feels normal, not to what was once said in a meeting six months ago.

Your reactions teach louder than your words. If your response to revenue is immediate and intense, but your response to customer confusion is calm and passing, you have just revealed what truly matters. Not because you said it, but because you felt it. People follow emotion faster than instruction. Emotion signals priority, and emotion signals survival. Emotion tells the pack what matters. Which means every spike of frustration, every surge of urgency, every visible shift in tone is a signal. And signals shape behaviour faster than any handbook ever could.

This is the part that stings a little because it removes excuses. You don't get the culture you talk about. You get the behaviour you let slide. Your team will mirror the level of ownership you insist on when it's inconvenient, the level of clarity you protect when you're tired, and the level of certainty you reinforce when deadlines stack up. Not in theory. In reality. In the normal week. In the messy moments. You do not get what you aspire to. You end up getting what you accept. If you accept blurred ownership because everyone is busy, blurred ownership becomes normal. If you accept defensive tone because someone is under pressure, defensive tone becomes normal. If you accept missed communication because the week has been chaotic, chaos becomes normal. None of that requires a formal decision, it just requires repetition.

Distance makes this more dangerous because distance makes everything look smoother than it feels. You can be five metres away and still be distant. You can be in the same room and still not feel friction because your route through the system is privileged. From your view the process feels fine, but from the customers' it may feel painful. And if you never deliberately step into that heaviness, you will never feel the urgency to remove it. Without urgency, priority fades. Without priority, reinforcement fades. Without reinforcement, standards drift.

THE UNCOMFORTABLE TRUTH

This is where everything in this book either holds or falls apart. Importance, understanding, emotion, expectation, effort, certainty, personalisation, and consistency, none of those survive on good intentions. They survive on behaviour being reinforced when it would be easier not to. If you say certainty matters but tolerate vague updates when busy, certainty quietly dies. If you say effort matters but reward speed over clarity, effort shifts shape. If you say importance matters but dismiss small frustrations because they are not dramatic, importance becomes conditional.

Culture is not what you say you stand for. It is what survives pressure. And whatever survives pressure becomes the version of your business customers trust or quietly question. The longer you allow pressure to redefine the standard, the more the temporary becomes permanent. What started as an exception quietly becomes the rule. What was once "just this week" becomes "how we operate". And no one even realises it moved. It just locks in.

That is why culture is not a mood. It is a muscle. It either strengthens under load or weakens under load. Muscles do not grow because you talk about strength, they grow because you lift something repeatedly that would have been easier to avoid.

This is where Service Rebellion stops being theory and becomes uncomfortable practice. It is not rebellious to shout about service. It is rebellious to refuse drift when it would be easier to let it slide. It is rebellious to pause and correct clarity when everyone is rushing. It is rebellious to insist on ownership when it would be faster to just fix it yourself. It is rebellious to taste your own process when you already assume it works.

Most businesses are not destroyed by lack of ambition. They are softened by what they allow to slide. And softness rarely feels dangerous until the market tightens and suddenly the small drifts matter more than anyone expected. You might not see yourself as a leader. You might see yourself as someone just trying to keep the wheels turning. But if people look to you when something wobbles, you are shaping the environment. And environment shapes behaviour long before any formal instruction does.

The uncomfortable truth is that silence is rarely neutral. When something slips and nothing is said, something is still learned. When ownership is blurred and no clarity is created, something is still learned. When tone drifts and no reset happens, something is still learned. Those lessons don't just sit there. They shape the business. Over time, your business becomes a reflection not of what you believe, but of what you repeatedly allow. When you leave the room, your influence does not leave with you. It remains in the patterns you have normalised.

It remains in the energy attached to different problems, and it remains in the standards that hold even when you are not watching.

If the experience your customers are having doesn't match the one you think you're delivering, the gap isn't strategy. It's repetition. It's what your business has learned from you. Those lessons shape the weight of the experience customers carry with them when they leave your office, close your email, hang up the phone, or walk out your door. That's not about blame, it's about control. If you've shaped it, you can reshape it. Once you understand that every reinforced behaviour either protects or erodes emotional weight, you realise culture is not about morale, it is about memory, and memory decides loyalty.

THE CONFRONTING QUESTION

Most business owners have never paused long enough to ask a confronting question: not "What do I want my culture to be?" but "What have I actually been training?" Those are not the same question. One lives in aspiration. The other lives in evidence. Have you trained urgency around sales but calm around service friction? Have you trained speed under pressure but blurred ownership when things wobble? Have you trained your team that escalation irritates you or that escalation informs you? These lessons are not written anywhere, but they are lived daily.

Most businesses – from two staff to two thousand – do almost no deliberate training on customer experience. They train for systems, compliance, and how to use the software, but very few train their people on how to handle a frustrated customer, communicate clearly under pressure, take ownership when something wobbles, or protect certainty when things get busy. Then they wonder why culture feels inconsistent. You cannot expect behaviours you have never deliberately taught. And you cannot expect standards to hold that have only ever been mentioned, not practised.

This is where it stops being theory and starts becoming a movement. The moment you react differently, the standard in the room changes. When clarity becomes non-negotiable – even when you're busy – the team adjusts. If you keep rescuing, you stay the owner. If you reset the standard, they start owning it. If you respond to a confused customer the same way you would a missed sales target, your team instantly sees what really matters.

You don't need a new strategy to do this. You need a new consistency. When you leave the room, what remains is not your intention, it is your pattern, and patterns are what scale into customer experience. They scale into tone, they scale into follow-through, and they scale into how heavy or light it feels to deal with you. Customers do not measure your strategy, they measure that feeling. The moment you see that, you realise something powerful. You are not at the mercy of culture. You are creating it every day.

Let's bring this down from theory into something you can actually see. Imagine you run a small service business. One of your team forgets to call a client back. The client emails you directly because they know you. You apologise, jump on the phone, smooth it over, and fix it yourself. The client leaves happy. You feel efficient because the crisis has been handled. But what did you actually reinforce?

You reinforced that when something drops, you will absorb it. You reinforced that follow-up matters to you, but not necessarily to the person who missed it. You reinforced that the quickest solution is rescue, not reset. The next time it happens, the same gravitational pull exists. Not because your team is lazy, but because the system has taught them who ultimately owns the consequence.

Now imagine a slightly different version. The client contacts you. You fix it, yes, but then you calmly reset the standard. Not angrily and not dramatically. Just clearly. “This is what we do when we say we’ll call someone.” The lesson lands differently because the rescue becomes temporary, but the standard becomes permanent. That difference compounds over time.

Or picture a growing company where a team member escalates a frustrated customer. The first response from the owner is subtle irritation. “Why didn’t we handle this earlier?” The tone isn’t explosive, but it carries weight. The team member leaves thinking, escalation equals trouble. Next time, they soften the issue. They delay it, they try to solve it quietly. Not because they don’t care, but because they are protecting themselves. Now imagine the first response is curiosity. “What happened? Walk me through their experience.” The energy is directed towards learning, not blame. Escalation becomes information, not a threat. Problems surface faster, ownership strengthens, and the culture shifts without a workshop ever being run.

Or take something even simpler. A vague internal update goes out. “We’re working on it.” You see it, you know it’s unclear, but you sigh and rewrite it yourself because it’s quicker. That rewrite teaches something. It teaches that clarity is optional until you intervene. Now flip it. You send it back and say, “Make this clearer. If you were the customer reading it, would you know what happens next?” It takes an extra three minutes, but it saves months of drift.

None of these moments are dramatic, and none of them look like strategy. They look like Tuesday. But Tuesday is where culture hardens.

This is the wake-up call most owners never consider: the stuff you brush off as "not a big deal" is exactly what teaches your team what a big deal really is. If ownership is clarified, ownership grows. If tone is corrected, tone stabilises. If follow-through is non-negotiable when busy, busyness stops being an excuse. Customers don't describe it as culture. They describe it as "These guys just get it". Or they stop describing you at all – not because you told them you value service, but because the lessons inside your business stopped contradicting that claim. Because whether you call yourself a leader or not, your business is learning from you right now.

This is where Service Rebellion either becomes real or stays theoretical. Everything earlier in this book – importance, understanding, emotion, expectation, effort, certainty, personalisation, and consistency – depends on what you reinforce when it is inconvenient. Because those levels do not survive on intention. They survive on pressure.

If importance disappears when you are busy, customers feel it. If understanding weakens when things get rushed, customers feel it. If emotion becomes transactional when you are tired, customers feel it. If expectations blur because no one clarified them, customers feel it. If effort drops under load, if certainty softens under stress, if personalisation gives way to process, if consistency collapses when no one is watching . . . none of that stays internal. It shows up in the experience.

The levels don't become your culture when you explain them. They become your culture when you refuse to let them slide.

Chapter summary

- If you own a business, whether you see yourself as a leader or not, people are learning from you constantly.
- Your understanding of and access within your business hides the friction your customers feel dealing with you.
- The emotional charge inside you shifts towards the things you actually feel – revenue, targets, deadlines, visibility, or whatever's making your day harder – and your team watches where that charge lives.
- What you focus on translates into how the customer feels dealing with you.
- Caring is internal and reinforcement is visible – your team cannot feel your internal standards, only your external reactions.
- Culture is not a mood – it is a muscle that either strengthens or weakens under load.
- Your staff look to you when something wobbles – you are shaping the environment and environment shapes behaviour long before any formal instruction does.
- Business owners, ask yourselves not "What do I want my culture to be?" but "What have I actually been training?"
- Most businesses – from two staff to two thousand – do almost no deliberate training on customer experience.
- Everything earlier in this book – importance, understanding, emotion, expectation, effort, certainty, personalisation, and consistency – depends on what you reinforce when it is inconvenient.

Chapter 21

TRAINING ISN'T ENOUGH

Before we go further into this chapter, let me be clear. I'm not anti-training. I speak at conferences around the world about customer experience and customer service, and I run in-house sessions for leadership teams and whole departments. I've stood in front of rooms where people are genuinely hungry to do better. I've seen the lightbulb moments, and I've watched teams walk out with energy and clarity.

I actually debated whether to include this chapter because I know a lot of business owners, small and large, don't see huge value in training. But this chapter isn't about training. It's about why behaviour doesn't change just because people understand something. You can have insight. You can have buy-in. You can even have intention and still go back to exactly the same habits.

Some businesses invest heavily in training, where others avoid it like it's optional. Most unfortunately misunderstand what it's actually supposed to do. They don't have time, and they don't see the value. They think culture just happens. But here's the part most owners miss: even if you never run a single session, your business is still being trained every day. It's just being trained by pressure, shortcuts, urgency, and whatever gets you through the week. So this chapter isn't about whether to train or not. It's about what your business is conditioning right now.

TRAINING AND THE ENVIRONMENT

Most businesses lie to themselves in a very polite way. They say "We just need more training" as if behaviour is a knowledge gap. As if the reason a follow-up didn't happen is because someone forgot that follow-up matters. As if the reason clarity disappeared is because someone doesn't understand the importance of clarity. That's almost never the problem.

The problem is the environment punishes the right behaviour and rewards the wrong one. Explain properly and you're "too slow". Escalate early and you're asked why you couldn't just handle it. Slow down to set expectations and you're told the queue is building. So what do you think people learn to protect . . . the customer or themselves?

People don't ignore training, they obey pressure. And pressure is a better teacher than any keynote speaker ever will be. That's why you can bring in someone brilliant, you can invest money, you can create a day of awareness, you can get genuine buy-in and still find yourself six weeks later wondering why nothing has really changed. Not because the session failed, but because the system wasn't adjusted to support it. Awareness competes with environment, and environment usually wins. By 10.17 am the rush has hit. Someone's called in sick. A delivery is late. A customer is irritated. The question isn't "What do we believe?" It's "How do we get through this hour?" That's when behaviour either holds . . . or drifts.

You can see this clearly in small businesses. I get asked to speak at a lot of pre-work staff meetings before the doors open. We talk about service, we talk about experience, we talk about ownership. Everyone agrees, and everyone genuinely wants to do better. But the part that makes it land isn't the talk. It's what the owner does at 10.17 am when something wobbles. Whatever behaviour helps people survive that moment is the behaviour that gets reinforced. If speed helps them survive, speed wins. If avoiding escalation helps them survive, avoidance wins. If pushing things to tomorrow helps them survive, drift wins. Not because anyone is lazy, but because humans adapt to what the environment rewards.

EMBED BEHAVIOURS FOR CHANGE

Businesses can confuse awareness with change. Awareness is knowing what good looks like. Change, however, is doing it when it's uncomfortable. Training creates awareness but conditioning creates change. Conditioning is what happens when behaviour is expected, supported, noticed, and backed up so often it stops being a decision. It becomes "how we do things here".

A wolf pack doesn't run a workshop on coordination. It survives because behaviour is embedded into how the pack moves every day. Drift isn't discussed. It's corrected. Formation isn't remembered from training. Formation is the environment. In business we often treat service like a topic, whereas the pack treats behaviour like survival. That difference is everything. If the lead wolf tolerates loose formation once because it is tired, the looseness spreads. If it corrects early, the correction spreads. The signal is constant and the reinforcement is daily. No one is waiting for inspiration.

You see this in small businesses just as much as multinational ones. A five-person trade company might bring in someone to talk about customer communication. Everyone agrees follow-up is important, everyone agrees clarity matters. Two weeks later, jobs are running late, someone forgets to update a client, and the owner jumps in to smooth it over personally. The client is happy and the day is saved, but the system has not changed. The behaviour has not been embedded.

The next time pressure hits, the same rescue pattern repeats. That pattern becomes normal. The owner becomes the bottleneck. The team becomes reactive instead of responsible. And the experience customers feel depends on whether the owner is involved.

Now scale that up to a multinational. They roll out a global service initiative: new language, new standards, posters everywhere, and new internal campaigns. It looks impressive. Six months later, customer feedback still shows inconsistency across locations. Why? Because the operating environment in each location still rewards output over clarity, speed over reassurance, internal convenience over external experience. The language travelled but the conditioning did not.

Small or large, the principle is the same. If the daily environment does not reinforce the behaviour, the behaviour fades.

This is also where many businesses misunderstand what real training should do. Training is not the finish line. It is the introduction. It sets the standard, it gives language, and it also creates awareness. But if nothing changes in the way behaviour is reinforced after that, the standard floats above the business instead of living inside it. You cannot expect staff to protect certainty under pressure if no one notices when certainty slips. You cannot expect ownership to strengthen if rescue remains the default response. You cannot expect consistency if leaders apply standards differently depending on mood or workload.

CONDITIONING

Conditioning is repetition made visible, in what gets praised without hesitation, what gets corrected early, what is allowed to pass, and what is quietly shut down before it spreads. Over time, those visible signals create an unspoken understanding: this is how we do things here.

Service Rebellion is not about enthusiasm, motivational language or people trying harder. It is about refusing to let the experience drift because the week got busy. That refusal cannot live in a once-a-year workshop. It has to live in the way leaders respond daily. It has to show up in how handovers are handled, how follow-up is checked, how tone is corrected, how expectations are clarified, and how customer friction is treated as seriously as missed revenue. That is conditioning the pack. When the lead wolf protects formation even when tired, the pack learns that formation matters. When the lead wolf ignores drift, the pack learns that drift is acceptable.

In business, if leaders treat customer experience as infrastructure instead of inspiration, behaviour changes. Not because people are inspired, but because the environment makes the right behaviour easier than the wrong one. That is how experience becomes DNA instead of discussion. Conditioning requires repetition when you're bored. Correction when you're tired. It requires backing the standard when you'd rather just get through the day.

That's why so many businesses default to training cycles instead. Training is intense but short. Conditioning is quiet but constant. Training feels like an event, but conditioning feels like discipline, and discipline is less glamorous than a workshop. But discipline is what builds reputation.

If you zoom out for a moment, you can see how absurd it is that we treat customer experience differently to safety or sales. No one says, "We did a safety workshop last quarter so we should be fine." No one says, "We trained our salespeople once so we don't need to reinforce it daily." Those areas are conditioned, and they are embedded. Drift is corrected early because the cost of ignoring it is obvious.

The cost-of-service drift is slower. It's the slow leak in confidence, it's loyalty thinning, and it's the move from "These guys are solid" to "Maybe we should get another quote". Inconsistency conditions the customer just as much as your systems condition your staff.

Conditioning is what makes behaviour hold when pressure rises and exposes the gap between what was trained and what was embedded. Calm days make almost every team look competent, but busy days reveal what is automatic. Customers and clients do not experience your calm days. They experience your pressure days. And if behaviour collapses under load, it was never conditioned. It was just borrowed from a training room.

PRESSURE VS CONDITIONING

No one runs training on checking your email or locking the door. No one reminds you to do those things. The environment expects it. People notice if it doesn't happen. The behaviour is conditioned. Service behaviour is rarely treated the same way. It's treated like motivation, not infrastructure. So leaders run another session, another reminder, another poster. And nothing really changes because the environment keeps teaching a different lesson.

This shows up clearly in follow-up. In some businesses, follow-up relies on memory and good intention. In others, it's built into the workflow. Ownership is clear. Someone notices if it doesn't happen. The first business hopes for follow-up. The second expects it. Customers feel the difference immediately.

Another sign of a training-led culture is when leaders say "We just need to remind people". That sentence sounds harmless, but it reveals the real issue. If something needs constant reminding, the environment is not carrying the behaviour. You see the difference when new staff join. Officially, they're trained in standards. Unofficially, they're conditioned by the people around them. If the team cuts corners, that becomes normal. If the team owns issues and communicates clearly, that becomes normal. Culture is learned faster from behaviour than from onboarding.

This is why inconsistency rarely comes from a lack of knowledge. It comes from a lack of conditioning. People already know that listening matters. They already know follow-up matters, and they already know clarity helps. Knowledge isn't the barrier, competing pressure is. Conditioning removes the internal debate. When behaviour is conditioned, people don't ask themselves whether they should update the customer. They just do it, like a seatbelt when they get in the car. It's automatic.

This is especially obvious in large organisations. You can run brilliant customer experience training, then send staff back into systems where customers repeat their story multiple times, get bounced between departments, and hear "I can't see that on my system" as if responsibility has vanished. Staff sit there knowing what good service looks like, but they are trapped in an environment that makes it hard to deliver, so they adapt. Not because they don't care, but because the system teaches them what really matters. That's not a training failure. That's a conditioning failure and conditioning is what makes consistency possible.

It's also where leadership comfort gets tested. Training feels safe, but conditioning requires noticing behaviour, correcting drift, and reinforcing standards in the moment. It's harder. It requires attention. It feels personal. But it's also where change actually sticks. You can't outsource conditioning to a workshop. It happens in meetings, in feedback, in what gets praised, in what gets corrected, and in what leaders react to. That daily shaping is what embeds behaviour.

When businesses rely on training, they're hoping people will choose the harder behaviour under pressure. When businesses build conditioning, they make the right behaviour the easier choice. Customers don't experience your training program. They experience your conditioning.

This is also why the so called "soft skills" label is misleading. Clarity, tone, ownership, reassurance, and follow-through aren't soft. They are the experience. Treating them like personality traits guarantees inconsistency. Conditioning turns them into operational standards.

You see it in handovers. In training cultures, people are told to "look after the customer". In conditioned cultures, responsibility doesn't disappear just because the task moved. Ownership stays until the next person has fully taken it. That's not motivation, that's structure. And structure holds under pressure.

Conditioning also changes what happens when things go wrong. In some businesses, mistakes trigger blame or silence, so people hide them. They delay them, and they hope they disappear. In conditioned businesses, mistakes surface early. Not dramatically, or emotionally, just early. And early problems are cleaner problems because cleaner problems are what customers feel.

There's a commercial angle here that's often missed. Conditioning reduces rework. Fewer follow-ups. Fewer escalations. Fewer "can you just check on this?" moments. The behaviours that seem slower in the moment often create speed overall. Training focuses on moments, but conditioning focuses on systems, and your customers or clients feel the system.

This is where Service Rebellion fits naturally. It refuses to treat experience as inspiration. It treats behaviour as operational muscle. The same seriousness given to safety, compliance, and financial control is applied to how customers are actually dealt with. Not to make it robotic, but to make it reliable. Reliability builds trust, and trust compounds over time. Fewer lost customers, more referrals, less effort replacing churn, and smoother operations because issues surface earlier.

Training can spark awareness but conditioning builds advantage. Without conditioning, businesses stay stuck reminding people to do what they already know. With conditioning, behaviour becomes the default, even when no one is talking about it.

And that's when customers start saying "These guys are so easy to deal with" without being able to explain why.

Right now, something is being conditioned in your business whether you mean it or not. If drift goes uncorrected, drift becomes normal. If rescue replaces reset, dependence becomes normal. If ownership blurs when it's hectic, blurred ownership becomes the standard. Conditioning works both ways. You can condition mediocrity as easily as you can condition excellence. The difference is what you notice, what you back up, and what you refuse to let slide when you're tired.

So don't ask "Do we need another session?" Instead ask "What is my business learning on a random Tuesday under pressure?" Because until the pack holds the standard without you watching, Service Rebellion stays an idea instead of becoming how your business actually moves.

Chapter summary

- Training creates awareness but conditioning creates change.
- If the daily environment does not reinforce the behaviour, the behaviour fades.
- If leaders treat customer experience as infrastructure instead of inspiration, behaviour changes.
- Conditioning is repetition made visible and over time those visible signals create an unspoken understanding: this is how we do things here.
- Conditioning is what makes behaviour hold when pressure rises and exposes the gap between what was trained and what was embedded.
- Inconsistency rarely comes from a lack of knowledge – it comes from a lack of conditioning.
- Training focuses on moments, but conditioning focuses on systems, and your customers or clients feel the system.
- Service Rebellion means the same seriousness given to safety, compliance, and financial control is applied to how customers are actually dealt with.

Chapter 22

THE STANDARDS YOU DEFEND

Every business defends something, whether anyone has ever stopped to define it properly or not. You don't see it in the values on the wall or the strategy document. You see it in what gets through. You see it in the rushed update that still moves forward. You see it in the handover that technically covers it but leaves the next person guessing. You see it in the behaviour that everyone notices but nobody pulls up because the day is busy and there are "bigger things going on". That's the real standard. Not what gets said. What gets allowed.

Once something is allowed to keep moving, it doesn't stay isolated. It repeats, then it settles, and then it becomes normal. So this chapter isn't really about awareness anymore. It's about ownership. It's about the uncomfortable point where awareness stops being interesting and starts becoming inconvenient.

TOLERATING THE SMALL STUFF

The truth is, most businesses don't have a standards problem in the way they think they do. They have a tolerance problem. They already know more than enough. They know the conversations that feel slightly off but keep moving anyway. They know the handovers that are just good enough to get through. They know the updates that technically answer the question but leave uncertainty sitting underneath. They know the people who create confidence and the people who quietly create drag. They know the parts of the business that feel tight and the parts that only hold together because someone capable is carrying too much in their head.

None of that is usually hidden . . . It's just tolerated. Not because the people in charge don't care, and not because the staff don't care, but because most of it feels too small to stop the day for. It feels manageable. It feels fixable later. It feels like something that can slide just this once because the team is under the pump, the phones are going mad, somebody's off sick, or the week has already gone sideways. That's how standards move. Not because leaders sit down and decide the line should be lower now, but because small moments that should have been interrupted are allowed to keep travelling forward.

That is the shift most businesses never feel happening. It does not arrive like a crisis. It arrives like convenience. One vague update gets through because everyone knew what was meant. One rushed handover gets accepted because the next person can probably work it out. One piece of ownership blurs because no one wants to waste ten minutes working out who should have done what. One customer has to follow up because the team was flat out, and – to be fair – nothing had gone dramatically wrong. Each moment in isolation looks minor, and because it looks minor, it doesn't feel worthy of leadership attention. But customers and clients don't experience these moments in isolation. They feel the pattern those moments create.

That's where standards live or die. Not in dramatic failures. In repeated allowances.

WHERE ARE YOUR STANDARDS BEING SET?

If you really want to know what your business defends, stop listening to what people say they care about and start watching what actually gets through. Watch what happens in a meeting when an update is unclear. Watch what happens when a customer situation is technically resolved but still feels messy. Watch what happens when someone hands over a situation without making the next step safer for the person picking it up. Watch how often language like "That should be fine", or "I think that's been handled", or "We'll deal with it if it becomes an issue" gets used and then just floats on by. That's your standard. It's not the thing you announced. It's the thing you accepted.

Most leaders think standards are set in big moments, in leadership sessions, performance reviews, strategy days, or town hall speeches. They're not. They are set in the moment you almost said something and didn't. In the slight hesitation where you noticed that something was thinner than it should have been, but you moved on because the room was full, the day was heavy, and there were more obvious fires to deal with. That's the moment the line shifts. Not on paper. In practice.

Once the line shifts in practice, people respond to that long before they respond to the words on the wall. That's the part a lot of owners and management seem to miss. People don't shape their behaviour around the stated standard. They shape it around the lived one. They shape it around what seems to get through, what seems to get rewarded, what seems to draw attention, and what seems to matter when the business is under pressure. If the loudest attention goes to speed, output, and recovery while the quieter behaviours that protect the experience are treated as background noise, then the priority list has already been written.

THE COST WHEN STANDARDS AREN'T UPHELD

That's when businesses become better at reacting than preventing. From the inside, that can look like hustle, agility, responsiveness, or people doing whatever it takes. From the outside, it feels unstable. Customers and clients feel the difference between a place that runs smoothly because the basics are protected and a place that keeps getting through the week by cleaning up issues after they've already created uncertainty. They might not describe it that way, but they feel it in their body. They feel when something is solid and they feel when they need to keep a closer eye on things than they should.

Once customers start keeping an eye on things, something important has already changed. They have stopped relaxing. That matters more than most leaders realise. Because customers rarely walk around consciously evaluating your business in the language you use internally. They're not thinking about alignment, behavioural drift, handover quality, or ownership architecture. They are simply reacting to how safe it feels to deal with you. They're reacting to how much work their brain has to do while moving through the experience. They're reacting to whether they feel guided or whether they feel like they need to supervise.

If the experience creates confidence, they stop looking around. If it creates low-level uncertainty, even slight uncertainty, they begin protecting themselves in small ways by following up sooner, holding back from referring, and comparing more often. They keep their options open.

None of those behaviours arrive with sirens, so most businesses misread them. They tell themselves customers are more price sensitive now. They say the market is tighter. They say people have too many options, which is true, but incomplete. What they usually don't say is that the experience has become just uncertain enough to make comparison feel sensible. That's what standards slipping actually costs. It doesn't always cost you a customer immediately. It costs you the ease with which customers used to commit, trust, return, and refer.

That is expensive. Not in a dramatic, overnight collapse sort of way, but in the slow, compounding way that drains a business without anybody naming it properly. Referrals slow, but not enough to make headlines. Decision cycles stretch, but not enough to feel like a crisis. Teams feel busier, but not obviously stronger. More effort starts going into follow-up, clarification, reassurance, and internal fixing. The business becomes heavier to run, yet leadership often responds by doubling down on output, speed, and pressure, not realising that a lot of the weight they're feeling has been created by earlier standards slipping.

That's the trap. Short-term relief becomes long-term strain. You let something go because the day is busy, and later you pay for it with more follow-up, more checking, more internal friction, more customer hesitation, and more emotional drag inside the team. What looked like practicality in the moment quietly becomes pressure later.

Most owners and managers don't mean to create this. They think they are being sensible. They think they are picking their battles. They think there are more urgent issues on the table. But what they are often walking past are the exact behaviours that stop those larger issues forming later:

- clear communication prevents confusion
- strong handovers prevent rework
- visible ownership prevents escalation
- tight expectations prevent emotional wobble.

If those are treated like optional extras instead of fundamental parts of the operating standard, then they will always be the first things to soften when the pace picks up. And when they soften, customers feel it. Not because they understand the mechanics, but because they feel the experience getting heavier.

ADDING TO THE MENTAL LOAD WITHIN

This is also where a lot of internal tension comes from, and most businesses completely miss that connection. When standards are solid, people inside the business don't have to burn as much mental energy trying to interpret each other, chase missing details, or protect themselves from loose ends. There's a confidence that comes from knowing how things are meant to be handled. There's a steadiness in the environment. People still work hard, but they don't feel like they are constantly compensating for things that should already be clearer than they are.

When standards become flexible, that steadiness disappears. Now people start checking more. They hesitate before responding because they're not fully sure how something will land. They leave little gaps because they assume someone else will pick them up. They protect their lane because protecting the whole experience feels too messy or too exposed. Over time, the emotional tone inside the business changes. You hear it in the language. "That'll do", "It's probably fine", "We can sort it later", "That's not really my area". None of those phrases feel dramatic, but they signal that the business is slowly moving from prevention to reaction.

Once reaction becomes the norm, the business starts operating in cycles of scramble. From the inside, that can feel dynamic. It can even feel like everyone is stepping up. But from the outside, it feels unpredictable. Customers don't want a business that gets good at cleaning up after itself. They want a business that makes them feel like they don't have to stay switched on in the first place.

DEFENDING THE STANDARD

Now the business has reached the point where defending standards becomes so important. Not defending them in the sense of speeches or policy documents, but defending them in the flow of real work. In the moment where the update is too vague and needs tightening. In the handover that technically passes the task but not the confidence. In the customer issue that was "fixed" but still left too much uncertainty hanging in the air. In the team conversation where someone is starting to normalise a lower level of care because everyone is tired and under pressure. That's where the line actually gets held. Or lost.

A wolf pack doesn't tolerate loose formation because the day is busy. It doesn't say "We'll tidy that up later once things calm down". It corrects early, not because it wants control, but because delayed correction creates risk later. That's what strong coordination looks like. It protects the formation while the problem is still small. It doesn't wait for the pressure to prove the importance of alignment.

Business is no different. If the standard is only protected when things are calm, it isn't really protected. If the line only gets held when leadership is in the room, then the system isn't strong, it's supervised. If quality only tightens after a complaint, then the business is learning too late.

That's why this chapter matters, and that's why it sits where it does in the book. Not because you need more theory – because by this point you already know enough to see it. The question now is whether you are willing to stop letting it through. That's the real decision.

Where in your business right now are you allowing something that you know should not be there? Not the giant issue – the obvious issue always gets attention – but the smaller one. The thing you keep telling yourself isn't worth stopping the day for. The thing you know creates drag, but not enough drag to force a conversation. The thing that feels easier to leave alone because pulling it up would create friction with someone who's already doing a lot, or because fixing it properly would require more discipline than the environment currently has. That's the one shaping the standard.

What gets tolerated today becomes what gets repeated tomorrow. And what gets repeated becomes the experience your customers live inside.

This is why "What you walk past becomes the standard" isn't just a line. It's the operational truth of how businesses drift. You don't teach people the standard only by what you praise. You teach it by what you allow to keep moving. You teach it by what no longer gets questioned. You teach it by what stops feeling worth addressing. And once a business gets used to living with slightly lower clarity, slightly weaker ownership, or slightly more customer effort, it stops noticing the line moved at all.

Meanwhile, customers are already feeling it. They don't know your internal reasons. They don't see who's off sick, who's overloaded, who's carrying more than they should, or which decisions got deferred because there wasn't time. They just feel whether the business seems easy to rely on or slightly harder than it should be. And that feeling shapes behaviour long before leadership sees anything obvious in the numbers.

INCONVENIENCE IS AN EXCUSE

So, no, protecting standards early is not being rigid. It's protecting momentum. It's protecting trust. It's protecting the pack. Because the moment customers have to compensate for you, trust starts thinning. The moment your team starts saying "That's probably fine" more often than "That's not how we do it", the line has already moved. The moment the business becomes more comfortable with rescue than prevention, you've started training the wrong muscle.

And once that muscle strengthens, the cost compounds. The business feels busier. Good people start carrying too much. Customers become more cautious. Referrals become less automatic. Leaders feel like they are pushing harder for the same result. None of that starts with a dramatic failure. It starts with tolerances that looked harmless while they were small.

That's why this chapter is not really about standards as an idea. It's about your willingness to defend them when it's inconvenient. It's about whether you are prepared to stop treating small misalignment as something that can wait until later. It's about whether you are willing to create a business where the line is held early enough that customers never feel the wobble. Because if you don't defend the standard, the environment will reset it for you. And it will always reset it lower.

Here's the part most people don't see straight away. You can't defend standards like this on your own. If the standard only holds when you're watching it, it isn't a standard. If it relies on one person catching everything, it isn't embedded. If it only tightens when pressure hits, it was never stable to begin with. This is where most businesses get stuck. They try to lift the standard through effort, through reminders, through pushing harder, through stepping in more often. But effort doesn't scale.

If you're honest, you can already see it. You know the exact part of your business where the standard is thinner than it should be. It's the thing that gets through because everyone is busy. It's the conversation that never quite gets finished properly. And it's the behaviour people notice but don't call out.

It's not hidden . . . it's just been accepted. And once something is accepted, it doesn't stay contained. It spreads! And that's where the next problem appears.

Chapter summary

- Every business defends something, whether anyone has ever stopped to define it properly or not – it's not what gets said, it's what gets allowed and tolerated.
- That's where standards live or die in repeated allowances.
- People don't shape their behaviour around the stated standard but around the lived one.
- If the loudest attention goes to speed, output, and recovery then the priority list has already been written.
- When a business becomes better at reacting than preventing, they learn that short-term relief becomes long-term strain.
- The behaviours that stop larger issues forming later:
  - clear communication prevents confusion
  - strong handovers prevent rework
  - visible ownership prevents escalation
  - tight expectations prevent emotional wobble.
- When standards are solid, people inside the business don't have to burn as much mental energy.
- The wolf pack corrects early, not because it wants control, but because delayed correction creates risk later.
- The moment the business becomes more comfortable with rescue than prevention, the wrong muscle is being trained.
- Defending standards successfully is about the willingness to defend them even when it's inconvenient.

— PART 5 —

THE WOLF PACK STANDARD

Chapter 23

WHY LONE WOLVES BURN OUT AND PACKS WIN

There is a belief sitting quietly inside a lot of businesses that strength comes from strong individuals – the dependable one, the fixer, the person who always steps in, always knows what is going on, always seems to catch things before they fully fall apart, and who everyone looks to when something gets complicated or urgent.

And on the surface, that belief makes sense. When they are involved, things move. When they are copied in, threads tighten. When they are present, problems shrink faster. But when they are away, everything feels slightly heavier, like the wheels are still turning but with more resistance than there should be.

FIXERS AREN'T THE ANSWER

Nobody consciously designs a system that's reliant on one or two fixers. It forms gradually because when someone proves they can handle it, everything starts flowing towards them. The capable person gets looped into more conversations. More decisions pass through them, and more context lives in their head. Eventually, a surprising amount of coordination starts sitting inside one or two brains instead of being built into how the business actually operates.

From the inside, that feels like having strong operators, but from the outside, customers and clients experience something very different. The customer's experience starts depending on who they land with, how stretched that key person is that day, and whether the invisible glue holding everything together is energised or exhausted. One interaction feels smooth and settled, the next feels slower, slightly uncertain, harder than it should be. Not because the others are incapable, but because the connective tissue of the experience is stored personally instead of structurally.

At first it looks like having a superstar, but over time it becomes a system balanced on one set of shoulders. You don't actually have consistency. You have someone compensating – compensation always looks impressive in the moment. They step in, they clean up, they close loops others didn't even see were open, they remember context nobody else was tracking, and they smooth over friction before it becomes visible.

From inside the business, that feels like strength. From the outside, however, customers and clients are experiencing something far more fragile: reliability that depends on who's in the room. It works brilliantly when the right person is involved, and it works well enough when that person is stretched. But it wobbles when they're not there. The wobble is subtle, but it's enough. Inside the business, that often gets framed as just needing the right people on the job. From the customer side, it feels like rolling the dice and hoping today is one of the good days.

PACK OR LONE WOLF?

Reliability cannot depend on personalities. And yet in many organisations, it quietly does. This is where the wolf stops being a metaphor and becomes a lens. A pack does not survive because one member is extraordinary. It survives because behaviour is aligned and awareness is shared. Signals are picked up early and responsibility is distributed. Movement happens because everyone adjusts, not because one wolf keeps rescuing the hunt. That's how strength is engineered.

When a business moves like a pack, customers and clients feel steadiness. They do not need to care who answers the phone or whose name is on the email. They do not feel like they are starting again every time a conversation shifts hands. The experience holds its shape because the behaviour is shared, not because one person is quietly carrying everything.

When a business moves like a lone wolf system, customers feel dependency without being able to articulate it. They feel that the experience is strong when the strong person is involved and thinner when they are not. They feel that something which should be smooth occasionally becomes heavier than it needs to be. They compensate in subtle ways. They follow up earlier, they double-check, and they keep mental notes. They start managing their own experience because they are not fully confident the system will carry it smoothly from one step to the next. Customers don't complain loudly. They compensate quietly. And compensation is expensive.

The lone wolf pattern reshapes internal behaviour as well. When certain individuals become the default problem-solvers, others adjust around that gravity. They defer more often, they check before acting, and they wait for confirmation. Not because they are incapable, but because the system has trained them to. Capability concentrates instead of spreading, and the rest of the team stops seeing the bigger picture. The more it concentrates, the more fragile the system becomes.

LONE WOLF SYSTEMS IN THE WILD

You can see this play out in real businesses every single day, although most owners don't recognise it for what it is because on the surface it looks like strength rather than exposure. Take a five-person trade company where the owner knows every client history, every pricing nuance, every job detail, and can quote faster than anyone else while smoothing over tension with one phone call – customers love this person. When they are in the middle of everything the business feels tight and responsive. But the day they are tied up on-site, in meetings, or simply exhausted, the rhythm shifts. Staff hesitate before responding because they are not fully sure of the context. Small questions stack up waiting for clarification. Nobody wants to get it wrong, so they wait. From the inside, that looks like "We just need them across it", but from the outside, it feels like friction, and it feels heavier than it should.

Now stretch that pattern into a larger organisation and it becomes even clearer. There is often an operations manager or senior account handler who knows where the sensitivities sit, which clients need reassurance, which suppliers wobble under pressure. This person carries the pieces that aren't documented but hold everything together, and they hold the pattern recognition, so all decisions flow through them, clarifications pass by them, exceptions land on their desk, and everything appears smooth while they are present. It works – until they take leave. Then response times stretch, ownership blurs, conversations circle longer than they used to, and customers feel the shift almost immediately. Emails require more explaining, calls take slightly more effort. Nothing catastrophic has happened, but the experience has thinned because the coordination was never shared.

This is the quiet risk inside lone wolf systems: they feel strong when the strong person is available and stretched thin when they are not. The strength is real, but it is concentrated rather than spread, and concentrated strength always carries pressure with it.

THE COST OF THE LONE WOLF SYSTEM

The deeper problem is that this pattern often gets praised precisely because it looks efficient. Targets get hit, problems get solved dramatically, and clients and customers are impressed with responsiveness. From the outside, it looks like a high-performing operation. But underneath, effort is covering structural gaps.

Every time someone saves the day, it's usually because something small was left loose. Every save postpones the correction that should have happened earlier. Every time someone says "Don't worry, I'll handle it", the system either strengthens the group or quietly weakens it, depending on whether context is being shared or allowed to sit with one person.

Over time, context begins living inside certain people rather than inside the operating rhythm of the business. Authority narrows. Awareness narrows. Decision-making bottlenecks without anyone naming it. Meetings become quieter when the key person is absent. Staff look around waiting for gravity to return. That silence is not about incompetence. It is about conditioning. The business has trained everyone where the answers sit, and customers feel the downstream effect of that training whether they understand it or not.

What customers experience in those moments is not technical failure. It is extra effort: they follow up sooner, double-check more often, and carry more of the coordination load themselves because they are not fully confident the system will hold without supervision. That quiet compensation is expensive, not in dramatic churn, but in the disappearance of ease.

This is where Service Rebellion intersects with the wolf pack principle in a very practical way. It refuses to let competence concentrate so tightly that the organisation becomes dependent on personal strain. If someone has to keep saving the day, that's not strength. That's a gap you haven't fixed yet. If one person being unavailable creates measurable wobble, the system was never coordinated. If one person leaving would make customers nervous, the structure was never strong.

The uncomfortable truth for many owners is that if you are the glue, you are also the bottleneck. If you are the memory, you are also the delay. If you are the safety net, you are also the structural weakness. Packs remove that fragility deliberately by distributing awareness, reinforcing alignment early, and correcting drift before it requires rescue. That is not slower, it is stronger. And it is what shifts a business from looking impressive in bursts to feeling steady over time.

In a coordinated environment, small signals get picked up early because awareness is shared. Someone notices a pattern forming, someone else joins the dots, and adjustments happen before issues become visible externally. In a lone wolf environment, signals often sit quietly until they reach the person with context. By the time they get there, the issue has grown heavier. Recovery takes more effort. Uncertainty has already seeped into the experience.

From the outside, customers do not see coordination gaps. They simply feel that something which should have been straightforward required more energy than expected. You rarely lose customers in dramatic exits because of this. You lose momentum and ease, and you lose that subtle confidence that makes someone tell others about your business without thinking twice.

This is also where praise patterns become dangerous. When the person who "saved the day" gets recognition while the people who quietly prevented the day from needing saving remain invisible, the signal lands clearly: firefighting is visible, but coordination is quiet, and reaction looks impressive, but prevention looks ordinary. Over time, people invest their energy accordingly. The business becomes excellent at recovery and average at stability. And when recovery becomes the thing that earns attention, prevention slowly becomes optional. People start waiting for problems instead of tightening formation early. They get good at solving instead of aligning. They learn to operate in bursts instead of building rhythm.

That rhythm is what customers trust. When rhythm disappears, even if competence remains, the experience starts feeling heavier than it needs to be. From the inside, that feels dynamic. From the outside, however, it feels unpredictable.

THE ANSWER IS NOT MORE LONE WOLVES

Burnout grows here as well, and not in the dramatic way most people expect. The strong operators begin absorbing more than their share. Every unclear handover circles back to them. Every messy situation waits for them to untangle it. Every grey area lands on their desk. Over time that load compounds. Stretch becomes normal, and holding everything together becomes expected. When effort becomes the glue, the system depends on strain, and strain is not sustainable. When those people get tired of it, disengage, or leave, the gaps they were quietly absorbing become visible almost overnight. Standards appear to drop suddenly. But they didn't drop – they were never structurally embedded. They were being propped up by individual effort.

This is where many businesses misread the situation. They think they need more capable individuals. What they actually need is shared awareness and aligned behaviour. Packs win for one reason: they distribute load and they distribute signal. When something shifts, the group adjusts. No one waits for one member to catch everything. Information flows rather than bottlenecks. Handovers feel like continuation instead of transfer because ownership does not evaporate when a name changes. And customers feel that difference immediately. They feel whether the experience is held by a system or by a person. They feel whether coordination exists beneath the surface or whether it depends on someone running hot behind the scenes.

Leaders sometimes worry that tightening coordination will slow people down. In the moment, alignment can feel slower because it requires clarity, expectation setting, closing loops properly instead of assuming someone else will. But over time coordination accelerates everything because fewer things need rescuing. Less energy goes into recovery. Less emotional friction leaks into the customer experience.

Lone wolf systems move fast in bursts and then stall under pressure. Pack systems move steadily and sustain momentum. Customers build trust with the steady one.

The pack system is not about flattening individuality. It is about preventing individuality from being the structural glue. Strong individuals still matter. They still contribute, and they still lead moments. But the experience cannot hinge on their availability or their memory. When behaviour alignment becomes the glue, the system holds even when individuals are stretched. Alignment means clarity does not disappear when someone logs off. Ownership doesn't blur when the conversation changes hands. Information does not bottleneck because someone is busy. It means the experience customers live inside is protected by structure, not memory. And structure outlasts energy every time. That is the difference between building a system and leaning on a person: one scales, one breaks.

SERVICE REBELLION STEPS IN

This is where Service Rebellion stops being language and becomes structure. Rebellion is not about energy or enthusiasm. It is not about louder customer service. It is about refusing to build businesses that depend on strain to feel strong. It is about refusing to let the customer experience live inside one person's memory. And it is about building formation instead of celebrating rescue. If you are serious about rebellion, then lone wolf systems have to go. Because rebellion is not emotional. It is operational.

If you are honest, you can usually see which pattern you are living inside. If two key people disappeared tomorrow, would the experience collapse? Would clarity thin out? Would ownership blur? Would handovers become heavier? If the answer is yes, you do not have a pack yet. You have talented individuals orbiting a central brain. And if you are honest, that central brain might be yours. That does not make you strong. It makes the system dependent on one person.

Dependency feels powerful in the short term because it gives you control, but control is not the same as coordination. Control centralises strain, and coordination distributes strength. If your business cannot move cleanly without you in the middle of it, you are not leading a pack yet. You are holding formation together with effort. And that brain is carrying more than it should.

Customers feel the difference between talented and aligned. Talented feels impressive but inconsistent. Aligned feels calm. Calm builds confidence. Confidence builds loyalty. Loyalty reduces the constant pressure to chase new business to replace trust that leaked out through inconsistency. This is not motivational rah rah. It is operational reality.

In a pack, a small misalignment is corrected early. Not aggressively, not emotionally, just early because delayed correction creates risk later. Alignment is protected when things are calm, so it does not fracture when things are chaotic. The pack does not wait for visible failure to prove the importance of coordination. It assumes coordination is the condition for survival.

Business is no different, even if the consequences feel less immediate. If coordination is loose during manageable weeks, it will fracture during chaotic ones. If ownership is blurred when the day is calm, it will collapse when the week is heavy. Strong packs are not built on inspiration. They are built on consistent signals, people staying aware of what's happening around them, and ownership that sticks instead of shifting. They are built on the understanding that the experience customers live inside cannot depend on who happens to be available.

You do not need more heroes. You need a system where awareness is shared instead of stored, where alignment is protected instead of assumed, and where no single brain is allowed to hold the entire experience hostage. You need reliability to matter more than rescue.

Because lone wolves burn bright, and brightness looks impressive in short bursts. But brightness without structure fades. Packs endure because their strength is not concentrated. It is coordinated.

If this chapter has done its job, it should have shifted something in you slightly. Not in a motivational way, but in a structural one. It should have made you look at where effort is carrying what alignment should be holding. It should have made you question whether your business feels strong because of individuals or because of formation.

You cannot build a pack accidentally. You build it by tightening coordination when it would be easier to rescue. By distributing awareness instead of centralising it. By reinforcing alignment even when things seem calm. By deciding that steadiness matters more than heroics. Because once customers feel that steadiness, they stop compensating, they stop second guessing, and they stop managing their own experience. And that is when trust begins to compound instead of thinning quietly in the background.

Chapter summary

- When you have a fixer, at first it looks like having a superstar, but over time it becomes a system balanced on one set of shoulders – you don't have consistency, you have someone compensating.
- A pack does not survive because one member is extraordinary but because behaviour is aligned and awareness is shared.
- When a business moves like a pack, customers and clients feel steadiness.
- When a business moves like a lone wolf system, customers feel dependency.
- The lone wolf pattern reshapes internal behaviour as well as external.
- In a coordinated environment, small signals get picked up early because awareness is shared.
- In a lone wolf environment, signals often sit quietly until they reach the person with context.
- Praise patterns become dangerous when the person who "saved the day" gets recognition while the people who quietly prevented the day from needing saving remain invisible.
- Burnout grows when strong operators begin absorbing more than their share of the business's strain.
- Over time a coordinated system accelerates everything because fewer things need rescuing.
- Service rebellion is about refusing to let the customer experience live inside one person's memory, and it is about building formation instead of celebrating rescue.
- Packs endure because their strength is not concentrated but coordinated.

Chapter 24

WHEN THE PACK MOVES AS ONE

By now the pack shouldn't feel like a clever theme. It should feel obvious. You've already seen what happens when coordination isn't built properly and effort becomes the thing holding everything together. You've seen standards slide when nobody pulls them up early. And you've seen businesses look strong on the surface while relying on a few people quietly carrying too much underneath. That's not strength, that's strain dressed up as competence.

The Wolf Pack Standard is what happens when you stop leaning on effort and start building structure. Wolves do not rely on the strongest one running harder when things get tight. They shift formation. They adjust spacing. They rotate position. The strength is in coordination, not in one animal carrying the hunt. It's what changes a business from looking capable to actually being stable. You'll walk into meetings and notice whether awareness is shared or sitting in one person's head. You'll hear a handover and immediately know whether it protects the next step or just shifts the problem. You'll feel whether clarity is built in or being assumed. That's the shift. Once you can see the standard, you can't hide behind effort anymore.

What changes here is not what you notice, it's what you tolerate. Because once the gaps are visible, silence becomes a decision. If awareness is sitting in one person's head and nobody challenges it, that is the standard. If handovers drop details leaving the next person to clean it up and everyone shrugs because it has always been that way, that is the standard. If clarity is assumed and confusion keeps reappearing in different forms, that is the standard. Standards are not declared once and laminated on a wall. They are reinforced in moments most leaders think are too small to matter. That is where the Wolf Pack Standard is either built or quietly dismantled.

RUNNING ON TASKS

If things only tighten when you step into the middle of them, you're still running on effort. Most businesses run on tasks. That is not a criticism, it is just reality. People open their inbox, respond to what is in front of them, complete their part of the job, tick it off, and move to the next thing. Departments operate in parallel. Roles are defined, and handover points exist. On paper it all makes sense, and often it works well enough to keep momentum moving.

But customers and clients do not experience tasks. They experience movement. Customers and clients don't care how you've structured your business. They feel whether things flow or stall, whether they have to repeat themselves, whether they're being looked after or pushed along, and whether one person owns it or it's being bounced between people who all mean well but nobody is actually holding the thread.

The Wolf Pack Standard begins when you accept that finishing your task is not the same thing as protecting the experience. In a task-driven set-up, the win is completion. In a pack-standard environment, the win is continuity. That sounds subtle until you see how much it changes behaviour. Completion focuses on whether the box is ticked. Continuity focuses on whether the next step is easier because of what you just did. That difference shows up in how people actually move.

In a pack, no one checks out just because they finished their part. Movement doesn't stabilise until the formation stabilises. It means answering the question is not enough if the answer leaves doubt underneath it. It means finishing your part is not enough if the next person has to rebuild context from scratch. It means handing something over is not a transfer of responsibility but a continuation of movement. It means you do not mentally close the tab simply because the issue technically sits with someone else now. Customers and clients feel that difference immediately, even if they cannot articulate it. They feel whether they are moving through a coordinated system or being passed between competent individuals who are each doing their best but not moving as one. The Wolf Pack Standard refuses to accept that as normal.

Operationally, that means a few things become non-negotiable:

- Handover must reduce friction, not relocate it.
- Communication must remove doubt, not simply answer the question.
- Ownership must remain intact even when roles change.
- Drift must be corrected while it is still small, not discussed once it is out of control.
- If those behaviours do not hold under pressure, the standard is not real yet.

IS COORDINATION WEAKENING OR STRENGTHENING?

In most businesses confusion doesn't arrive dramatically. It seeps in through vague updates, thin handovers, and assumptions that technically close a task but leave doubt underneath. Those moments feel too small to interrupt, which is exactly why they compound.

In a pack standard environment, those moments are noticed early, not because people are perfectionists, but because awareness is wider than individual workload. Someone hears the words and realises the customer is still unsure. The box might be ticked, but the confidence isn't there. Someone realises that the next step has not been framed clearly enough. Someone sees that a pattern of follow-ups is forming and tightens the process before it becomes visible externally. That tightening is not drama, it's not a workshop, and it's not a values discussion. It is simply how the group moves.

When awareness narrows, coordination weakens. And when coordination weakens, customers feel it. The Wolf Pack Standard doesn't tolerate that. It changes the question from "Is my part done?" to "Is the experience stronger and better because of what I just did?" It changes the mindset from protecting your task to protecting the experience. And formation protection becomes visible under pressure.

The real test of structure is what happens when strain enters the system. When phones do not stop ringing, when inboxes get full, when someone is off sick, when timelines get closer.

In lone wolf environments, pressure pushes people deeper into their own lane. Focus narrows, clarity drops, and handovers become quicker and less deliberate. Ownership fragments because everyone is trying to survive their own list.

Under pressure, wolves don't scatter. They tighten. In a pack standard environment, pressure widens awareness instead of narrowing it. People pay closer attention to what is happening around them because they understand that strain in one part of the formation eventually becomes strain for everyone. They don't cut corners on communication when things get busy, they actually get clearer because when everyone's busy and nobody really owns it, the cracks show fast. Busy doesn't create cracks, it reveals them. And the Wolf Pack Standard doesn't let busy become an excuse for letting them widen.

Here's the part that makes people uneasy: in most businesses, responsibility stops at the edge of someone's role. But in a pack standard environment, you don't get to say "That's not my job" if the experience is wobbling. Ownership still exists, but protecting the customer comes first. The priority is sorting it out, not working out whose fault it technically is. From the outside, that feels seamless, and from the inside, it requires people to get out of their own way. It requires people to act in service of the formation rather than in protection of their lane.

That is where the cultural shift becomes visible. In strong pack environments, drift is corrected early, and it is corrected without theatrics. If tone slips, someone brings it back. If ownership blurs, someone re-anchors it. If communication thins, someone strengthens it. Not because they want control, but because they care about how this runs. In other environments drift becomes the new normal quietly. A slightly lower standard gets through without comment, then the next one feels easier to let go as well. Before long what used to be tight becomes average, and lifting it again feels like a push instead of a return. The Wolf Pack Standard interrupts that slide before it resets the baseline.

STEADINESS RELAXES CUSTOMERS

This is where Service Rebellion becomes practical rather than inspirational. Rebellion was never about louder customer service or more enthusiasm. It was about refusing to let drift become culture. It was about refusing to allow effort to substitute for structure. And it was about refusing to build businesses that only hold together when people are pushing too hard. Here Service Rebellion stops being a nice idea and becomes a standard you hold people to. Not in speeches, but in behaviour, in handovers, in tone and especially in follow-through.

It says we don't celebrate the save without asking why it was needed. It says we do not allow one person to quietly hold the entire experience in their head – if it only lives in someone's head, it's not real. It says we'd rather not need the rescue in the first place. When steadiness becomes visible, customers relax.

That relaxation is measurable even if it is not always tracked. Customers who feel steadiness hesitate less. They question less, they refer more confidently because they trust the experience will hold for someone else, not just for them on a good day. They are less price sensitive because they are buying certainty as much as outcome. They stay through small issues because the baseline confidence is strong. And this isn't just culture talk. It hits your bottom line. It reduces rework, it reduces escalation, it reduces mental strain internally, and it reduces the need to constantly replace lost trust with new marketing. Momentum builds because what you create actually sticks.

PACK TEAMS WORK BETTER

In pack environments, awareness is shared. That means signals get picked up earlier, pressure doesn't concentrate, and issues are tightened before they become visible externally In strong teams, leadership isn't fixed. It moves to wherever it's needed. The experienced ones move to the front when direction matters, and they fall back when protection is required. It's fluid, but it is never absent. Someone is always watching the formation.

You can also see the Wolf Pack Standard in how new people settle. In lone wolf systems new employees struggle because knowledge is informal and centralised. They have to discover who really knows what, and they have to work out the unwritten rules on their own. In pack environments expectations are visible. The standard is reinforced daily through action. People learn faster because they don't have to guess what "good" looks like. That protects consistency as you grow.

Another practical marker of the Wolf Pack Standard is how problems are discussed. In defensive cultures, the first question is "Who missed this?" In coordinated cultures the question is "What signal did we miss and how do we tighten earlier next time?" Accountability still exists, but it is aimed at strengthening formation rather than protecting ego. When people aren't worried about protecting themselves, they call things out earlier. And fixing something early is always easier than cleaning it up later.

Leadership shifts inside this standard as well. Leadership stops being about pushing output. Instead it's about protecting alignment. That does not mean targets disappear. It means speed does not outrank clarity. It means progress does not outrank stability. And it means someone is always watching for drift under pressure. In pack environments leadership is not always at the front. Sometimes it is at the back, ensuring nobody drops off. Sometimes it is in the middle, reinforcing rhythm. Sometimes it is directional, sometimes protective. But it is always aware of formation. That awareness is what customers feel as confidence.

The Wolf Pack Standard is not about being perfect. It is about being intentional. It is about deciding that the experience customers live inside cannot depend on who happens to be available. It's about keeping things clear when it's busy. It's about ownership sticking so the experience doesn't shake when it moves. And it's about realising strength isn't someone carrying the load, it's the load being shared properly.

COORDINATION AND STRUCTURE

You now have a choice. You can keep running on effort and hope your strongest people never leave, never burn out, never disengage – or you can deliberately build formation. You can keep celebrating rescue and telling yourself it proves strength – or you can tighten coordination so you're not constantly stepping in to fix things. You can allow drift because everyone is busy – or you can decide that busy is precisely when standards matter most. It's shared awareness. It's ownership that doesn't evaporate, and it's coordination that holds when it matters. When that formation is real, customers stop feeling like they're navigating a process and start feeling looked after. That's when trust holds. That's when momentum gets easier.

When coordination is strong, effort goes into forward movement instead of constant repair. Teams feel calmer internally because they are not mentally carrying the entire experience in their own head. They have enough space to notice tone shifts, subtle uncertainty, and brewing issues because they're not overloaded trying to remember everything.

The mistake many businesses make is assuming that internal calm is personality-driven. It is not. It is structural. It comes from the whole team knowing what's happening, not from one or two people carrying the load. If you remove the metaphor completely, the Wolf Pack Standard simply means no single person should be required to remember everything in order for the experience to hold. No customer should feel the difference when one name changes to another.

This is where the chapter needs to shift you, not emotionally but structurally. If your business feels strong because of individuals, you are exposed. If your business feels steady regardless of who is present, you are coordinated. If the thought of two key people disappearing creates anxiety about the experience collapsing, then awareness is not yet shared. And if you are the one carrying most of that awareness, the business is leaning on your effort instead of building formation. That is not strength. It is concentration, and concentration always carries strain.

This isn't about wolves. It's about whether your business holds when it's tested. It's about tightening things before they slip. It's about fixing drift instead of celebrating saves. And it's about building something that lasts without someone having to carry it.

If your business still depends on effort to feel strong, you already know where the risk sits. If coordination only tightens when pressure rises, the structure isn't there yet. Packs don't wait for collapse to prove the point. They tighten before it happens. The Wolf Pack Standard isn't a philosophy. It's a choice.

And once you see it, you don't get to pretend you don't.

Chapter summary

- The Wolf Pack Standard is what happens when you stop leaning on effort and start building structure.
- Most businesses run on tasks, but customers and clients do not experience tasks, they experience movement.
- In a task-driven set-up, the win is completion – in a pack-standard environment, the win is continuity.
- When awareness narrows, coordination weakens, and when coordination weakens, customers feel it.
- The Wolf Pack Standard changes the mindset from protecting your task to protecting the experience.
- In lone wolf environments, ownership fragments under pressure because everyone is trying to survive their own list.
- In a pack standard environment, pressure widens awareness instead of narrowing it.
- Service Rebellion is about refusing to let drift become culture.
- When steadiness becomes visible, customers relax.
- In lone wolf systems, new employees struggle because knowledge is informal and centralised.
- In pack environments, expectations are visible.
- In pack environments accountability still exists, but it is aimed at strengthening formation rather than protecting ego.
- The Wolf Pack Standard is about being intentional, not perfect.
- Internal calm is structural, not personality-driven.

Chapter 25

SERVICE REBELLION: THE LINE IN THE CONCRETE

At some point you have to decide what business you are actually in, and I do not mean what your website says, or what your strategy document claims, or what your job title suggests. I mean what business you are truly in when a real customer interacts with a real person in your organisation on a random Tuesday afternoon when nobody is watching, when there is no owner or executive in the room, and when the only thing shaping the experience is the behaviour of the person standing in front of them.

YOU ARE IN THE BUSINESS OF BEHAVIOUR

After 30 years in business building companies from nothing, watching them scale, watching others struggle, stepping inside organisations of every size and industry, I can tell you this with certainty: most businesses think they are in the product business, or the service business, or the technology business, when in reality they are in the behaviour business. That is what your customers actually experience.

They do not experience your strategy, your quarterly planning session, your carefully worded values statement, nor your leadership alignment day. They experience behaviour, tone, effort, and the feeling they get when they deal with you. That feeling is shaped moment by moment by the small behaviours that either build trust or quietly erode it. Your customers experience how quickly someone responds to them, whether they are spoken to like a person or processed like a transaction, whether someone takes ownership or pushes them somewhere else, how hard they have to work to get what they came for, and whether they feel important or invisible.

That is your brand in the real world. Not the marketing slogan you blast out. Everything in this book has been pointing to that, even when it did not sound like it at the time. This has not been about being nicer or adding warmth to scripts or running a training day and hoping inspiration carries the culture forward for a few weeks. It has been about alignment. Alignment between what you say matters and what actually happens when the pressure is on. Alignment between what you promise in your marketing and what your customers feel in your operations. Alignment between what you tolerate quietly and what you claim publicly.

Every business already has a culture. You do not get to opt out of that. Culture is not something you decide to install, it forms whether you lead it or not. The only question is whether it forms deliberately because you shaped it, or accidentally because you allowed it to drift. If you reward speed but ignore sloppiness, that becomes your culture. If you talk about customer first but reward internal performance over customer impact, that becomes your culture. If you say loyalty matters but you make customers repeat themselves, chase responses, navigate confusing processes, and defend their own legitimacy, that becomes your culture.

Over time those behaviours stop feeling like exceptions and start feeling normal, and once they feel normal, they are very hard to reverse. You are already teaching your customers how to feel about you. You are already teaching your team what matters, and you are already reinforcing a standard every single day, even if you never speak about it directly.

Every part of this book points to the same thing. The small moments where customers decide whether they matter . . . or whether they're just another number. They're the moments where experience either strengthens . . . or leaks. Importance, understanding, emotion, expectation, effort, certainty, personalisation, consistency, recovery, and connection – none of these live on a slide deck. They live in behaviour.

This is why so many businesses feel stuck. They upgrade their systems, invest in technology, redesign their branding, automate more of their communication, and on paper everything looks sharper and more advanced than ever before. Yet customers still leave, complaints still appear, staff still feel drained, referrals still fluctuate, and loyalty still feels fragile. You can upgrade your systems, you can automate more, you can redesign the brand, but none of that fixes behaviour.

MISALIGNMENT

Small businesses feel the impact of misalignment quickly because friction hurts immediately when you operate close to your customers.

If you are a local operator and you ignore someone or treat them poorly, the feedback loop is fast. Word spreads, people talk, and you end up feeling it in your bookings and your revenue.

Larger organisations often do not feel it straight away, and that is where the danger sits. Scale can hide behavioural cracks for a while, but just because customers haven't left yet doesn't mean they're happy. It can just mean they haven't had a reason strong enough to move. Underneath, though, experience is still shaping perception, and perception eventually shapes behaviour. Customers do not stay loyal because you are big, they stay loyal because they trust you, and trust erodes quietly long before it collapses publicly.

This is where mediocrity becomes normal. Customers stop complaining and simply disengage. Staff stop challenging and start protecting themselves. Leaders become insulated from the frontline and begin believing their own reports instead of reality. When business owners and business leaders no longer experience their own customer journey in its raw form they start making decisions based on assumptions instead of lived experience.

You can have dashboards filled with green indicators and still be bleeding loyalty. Numbers can tell you what happened, but behaviour tells customers how it felt. And how it felt is what they remember. Customers today are not comparing you only to your competitors. They are comparing you to the best experience they have had anywhere recently. If a café remembers their name, if a retailer handles a return effortlessly, if an airline owns a mistake without drama, that becomes the standard they subconsciously carry forward. They do not reset their expectations when they walk into your business. They carry them with them. Your industry does not get a discount on expectations.

There is another layer here that most businesses underestimate, and it is critical. Customers are not just calculating value for money. They are calculating value for effort. Even if they never say those words, they are asking themselves whether what they received was worth not only the price they paid but the energy they had to spend. Effort magnifies cost, and friction amplifies frustration. When dealing with you feels heavy, customers reassess the relationship. You are competing on energy as much as you are competing on price or product. The energy your customer has to invest to engage with you. The energy your staff have to spend navigating internal complexity. The energy your leaders burn managing avoidable issues that only exist because behaviours were never addressed directly.

The businesses that grow sustainably are not always the cheapest or the loudest. They are often the ones that feel easiest. They remove unnecessary effort, they create clarity, they reduce confusion, they own mistakes quickly, and they align behaviour with promises. And over time that alignment compounds into trust.

YOUR RESPONSE IS YOUR CHOICE

This is the line in the concrete. You either decide that behaviour matters enough to shape it deliberately, or you allow drift to define you. Drift does not feel dramatic. It feels gradual, it feels like small compromises that seem harmless at first – tolerating a behaviour because addressing it would create tension, postponing a conversation because you are busy, or allowing a process to remain clunky because changing it would take effort. But drift builds up. Over time the gap between what you say and what customers experience widens. That gap becomes reputation. Then that reputation becomes positioning. And positioning determines growth.

This is not about perfection. Mistakes are inevitable, systems will fail, people will have off days, customers will sometimes be unreasonable – some very unreasonable – but none of that defines you. What defines you is your response. When something goes wrong, do you default to policy or to ownership? Do you protect ego or protect the relationship? Do you treat a complaint as an inconvenience or as insight? Do you focus on defending the business or strengthening the trust? Your response teaches your team how to behave. It signals what matters more: being right or being responsible. Over time those signals form culture far more powerfully than any formal declaration.

If you want customers who talk about you positively, then the experience you create must be worth talking about. If you want referrals to flow naturally, then people must feel confident attaching their name to yours. If you want staff who care, then you must create an environment where care is not punished by bureaucracy or indifference. Culture does not shift because you launch new values. It shifts because behaviour changes repeatedly and visibly, especially from those in leadership positions. When leaders close the gap between promise and practice, teams follow. When leaders tolerate misalignment, teams adapt downward.

MAKING THE DECISION

By now, if you've read every chapter. You already know where the friction lives in your business. You felt it as you were reading. It wasn't theoretical, it wasn't abstract. It was that one process everyone complains about quietly but nobody owns. It was the tone that creeps in when pressure rises. It was the approval layer that makes sense on paper but drains momentum in reality. It was the person who performs well financially but leaves tension behind them. It was the gap between what you say you stand for and what actually happens on a random Tuesday when nobody senior is in the room. You didn't need me to point it out because you recognised it because you're close enough to the truth to see it. That's the part that matters.

Once you recognise it, you can't pretend it's just the market tightening or growth stretching you or the industry being messy. When you see that behaviour is shaping the experience far more than your strategy ever will, the responsibility doesn't sit out there somewhere. It comes straight back to you. That's why this is a line in the concrete. Not because everything must change overnight, and not because you need a dramatic overhaul, but because from here on, drift isn't invisible anymore. Every time something misaligned happens and you let it slide, you will know you let it slide. Every time a customer has to work harder than they should, every time ownership blurs under pressure, every time standards soften because it's inconvenient to hold them, you will recognise it for what it is. That awareness forces a decision.

If you run your own business, the decision sits in your daily behaviour. It sits in how you respond when you're tired, in whether you close a loop properly or assume someone else will handle it, in whether you protect clarity when you're busy or sacrifice it for speed. Your discipline becomes the culture faster than any policy ever will.

If you lead a team, the decision sits in what you tolerate. People watch what you correct and what you excuse. They watch whether you protect alignment or protect comfort. Over time they mirror you, not your speeches.

If you manage a department, you decide whether customers experience your internal gaps or whether you take responsibility for closing them. Get your team living this properly, and the tone of the whole place starts to shift.

If you're leading thousands of people, it's easy to live in reports. The real question is whether you're close enough to feel the experience yourself. Because distance creates distortion, and distortion makes drift look normal.

None of this is dramatic. It just needs to be deliberate. You don't need ten initiatives, a cultural rebrand, and a new slogan. You just need to choose one behaviour that contradicts what you say you stand for and stop tolerating it. Hold the standard long enough that it stops feeling like enforcement and starts feeling like how things are done here. Then move to the next one.

Because what changes businesses isn't inspiration. It's consistency. It's the quiet refusal to let misalignment become normal. It's the discipline to close the gap between promise and practice again and again, until the gap stops appearing.

You cannot drift into the business you say you want to build because drift only ever lowers the bar. You can say all the right things and still be drifting. You can work ridiculous hours and still be misaligned. And you can grow fast and still feel fragile. If behaviour isn't being corrected and reinforced consistently, none of it is strength. It's just activity.

FUTURE PROOFING

There is one more reality that needs to be faced before you close this book and move back into the rhythm of your day. Every business believes it will respond well under pressure. Every leadership team believes that when things tighten, when the unexpected happens, when a client escalates or a mistake becomes visible, the culture will rise to meet it.

But culture does not rise in pressure. It reveals what has been rehearsed quietly for months or years beforehand. If drift has been tolerated in small moments, pressure does not correct it. It magnifies it. If ownership has been blurred on calm days, it disappears completely when timelines compress. If communication has been allowed to thin when everyone is busy, it fractures when everyone is stretched. None of this is dramatic in isolation, but under load it becomes visible very quickly, and customers feel it before leaders do.

That's the part that should unsettle you slightly. Because the market over the next decade is not going to offer long, calm periods where you can gently refine alignment at your leisure. The pace will not slow. Technology will accelerate expectations rather than soften them. Switching will remain easy. Customers will not announce that their tolerance has shifted. They will simply adjust their behaviour, diversify suppliers, reduce reliance, become more cautious in who they recommend, and quietly test alternatives. Internally everything still looks steady but externally, people are already pulling back. It's not dramatic failure. It's small compromises that quietly reset the baseline.

In the beginning it feels reasonable, it feels practical. You tell yourself now isn't the right time to tighten standards because revenue needs focus. You tell yourself one behaviour isn't worth the internal friction it would create. You tell yourself you'll deal with it once things settle down, once growth stabilises, once the next quarter is secure. But things don't settle and later doesn't show up.

What arrives instead is a slightly heavier business to run. Slightly more effort required to generate the same momentum. Slightly more noise needed to drive referrals. And slightly more strain placed on the same reliable people who carry the whole job in their heads because the system does not. That extra strain becomes culture, and that culture, once it settles, feels justified.

Nobody sets out to be average. It just slides a little at a time until what used to feel off now feels fine. You don't feel the hit all at once. It shows up in small ways. A client leaves a little earlier than they should have. Or a team conversation gets defensive instead of honest. A good staff member gets tired because they're always covering gaps the system should be handling, or a leader looks up one day and realises loyalty isn't as solid as they thought. Nothing explodes, it just adds up.

If you read this book and recognised parts of your own organisation in those patterns, that recognition is not accidental. It is exposure. Seeing it is uncomfortable because once you see it, you can't pretend it's not there.

From this point forward, you know that behaviour is shaping everything. You know that drift compounds, you know that alignment does not install itself automatically, you know that ownership either lives in people's heads or it lives in how the system moves. You also know that customers calculate effort as much as price, and you know there's only so much energy in the tank, for your team and for the people you serve. Once you see it, you don't get to sit on the fence. Doing nothing is a choice. And decisions, especially repeated ones, shape destiny more than strategy ever will.

So this is the decision point. Not someday, not when things calm down, not after the next quarter, not when "we get some better staff on board". Now! Every day you leave it alone, you are choosing the business you will become. And every day you shape it deliberately, it becomes strength.

You don't build a reputation in a big moment. You build it in the small ones you either correct . . . or excuse. A pack doesn't wait for collapse to tighten formation. It adjusts early. Quietly. And without drama. It protects alignment before pressure hits. It corrects drift before it becomes normal. No wolf waits for another to carry the weight alone because survival depends on shared awareness, not individual strain.

Business is no different. If your business only holds together when certain people push harder, you don't have strength. You have effort, and effort burns out. But formation endures.

From here, you either tighten formation . . . or you drift. You either protect the standard . . . or you lower it. You either build a pack . . . or you burn out your strongest people pretending you already have one. There is no neutral. Because behaviour is already shaping your future. And from this point forward, you can't say you didn't know. The line is in the concrete now.

Remember: if nothing changes . . . nothing changes.

Chapter summary

- Every business is in the behaviour business.
- Your business does not get to opt out of culture – it is not something you decide to install, it forms whether you lead it or not.
- You can't fix behaviour by upgrading your systems, automating more, or redesigning your brand.
- Small businesses feel the impact of misalignment quickly because friction hurts immediately when you operate close to your customers.
- Larger organisations often do not feel misalignment straight away, and that is where the danger sits.
- Customers are not just calculating value for money, they are calculating value for effort – you are competing on energy as much as you are competing on price or product.
- Over time the gap between what you say and what customers experience widens, and that gap becomes reputation, which becomes positioning, which determines growth.
- Your response teaches your team how to behave – it signals what matters more: being right or being responsible.
- When leaders close the gap between promise and practice, teams follow.
- When leaders tolerate misalignment, teams adapt downward.
- You just need to choose one behaviour that contradicts what you say you stand for and stop tolerating it.

ABOUT THE AUTHOR

At 25 years old Justin Herald took 50 Australian dollars and turned it into the multimillion-dollar global brand, Attitude Inc. Since then, he has spent more than 25 years building businesses from the ground up, mentoring business owners, working with leadership teams and speaking with frontline staff about what it actually takes to raise performance, tighten standards and improve the way customers experience a business.

He is an eight-time international bestselling author whose ninth book *Service Rebellion, The Wolf Pack Standard* is his most recent work and represents the culmination of more than two decades of observation, experience and work inside businesses of every size and industry. It is the framework Justin has been building toward his entire career.

Over more than 25 years Justin has delivered more than 600 presentations across Australia, New Zealand and internationally, speaking at more than 80 conferences and events each year to business owners, executives, leadership teams and frontline staff across virtually every industry.

Built on real world experience not theory, Justin's work addresses simple but uncomfortable business truths. Busy quickly replaces discipline. Small compromises rapidly compound. And customers feel the drift long before leaders do.

Working with businesses that understand the risk of mediocrity, Justin helps tighten execution, eliminate behavioural drift and maintain the standards that keep customers loyal before the damage shows up in retention, reputation or margin.

Because customers do not experience your strategy. They experience your behaviour.

Justin lives on the Gold Coast with his wife and five daughters and has spent more than 25 years watching great businesses drift and exceptional ones hold their standard. Service Rebellion is his attempt to close that gap for good.

JustinHerald.com
ServiceRebellion.com

www.ingramcontent.com/pod-product-compliance
Lightning Source LLC
Chambersburg PA
CBHW021230060726
47590CB00005B/1701

9781923765030